PETER SCOTT
AND THE BIRTH OF
MODERN CONSERVATION

PETER SCOTT
AND THE BIRTH OF
MODERN CONSERVATION

Chris Moore

Quiller

For Katherine, Matt, Alice, Leo, Charlie and Alfie

First published 2022

Quiller
An imprint of Amberley Publishing Ltd
The Hill, Merrywalks, Stroud, GL5 4EP
Tel: 01453 847800
E-mail: info@quillerbooks.com
Website: www.quillerpublishing.com

British Library Cataloguing in Publication Data.
A catalogue record for this book is available from the British Library.

ISBN 978 1 8468 9364 3 (hardback)
ISBN 978 1 8468 9365 0 (ebook)

1 2 3 4 5 6 7 8 9 10

Typesetting by SJmagic DESIGN SERVICES, India.
Printed in the UK.

Contents

Foreword

'Make the boy interested in natural history ...', wrote Captain Scott in his last letter to his wife, Kathleen, as he lay blizzard-bound and dying in his tent in the Antarctic. He and his companions did not survive their journey back from the South Pole in March 1912, and he became a national hero. Kathleen took this message to heart and found ways, sometimes subtle, to encourage her small son, Peter, to become interested in nature. As it turned out, she succeeded beyond expectation. Being an artist herself, and a sculptor, she also encouraged him to draw. From a young age, he would lie on her studio floor drawing while she was sculpting. Peter grew up in an atmosphere of confidence and positive thinking and this led him to be confident and optimistic throughout his life. He was willing to try things and to work hard to achieve goals. He was also a perfectionist but with a practical nature.

The twin strands of nature and art ran through his whole life. As a student, he was unsure about his career – whether it should be in natural sciences or in art. In the end, art won, and he became a successful wildlife artist, combining his interests. He would draw or paint something almost every day and his home was built to look out on a lake where wild swans come to rest and feed. However, before the Second World War, it was becoming clear to him that humans were having an increasingly destructive effect on nature. In particular, the birds he loved most at that time, wild geese, were rapidly declining in numbers. As a result, when he was demobbed from the navy in 1945, he set up a research organisation with a small collection of birds at

Slimbridge on the Severn Estuary in the west of England to discover the scale of mortality in the geese, the reasons for the decline and to find out what could be done to redress it. This organisation has grown into the Wildfowl and Wetlands Trust, an international charity which aims to conserve, restore and create wetlands, and save wetland wildlife.

In the 1950s, it was becoming clear that nature was under threat worldwide, and Peter became involved with setting up Worldwide Fund for Nature (WWF) and subsequently with many other conservation endeavours. In his later years, much of his time was dedicated to conservation, although he was still painting for exhibitions and commissions.

The sons of famous men often suffer the problem of great expectations. This book tells the story of how my father escaped this problem and lived a life full of achievement and creativity. Not only did he produce many evocative paintings of wildlife, set up several conservation organisations, and succeed in conserving many wild species, but he was also a successful author and broadcaster, and he excelled in a number of sports including dinghy sailing and gliding. Chris Moore describes my father's many adventures in these fields. The author has been closely involved with the transition of Peter's house at Slimbridge into a museum and tells the story of his extraordinary life in an informal and readable fashion.

Dafila Scott

Introduction

By whatever standards you might wish to apply, Peter Scott was a remarkable man who led an extraordinary life. Writer, artist, broadcaster, conservationist, scientist, sportsman; in any one of his chosen fields he would have been remembered as someone who made a difference. That he excelled in all of these is perhaps the main reason why his life remains an inspiration to others over thirty years after his death. To his chosen fields, Peter brought a restless energy, boundless enthusiasm, integrity and determination to succeed. All who met him remembered his charm and personality, and there are many examples of the kindness and assistance he gave to others.

Through his enthusiasm and energy, Peter was able to persuade countless others to help him in his work. He cared passionately about the natural world and was deeply concerned about the harm that humanity was inflicting upon it, at a time when hardly anyone else was thinking about such matters at all. It was his single-minded determination to do something about this crisis that led Sir David Attenborough to call him the patron saint of conservation and Slimbridge its birthplace. A central tenet of Peter's philosophy was that if you made people care deeply about something and that something was in need of aid, those people would want to assist in whatever way they could, without needing to be persuaded.

Never a wealthy man, Peter was adept at sourcing funds for the projects that were closest to his heart. It was said he could talk to kings and dustmen with equal charm and fluency and the list of names of the great and the good who came under his spell is a very long list indeed, including as it does royalty, presidents, prime ministers, statesmen, captains of industry, legislators, heads of faiths, sportsmen, stars of stage and screen and people from many other walks of life.

Throughout his life Peter travelled extensively to all parts of the globe, ever curious, ever restless, always wanting to see more of the great pageant of the natural world that he feared was disappearing before his eyes almost faster than he could do anything to save it. He wrote and spoke repeatedly about what he saw in the hope that others too would come to love and appreciate the beauty of nature as much as he did.

This then, was a great life well lived. It has been difficult to encapsulate it in a book as modest as this one. Hopefully it does him justice.

1

The Youngest Fellow

The British Empire had just passed its high-water mark when Peter Scott was born, though at the time it would not have seemed to the people of Britain that the Empire was in decline. Britain's place in the world was assured, its dominions covered 25 per cent of the land surface of the globe and it seemed that there was nowhere that its influence didn't reach. Most recently this now included Antarctica, that hitherto unknown and unexplored landmass at the other end of the world. Twenty years previously, nobody had been known to have set foot on the white continent even though, in the mid-nineteenth century, parts of the coastline had been mapped by British expeditions, and landfall had been made on some of the offshore islands. In 1902, Robert Falcon Scott had led a party south onboard *Discovery* and set foot on the continent itself. He had returned a national hero and had caught the eye of the eminent sculptor Kathleen Bruce whom he promptly married. Now, seven years later, the race was on to be the first to reach the South Pole itself. Another expedition would be mounted, and Robert Falcon Scott would be its leader once again.

Peter was born on 14 September 1909 in a house at 174 Buckingham Palace Road. He later wrote of having a vague recollection of his father, a man sitting in the living room at home, though it may well be that he was remembering what his mother subsequently told him about those very early months of his life. Certainly the infant Peter had little time to get to know his father, for he departed on his second Antarctic journey when Peter was just one year old. The story of that expedition, the triumph of reaching the South Pole only to find that the

Norwegian, Amundsen, had got there first, the long march back beset by violent storms and the final tragic death of the last three members of the expedition in their tent just eleven miles from safety, became the stuff of legend. By dying in such circumstances, Peter's father achieved a level of fame and glory that might have eluded him had he returned safely home.

There is no doubt that these events had an impact on Peter's life as he was growing up. Even before news of the death of his father reached England, the press were keen to exploit every aspect of the Scotts' family life. After Robert Falcon Scott's departure for Antarctica, Kathleen Scott kept a diary addressed to her absent husband, and in an entry on 19 November 1911 she wrote:

> I worked all the morning. Then a 'Daily Mirror' man came to see me and upset me greatly. He said if I would allow a photograph of the infant writing a letter asking for money for you to appear in the 'Mirror' he was convinced he could get £4000 [an appeal for additional funds for the expedition was ongoing]. My dear, I do humbly beg your pardon if I have done wrong, but I said no.

At the age of two, Peter was apparently not totally unaware of events surrounding his father. In her diary entry for 11 March 1912, Kathleen recorded the following:

> Peter said this morning. 'Mummy, is Amundsen a good man?' I said, 'Yes, I think he is.' Then he said 'Amundsen and Daddy both got to the Pole. Daddy has stopped working now.'

This occurred four days after news of Amundsen's success had arrived in England; there was no news of Scott and his companions. On that same day, lost in the wilderness, Scott wrote in his journal, 'Titus Oates is very near the end, one feels. What we or he will do, God only knows.'

After news of Scott's death became known, his mother worked even harder to shield Peter from the prying eyes of the press and the public, all keen to romanticise the story of the young boy left fatherless by such a tragic turn of fate. In the main she succeeded, and Peter's boyhood was not over-shadowed in the way it might well have been had his mother been less diligent. There was, however, one aspect of the tragedy that would have a significant impact on Peter's future life. As he lay dying in his tent, Robert Falcon Scott wrote a last letter to his wife. In it he mentioned Peter and gave Kathleen the following advice: 'Make the boy interested in natural history. It is better than games. They encourage it at some schools.' It is probable that he had in his thoughts his close friend and companion, Edward Wilson, who now lay dead at his side. Wilson was the naturalist on both of Scott's polar expeditions and the man who Robert Falcon Scott seemed most to admire amongst his team. He wrote in his journal, 'Words must always fail me when I talk of Bill Wilson. I believe he's the finest character I ever met.' When he was dying in his tent, with the body of Wilson beside him, Scott found time to write a letter to Wilson's wife in which he wrote, 'He died as he lived, a brave, true man – the best of comrades and the staunchest of friends.'

The Scotts were not wealthy. Robert Falcon Scott had been a sea captain on a modest salary, though his fame had made him a national figure in the years after his return from the *Discovery* expedition. Kathleen was an accomplished sculptor (she would never accept the term sculptress), having trained in Paris under Rodin. Her work was very much in demand. She created busts and statues of many eminent figures of the period, as well as being a lively and engaging society figure. Scott died in considerable debt, a circumstance which might have given Kathleen serious problems. However, in light of the nature of Scott's great achievement and his tragic death, a government fund was established to pay off the debts and provide a living for his widow and young son. The residue of this fund would eventually be used to help found the Scott Polar Research Institute in Cambridge.

Kathleen Scott grieved in private but didn't allow her feelings to affect Peter. She was fiercely determined that the tragedy that had befallen the family would not impact on his development. As an only child, Peter was used from an early age to conversing with adults, and it seems they treated him like an adult too. It is highly probable that this early assurance in the company of all sorts of people was the source of his ease and confidence in the company of others in later life. Many famous people visited the house either to have their likeness captured in stone or bronze, or as friends of Kathleen; the Scotts may not have been wealthy, but they moved in the very highest of circles. The Prime Minister, Herbert Asquith, often came to tea, and Peter played regularly with Michael and David McKenna, the children of the Chancellor of the Exchequer. Yeats, Galsworthy and Charles Rolls came to the house to have busts sculpted, George Bernard Shaw was a close friend, as was H. G. Wells, while T. E. Lawrence and Julian Huxley often came to visit. Apart from Asquith, Kathleen was friend or confidante over the years to five other prime ministers: David Lloyd George, Bonar Law, Stanley Baldwin, Ramsay MacDonald and Neville Chamberlain. Kathleen may only have been half-joking when she wrote in her diary in August 1912, 'Today I introduced Peter to Bonar Law so as not to bias his political tendencies.'

One of Peter's earliest memories was of attending a garden party at Buckingham Palace and playing trains with Queen Alexandra. Of another visit to the palace Kathleen noted, 'We stayed an hour and the Queen photographed Peter and me.' Kathleen was a formidable woman with strong views on politics and the big issues of the day. In 1915 she went to work at the Vickers factory in Erith in Kent, assembling electrical equipment for the war effort. A diary note for December 1915 records, 'I came back from Vickers to find the P.M. had been twice.'

From the beginning, Kathleen made sure that Peter had a number of mentors or father figures who could, as far as was possible, make up for the loss of his own father and guide the boy during his early years. Among these were zoologist Sir Arthur Shipley who was vice-chancellor of the University of Cambridge at the time he took Peter under his wing. Another influence was Sir Ray Lankester, the former director of the Natural History Museum. Peter used to visit his home where they talked about all manner of things. Peter remembered he was often given something to bring home with him, a fossil, an exotic feather or an animal bone.

Kathleen wrote of these visits in her diary in 1916:

I took Pete to lunch with Ray Lankester and them two scientific gents argued and agreed and gloated together till four. It was very delicious to see the big old man entering absolutely into the mind of the little boy, each finding the other good company.

And in an entry a week later:

Pete and I called for Sir Ray and went to the South Kensington Museum and home with him for tea. They were engrossed in each other, and in snails' eggs, octopus suckers, eel spawn, tsetse fly bacillus, pearls, puffins, peacocks, fox-cubs and badgers, and crystals at his house and flint implements, sea-urchins, radium, and a flint which when it came to rest after spinning one way began to spin another, all a feast for Pete. They were lovely together and how much better a game for him than soldiers or trains.

It is not difficult to see where Peter's love of natural history came from.

Peter had two godfathers. Sir Clements Markham was a former president of the Royal Geographical Society and gave to Peter his middle name of Markham. He may well have felt some sense of responsibility for the boy's fate as it had been he who had first recommended Robert Falcon Scott for the *Discovery* expedition in 1902. J. M. Barrie, author of *Peter Pan*, was Peter's other godfather, and Peter was named after Peter Pan. As a christening present, Barrie gave his godson a life fellowship of the London Zoological Society; Peter was the youngest person ever to receive such a fellowship. Kathleen was clearly determined to see that Peter's father's dying wish for him would be fulfilled.

Kathleen took an extended trip to New Zealand in 1912, expecting to be reunited with her husband on his return from the South Pole. In her absence, Sydney Holland, Viscount Knutsford, was appointed Peter's guardian. The little boy was dispatched to Holland's home at Kneesworth Hall near Royston in Hertfordshire while his mother was away. Sydney Holland kept a flock of ornamental ducks on a lake which the infant Peter must have seen on his daily outings in the park and perhaps was allowed to feed. Viscount Knutsford continued to play a significant role in his development in later years, and Peter often spent holidays at the Holland family home. Baden-Powell, the founder of the Scout movement, suggested to Kathleen that Peter would benefit from being ambidextrous, so Kathleen, anxious to give Peter every advantage, took his advice and made Peter write with his left hand. Unfortunately she pushed it too far, with the result that he became permanently left-handed, though this never impeded him at any stage in his life and indeed, on occasion, was to be an advantage.

Peter grew up with a passion for natural history and started to paint and draw at a young age. Lizards were an early obsession and then hawk moths, insects for which he retained a fascination for the rest of his life. Kathleen owned a small cottage by the sea at Sandwich in Kent, and Peter had fond memories of holidays spent playing on the beach and looking for creatures in the sand dunes nearby. It was obviously a special place for both Peter and his mother; when she died in 1947 he and his brother scattered her ashes there. During the First World War there were German air raids along the Kent coast; Peter remembered sheltering in a cupboard during the bombardment. In 1918, Kathleen was working for the Ministry for Pensions when she was seconded temporarily to work in France to deal with matters relating to British residents there. As a result, she and Peter lived in Paris for a while. As the Germans approached, the shelling of the city increased, so they returned to England for safety. After the war Kathleen took holidays abroad, always accompanied by her son. Peter thus visited France and Italy at a time when very few English people were travelling abroad and even fewer children of Peter's age. There is little doubt that Peter's upbringing, surrounded by adults, some of them the cleverest and most prominent of the age, treated like an adult himself from the start and shielded from the prying eyes of the press, developed in him a restlessly enquiring mind, an inner strength, emotional maturity, a resolve to forge his own path in life and possibly too, a certain reserve when it came to being in the spotlight.

When Peter was ten, he was sent to West Downs Preparatory School near Winchester. It is hard to say if he enjoyed his years there; tolerated them might be a better description. Though he was to take great pleasure in various sports in later life, he was not keen on, or good at, team games. As a result, he never shone at football and cricket, games in which ability would be a ready ticket to social acceptance and popularity. He admitted to being slow to learn to read and write and was for the rest of his life a slow reader, indeed he claimed to read no more than two books a year. Nevertheless, he was socially adept and could talk to people with ease, so his days at prep school were not too painful. His letters home show that he was already a keen birdwatcher, and he often described to his mother the different birds he had seen on his walks.

Though Kathleen continued to grieve privately for the loss of her husband she gained great solace from seeing her son flourish and develop. Her work too brought her great satisfaction, and she enjoyed a busy and active social life amongst the highest circles of British society. She had little time for the civilised chatter that she encountered in many women's drawing rooms, preferring to talk politics or science with the men; indeed she clearly preferred the company of men to women, most of whom she regarded as rather empty-headed. Given her views, it is perhaps not surprising that she was in the forefront of the movement to stop the voting age of women being reduced to twenty-one. Men admired her and in some cases were intimidated by her, but she was a good and loyal friend to many of those who sought her company and her advice. It was inevitable that in the end she would remarry, but to whom? Whoever she chose would become a father to the person she idolised more than anyone, her son, and only men of the highest character and standing would be eligible. One suitor in the early 1920s was Colonel Thomas Edward Lawrence, whose exploits in Arabia had made him a household name. He was attractive and amusing, and Kathleen was sorely tempted, but in the end she chose a more steadfast and reliable alternative, an MP and rising star in the Conservative Party, Edward Hilton Young, a war hero who had lost an arm during active service in France. The wedding took place in 1922, in the crypt of the House of Commons. Peter clearly got on well with Edward Hilton Young from the start. His soon to be stepfather was keenly interested in birds, and Peter hugely enjoyed the birdwatching expeditions they shared. One can't help imagining that this would be a plus point for Kathleen when considering a future stepfather for her son. Edward Hilton Young later wrote a book on birds entitled *A Bird in the Bush*, published in 1936 with illustrations prepared for the book by Peter.

Anyone hoping to visit Peter's birthplace in Buckingham Palace Road and find a blue plaque on the wall will be disappointed, for the house was pulled down to make way for the Green Line Coach Station. The family moved from Buckingham Palace Road to a house called Leinster Corner at 100 Bayswater Road. It had a separate building in the grounds which Kathleen converted into a studio. By a curious coincidence, the house had once belonged to J. M. Barrie, and it was in this garden room that he had written *Peter Pan*. By this time, Peter had a half-brother, Wayland, who had been born in 1923. It was around the time of the move to Leinster Corner that Peter was introduced to Evelyn Cheeseman, curator of insects at London Zoo, who fed his interest in natural history and insects in particular. She must have been impressed by his artistic skills as she invited him to make a drawing of the caterpillar of the privet hawk-moth to illustrate a book she was writing. This was the first time that a drawing of Peter's would be reproduced in print.

It was the author, H. G. Wells, who recommended to Peter's mother that he should attend Oundle School. Oundle had a good reputation for both engineering and natural sciences and seemed to Kathleen to be a place where Peter might thrive. The headmaster was Kenneth Fisher whose son, James Fisher, was to become a good friend of Peter's in later years. Shortly before starting at the school in 1932, Peter attended a field course organised for pupils of Oundle at the Marine Biological Association at Plymouth, where they studied the rich marine life of the foreshore. Peter was fascinated by the huge array of lifeforms that teemed in the rock pools. Here he had his first intimation of the vast web of life that connects all living things. It may also be the case that this new-found fascination with marine life was the catalyst for the enthusiasm with which he took to scuba-diving in later years.

Once installed at Oundle, he threw himself into school life, though he found it hard to conform to some of the school traditions, particularly where sport was concerned. He wrote in his autobiography *The Eye of the Wind*:

> I had a strong aversion to watching other people play football. I have never enjoyed watching other people doing anything so much as doing it myself. In this context I became a violent rebel. I could not bear standing frigidly on the touchline shouting wanly 'Come on, Ound-erl' in unison with a lot of equally bored contemporaries.

His attempts to avoid the tedium led to corporal punishment on a good number of occasions, indeed he claimed to be more beaten than any other boy in his house.

His preferred way of spending free time at school lay not in watching team sports but in doing anything related to natural history. One early passion was coarse fishing, for which there were excellent opportunities nearby. He turned out to be rather good at it, but unlike most boys who fished, Peter would make careful drawings of his catch, which he would later send to the Natural History Museum. Several very large specimens that he caught found their way to London Zoo. Already, at an early age, it seemed natural to him to be in contact with the leading scientific organisations in the country and to be sending them drawings and specimens. With his friend Michael Dilke, he made a collection of animal skins, starting with two badgers that had been killed on a nearby railway line. He also collected caterpillars of moths, particularly hawk moths and kept them on his windowsill, where they eventually hatched. Various animals and birds were kept in his room, including rabbits, three species of owl and pipistrelle bats. Ferreting for rabbits was another pastime, one which augmented his pocket money.

Kenneth Fisher, the headmaster, used to lead birdwatching trips for a small group of pupils. Visits were made to the floodplain of the River Nene where Peter had his first encounters with wildfowl. In winter, the wet fields harboured thousands of teal, wigeon, mallard and shoveler and, most thrillingly for Peter, small numbers of grey geese, in particular white-fronted and pink-footed geese. This was Peter's first introduction to these birds which were to have such a profound influence on his later life.

He and Michael Dilke produced a book entitled *Adventures Among Birds*. Michael wrote the text and Peter produced the illustrations. It might have languished in a drawer as a school project, but a fellow pupil, John Brereton, had connections with a publisher so the book was printed and published and went on sale. The authors were described as 'three schoolboys' as Peter did not want any success the book might have to be as a result of his famous name.

Fortunately too, Oundle was a school with a strong tradition in art. Apart from formal lessons there was an art club with its own studio, an old tin shed that had been converted from a chapel. Here, free from the strictures of formal tuition, the boys were free to engage in whatever medium and subject they chose, and Peter clearly took advantage of the facilities. His friend, painter Keith Shackleton, who attended the school some fourteen years later, wrote of finding in the shed a series of etchings that Peter had made during his time at Oundle. They were remarkably accomplished, and prints were taken afresh from the plates. Images included a lizard, a hawk moth (of course), a kingfisher and a trout.

Holidays from Oundle were to prove equally formative in different ways. On a school holiday in the Pyrenees, Peter first learned to ice skate and took to it, as to so many other pursuits, with single-minded intensity. His proficiency on the ice led him to take up ice dancing, and Christmas holidays were taken in St Moritz to improve and develop his technique. Though always happy to be demonstrating his skills alone in the middle of the ice, pairs skating brought him into contact with a succession of pretty girls or 'the juvenile females of my species' as he described them. It was on the ice at the Ice Club in Westminster that he collided with someone who would, in future years, become a close friend and supporter, the actor James Robertson Justice.

On a summer holiday on the Norfolk Broads, he was taught to sail by his stepfather, very quickly becoming adept and able, by the end of the holiday, to handle a sailing boat on his own. Other holidays were taken at Fowey in Cornwall where for three years they rented Menabilly, the house that would eventually belong to Daphne du Maurier. Partly ruined, the house had extensive grounds to explore and a colony of greater horseshoe bats in the roof. Fowey offered further opportunities for sailing, particularly during regatta week. Peter's stepfather owned a thatched cottage called The Lacket, near Marlborough. Holidays there, meant long walks over the downs where Peter took an interest in the wild flowers that grew in profusion and made a series of watercolour paintings of them. When Peter was seventeen, his guardian, Viscount Knutsford, invited him to join him for a holiday at a shooting lodge he had rented at Inverewe in northern Scotland. Here, Peter learned the art of deer stalking and shot his first stag, something that made quite an impression on him.

Oundle School had been a good choice for Peter; it offered him a substantial opportunity for free expression, allowing him to unlock some of the passions and pursuits that would occupy him in later years. That pupils were encouraged to develop their personal interests alongside more formal tuition suited Peter's temperament perfectly, and the school provided a good preparation for his forthcoming adult life. H. G. Wells had offered sound advice.

2

A Fire Ignited

In September 1927, Peter went to Trinity College, Cambridge, to study natural sciences, a subject which would include zoology, biology, physiology and geology. His previous life at boarding school made the transition to university life a relatively easy one. He was fortunate to be granted rooms in the Great Court where he quickly created an aviary in his room, presumably with the agreement of his room-mate Humphrey Trevelyan, whose father was a friend of Peter's stepfather.

It seems that in the early days he settled well to his studies. For recreation, he joined the Trinity Foot Beagles, whose activities would have taken him out into the surrounding countryside. A fellow beagler, Francis Wayne, mentioned to Peter that he knew where they could go snipe shooting, so Peter sent home for his father's old shotgun which he had purchased when invited to shoot at Sandringham. On their first outing, Peter put up a snipe in front of him and managed to kill it with his first shot. He regarded this as something of a fluke, this being his first ever attempt at shooting at a flying bird. Fluke or not, it was a shot that set him on the road to becoming a wildfowler. Here was a way of combining his longing for excitement and adventure with his passion for birds and the wild places where they lived.

Soon, Peter was returning regularly to the fens with a group of friends that included Michael Dilke, an old friend from Oundle and fellow undergraduate Christopher Dalgety. In winter, the rivers that drained the fens through Cambridgeshire overflowed, forming vast expanses of flooded meadowland called the Washes. These teemed with wild duck and other waterbirds which provided exciting sport for the group of friends. Any type of bird was a suitable quarry; the list of species they shot included wigeon, teal, coot, goosander, lapwing and redshank. Peter began to keep a diary full of detailed records of their activities and the birds they shot. Peter later wrote of this diary in *The Eye of the Wind*:

> The diary is by and large – and I have faced it – a rather tedious document; it is concerned too much with the very precise details of our movements … The diaries record much irrelevant detail … They fill six thick volumes covering the next six years – a fascinating monument to the misapplication of time. Yet perhaps they have some bearing on the kind of chap I was at the age of eighteen.

Christopher Dalgety owned a second-hand punt called *Penelope* (the Latin name for wigeon), on which he had mounted a borrowed punt gun and which he kept at Sutton, a village in the fens. He invited Peter to join him on duck shooting excursions, and Peter was entranced. Here was an entirely different but extremely exciting form of wildfowling. It took considerable skill to propel the unwieldy boat while lying flat in the bottom out of sight of their quarry, bringing it to a close proximity to the resting birds before letting fire with the gun mounted on the front. Often a protracted stalk in the punt would lead to nothing. On other occasions everything fell into place, and they would kill a large number of duck with one shot. On one occasion they saw three grey geese and attempted unsuccessfully to bag them. Peter realised that to be proper wildfowlers they would have to include geese among their quarry, so at Christmas 1927 he went to Wells-next-the-Sea in Norfolk, where large flocks of pink-footed geese wintered and were hunted.

Just as the snipe he shot back in September proved a pivotal moment, so did his visit to Norfolk. He had no success in shooting any geese, but he clearly fell under their spell, writing lyrically of the sight of skein after skein of geese arriving in vast numbers overhead, with the sound of their calls filling the sky. Perhaps here, for the first time, he fell truly in love with the birds that would remain a passion for the rest of his life. It would be some time before he gave up wildfowling, but now the lure was not just the thrill of the hunt; his desire to kill wildfowl was inextricably mixed with his love for the birds and the wild places in which they lived. It might be supposed that these two conflicting desires would present Peter with a moral dilemma. How could he want to kill and maim the very creatures for which he had developed such a passionate regard? He was clearly aware of this conflict, but in the early days he was able to rationalise his feelings without difficulty. In *The Eye of the Wind* he wrote:

> If anyone asked me, and they frequently did, how I could equate the killing with my evident love of the living birds, my answer was given without hesitation. They were man's traditional quarry and it was part of man's instinct to hunt; it was part of the bird's instinct to be hunted. My delight and admiration for the wild geese was based as much upon their supreme capacity to remain watchful and to look after themselves as it was upon their beauty and grace. There was nothing sentimental about my regard for them.

At the beginning of 1928, Peter went with Christopher Dalgety to Terrington Marsh on the edge of the Wash, which turned out to be such an excellent place for wildfowling that they used the code name 'Sandbanks' when talking about it, to prevent others from knowing where it was. Here, in February, Peter shot his first wild goose, a bean goose, a species that was as uncommon then as it is today.

The punt *Penelope* was subsequently deemed inadequate for their needs, so Peter and Christopher Dalgety had a new punt built by a boatbuilder in Cambridge and bought a second-hand muzzle-loading punt gun to mount in it. Christened the *Grey Goose*, the punt was sailed and rowed down into the fens to be kept at Oxlode on the Washes, just a little over five miles from Welney, where in years to come Peter would establish a wetland reserve to create a safe haven for thousands of wintering whooper and Bewick's swans, as well as countless numbers of other species of wildfowl. Now, Peter was away in the fens all the time, spending whole nights out hunting, often without any success, getting wet and muddy and snatching a couple of hours' sleep in the car or a hayrick. His passion was close to becoming an obsession.

It was around this time that Peter started painting ducks and geese in the wild, mostly in watercolour and in quite modest dimensions. In *The Eye of the Wind* he wrote:

> Basically I was painting on the roof of my cave, just as the Cro-magnon hunters had painted their quarry on theirs. Perhaps, like them, I was seeking some kind of magic which could be exploited to bring wildfowling success if the paintings were good enough.

He began to sell small paintings to college acquaintances, developing an aptitude for simple pencil or pen portraits of his friends which he could dash off in half an hour or so. His talent began to be known, and he was invited to mount an exhibition of about twenty of his watercolours at Bowes & Bowes, a bookseller in Cambridge, managing to sell a number of pictures for five guineas apiece. He had no idea that he could make a living from painting. He simply liked doing it, and the proceeds at least paid for his petrol as he drove to and from the fens. Peter's interest in ice skating continued, but there was no rink near Cambridge so it became an activity reserved for Christmas holidays when staying in London with his parents as there was a rink close to their home at Leinster Corner.

Another passion was sparked at this time. In the late 1920s, dinghy sailing was in its infancy but was adopted as a sport at Cambridge University where it came under the wing of the Cambridge University Cruising Club. It was at this point that Peter met Stewart Morris, an expert sailor who would go on to win an Olympic sailing gold medal in 1948. Morris was a founder of the Oxford and Cambridge Sailing Society. Races between the two universities became an annual event for which, in future years, participants would be awarded a half-blue. Peter was good enough to be selected several times to represent Cambridge in these races, and he crewed regularly for Stewart during summer regattas on the Norfolk Broads. Sailing came to fill the summer days while winter was reserved for shooting.

In the summer of 1930, Peter crewed for Morris in his sailing boat *Clover* which had been entered for the Prince of Wales Cup at Lowestoft. The Prince of Wales Cup, the British championship race for a class of fourteen-foot dinghy known as the International Fourteen, was first contested in 1927, becoming the premier event for dinghy racing in the United Kingdom. The racing in 1930 was problematic in very light winds, and *Clover* eventually came eleventh. Though not a particularly convincing performance, that year's racing introduced Peter to dinghy sailing at the very highest level, a sport that he would pursue with vigour in the coming years.

However, it was the autumn and winter that Peter lived for and the opportunity to return to the wild places that had become such a magnet for him. If the Washes were a wilderness, Terrington Marsh on the edge of the Wash was a much wilder landscape still. Here, huge expanses of mudflats lay exposed under enormous skies; Peter could be out all day and never see another living soul. The wildness and beauty of the place drew Peter beyond the fens, and he began to spend whole days and nights out on the salt marsh. *Grey Goose* was not a sea-going punt, so he and Christopher Dalgety now had a second, larger boat built, again in Cambridge. Named *Kazarka*, the Russian name for the red-breasted goose, this new vessel was twenty-four feet long with a twelve-foot cockpit and capable of being taken to sea, at least within the confines of the Wash. Peter and Christopher Dalgety took the boat down to Norfolk where their first sea-going voyage nearly ended in disaster. Starting out far too late in the day, they attempted to sail the boat from King's Lynn to the mouth of the River Nene. Darkness overtook them, and on a rising tide and in heavy seas they came close to foundering on the edge of the mudflats as they tried to find their way. After many hours they arrived in the mouth of the River Nene, making landfall a few yards from the lighthouse at Sutton Bridge which Peter would call home in years to come.

Because of her size and the nature of the creek where she was kept, *Kazarka* could only be launched one hour either side of high tide. This meant that any excursion had to be shorter than two hours in length or the punt had to be taken out on one tide and brought back on the next, meaning that it was necessary to spend ten to twelve hours on the boat. This fact, coupled with the distance between Cambridge and Terrington Marsh, meant that Peter would be away from college for a couple of days or nights at a time. Escaping from college required scrambling fifteen feet up a narrow gap between two walls to drop down into the street on the other side. For night after night, Peter would be out in the dark, sometimes lying on a mudbank for hours at a time in pursuit of his elusive quarry but always with the wild geese and their thrilling calls for company and the possibility of a successful shot and the excitement that came with it, to draw him on.

It was inevitable that all this activity would impact on his studies. Peter was staying out of college far longer than was actually permitted, climbing the college wall to get away and back, unseen. During the day his work would be impeded by tiredness while the mundane routine of study and reading which he found boring, paled by comparison with the excitement of his other life out in the wild. In retrospect, it is surprising that matters did not come to a head sooner than they did, but eventually the inevitable happened. A letter was sent to his parents, and Peter received an admonishing letter from his stepfather. Edward Hilton Young had attained a first at Cambridge and had been President of the Student Union, so his frustration with his stepson must have been all the greater.

Peter's reply gives a clear insight into his thoughts about his studies at the time.

> Somehow or other being out in the wilds seems so much more necessary to me than learning the fossils of the Devonian period that I cannot quite manage to 'put it from me'. It's such a rare thing to be able to enjoy and understand a wild place. That sounds stupid I know but it's what I feel. Anyone can learn the names of fossils and the classification of animals but I don't want to do things that anyone can do. Anyone can't paint – and I suppose that's why I like it, and anyone can't understand ... and get the best out of the element and the wastes – the places where 'anyone' wouldn't even want to go. I suppose it's scope for imagination that I want and there isn't any that I can find in the inside of a dogfish.

There is a certain irony in the fact that Peter's stepfather's brother was Geoffrey Winthrop Young, a leading British mountaineer before the First World War. He too had studied at Trinity College and had written a short climbing guide, *The Roof-Climber's Guide to Trinity*, a volume which Peter had no doubt found useful when planning his illicit scrambles in and out of college. Peter indeed produced several drawings for the second edition of the book.

It was not laziness that impeded Peter's studies. It was simply that, for him, he couldn't see the point of the work he was required to undertake at university while at the same time, the lure of the wild places was irresistible to him. He was passionately interested in the birds and animals of the saltings and marshes, how they behaved and interacted. The sciences of ethology (the study of animal behaviour) and ecology (the inter-relationships of people, animals and plants in their environment) were barely recognised at the time. It is interesting to speculate whether Peter would have applied himself more rigorously to his university work had these sciences been available to him as legitimate areas of study.

It could be argued that the influence of his father cast a long shadow over Peter's struggle to find his path in life. His was an example that Peter could not emulate directly for fear of never matching up to an impossible level of expectation; Peter could never become an explorer, polar or otherwise. But the desire to be different, to strike out alone where others would not or could not follow, to try to be the best at whatever he undertook, this was his father's legacy, a legacy which would influence his choices again and again in later life. The boy had indeed become interested in natural history, a fire had been ignited and it was going to be impossible to put out the flames.

In the meantime, something had to be done. As things stood, Peter was at risk of failing to obtain his degree. Kathleen was deeply disappointed with Peter's academic performance and blamed herself for indulging him. She wondered whether she had spoiled him too much when she had let him take her car to Cambridge while she walked or took the bus instead. She worried why he seemed so indifferent to his studies and decided that she had sent him to Cambridge too early, though he was much the same age as all his fellow undergraduates.

There was, of course, something else for which Peter held a keen interest. All through his time at university he had never stopped painting altogether. He had had his small success with the exhibition at Bowes & Bowes and had made a little money from his work. Could this be the solution to his problems? Certainly, if he turned to art full time, he might be able to combine his pleasure in painting with his love for the wild places and the geese for which he had developed such a passion. A decision was made. He would switch to a degree which combined zoology, botany and the history of art.

To be able to make the change in his field of study, Peter had to stay on at Cambridge for an extra term in the autumn of 1930. The gravity of the upheaval must have hit home because Peter rented a shoot at Fulbourn Fen, just three miles from Cambridge. In this way he could continue with his sport close to home without the risk that he would be once again neglecting his studies through long trips out to the Wash. Though *Kazarka* was back at her moorings on Terrington Marsh, he went there rarely. It was during this final term at Cambridge that Peter met Michael Bratby who invited him to go pigeon shooting with him. A friendship developed which was to last a lifetime; Michael would provide staunch support to Peter during the early days of the Severn Wildfowl Trust after the war. Peter undertook extra studies during the autumn term, realising that it was the only way to successfully graduate, given the change in direction. He finally got his degree at the end of 1930, no doubt breathing a huge sigh of relief. What he may not have realised at the time was just how valuable the scientific components of his degree would be in the coming years. On the afternoon of his final exams he went snipe shooting to celebrate. Pursuit of the snipe then, represented the beginning and the end of his shooting days at Cambridge.

3

A Bird in the Hand

At the time he made his momentous decision to change his degree to include the history of art, Peter wasn't sure that he would ever be able to make a living from painting. For him it was another of his passions, the thing he most enjoyed doing when he wasn't outdoors. In 1929, following his modest success with the exhibition at Bowes & Bowes in Cambridge, he had had some watercolours of wild geese reproduced in black and white to accompany an article on shooting he had written for *Country Life* magazine. There was no indication however that there was a wider public interest in paintings of waterfowl in flight, and he still wasn't sure if he could make his living in this way. During his Cambridge years, he had produced a series of portraits of well-known university figures which were published in *Granta* magazine. Here, possibly, might exist a way of earning money in the future; but first he needed formal training in painting. With the portfolio he had already established, he was able to gain a place at the Royal Academy in London to study fine art, beginning in the autumn of 1931. Before that, it was arranged that he would study at the Munich State Academy in Germany.

Peter wrote of his time in Munich with great affection. He lodged with the family of one of the professors at the academy, Professor Angelo Jank, who specialised in painting animals. On arrival, Peter spoke no German at all, so took lessons twice a week. This, combined with his immersion in a German-speaking household, brought reasonable proficiency in a fairly short space of time. As at Cambridge, he flung himself into the pursuit of a range of interests, some old, some new. During the early part of 1931 there were plenty of opportunities to go ice skating. The World Ice Skating Championships were held that spring in Berlin, and Peter flew there to attend and enjoy the performances. There he ran into his old tutor from England, Bernard Adams, who told him that if he gave him two years of his time, he could make him world champion. Peter was momentarily tempted but in the end declined. He wasn't sure that he could give up two years of his life in pursuit of something which, in the end, he regarded as an art form and not properly a sport. As the year progressed, ice skating was replaced with ballroom dancing, another activity which gave him the opportunity to meet young women. There was one girl in particular, one of the younger sisters in the household, to whom he formed a particular attachment, which it seems was reciprocated.

As a student, Peter was entitled to half-price tickets at the Opera House. Despite his love for classical music, Peter had never taken to opera, possibly because there were few opportunities to see it performed in Cambridge. Now his eyes were opened. He became a real enthusiast, returning to see performances two or three times a week. Wagner was a particular favourite; he saw the *Ring Cycle* four times during his stay in Germany. Another favourite was Richard Strauss's *Rosenkavalier*. On a memorable occasion, Strauss came to Munich to conduct the opera himself. A friend of Peter's who was a music student knew the family where Strauss was staying and took Peter to meet the great man. Strauss, it turned out, had a particular passion for the game of poker, and the two students were invited to join a game with the great man.

As winter turned to spring, Peter began to spend time in the village of Oberau in the Loisach valley which lay in the foothills of the Alps, south of Munich. He went with fellow Englishman Stevie Johnson who was learning German and was a keen fly fisherman. As spring turned to summer, the valley became carpeted with wild flowers, the meadows teemed with life, and Peter realised how much he missed the wild places which had played such an important part in his life during his Cambridge years. There were fish to be caught in the streams, miles of paths through beautiful, empty countryside and later, fresh wild strawberries and the smell of new-mown hay. Peter's descriptions of the valley that summer are as lyrical as any he wrote about his beloved marshes back in England; he clearly remembered his time spent in the German countryside with great affection.

Back at the academy in Munich, things were not going so well. Peter loved painting and drawing, and had done so as long as he could remember, yet he struggled with the discipline required to develop the techniques it was considered one had to master to become a serious artist. His mother held the view that an artist was born not created; all you needed to develop your artistic skills were endless time, materials and suitable subjects on which to practise. Peter recalled that his first ever painting in oils, created in Munich, baffled his teacher. It was of a flight of geese silhouetted against a fiery sky, a subject which the professor could not conceive as a suitable choice for a painting. Peter nevertheless stuck at it. After all, he had made a big decision the previous year to train as an artist. If he gave in now, what would be left? His studio painting of a horse he described as 'inescapably a horse ... inescapably that horse. As a portrait it was really quite a good likeness, but as a painting it was dull and pedestrian to a sad degree'. The painting was described by his teacher as 'technically, not too bad'. In Peter's world 'not too bad' was no different than 'terrible'. He wanted to be the best and this seemed not to be the way to achieve it. During his time away, Peter had painted from memory some of the animals and birds he had encountered in the Loisach valley. His teacher noted with some acuity that these seemed to interest Peter far more than the horse. The clues were all there in front of Peter, but at that stage he was unable to see the essential truth, that the skill had been there all the time; all it needed was the passion for his subject to unlock his ability. But that insight was still a couple of years away.

During the early part of the 1930s, Germany was a popular holiday destination for the British who went in large numbers, attracted by the scenery, the food and the culture. Very few took much notice of the rise of the National Socialist German Workers' Party and its fanatical leader, Adolf Hitler. Peter was certainly aware of its existence, indeed he went with one of the sons of the family with whom he was staying to see Hitler speak at a *bierkeller* in Munich. He recalled he was impressed with his oratory but felt that nobody could take him seriously. A more ominous note was sounded when the son of a family friend got engaged to a Jewish girl. Frau Jank, Peter's landlady, a woman who had been nothing but kind, charitable and friendly during his stay, was horrified that this youth was, in her view, throwing his life away. How could he be so foolish and so unkind to his parents in this way? The matter gave Peter pause for thought and he found the family's attitude disturbing and alarming; until this moment he had had no experience of any sort of prejudice. What he could not have foreseen at that time was that the ranting man in the *bierkeller* and the sinister prejudice of his hosts, would lead in just a few years to a maelstrom into which he, and everyone he knew and loved, would be swept.

Back in England, in the autumn of 1931, Peter began his first term studying fine art at the Royal Academy Schools in London. He quickly settled into the new routine; this time he clearly enjoyed the practical aspects of the work and was interested in the theory too; after all, the course was going to make him better at something he loved doing. In *The Eye of the Wind,* he recalled being amazed at the skill of his fellow students and felt that he lagged some way behind when it came to technical ability. Not surprisingly perhaps, the artworks he felt most satisfied with were a series of decoy geese made out of rolled-up wire, covered with canvas and painted. As part of their training, students had to study the works of the great artists and undertake practical studies to show they understood the theories and techniques their works embodied. One such exercise was to create a painting with a classical motif, in Peter's case, the baptism of Christ in the River Jordan. In Peter's version, two tiny figures stood in the river in the far distance. In the foreground, flocks of geese and ducks fed on the rich vegetation on the banks of the Jordan. His final assessment of his time at the Royal Academy was that the training was of great value to him. Nevertheless, despite his interest in the work he was doing, his main focus was, once again, elsewhere.

Being back in England meant that Peter was able to return once again to his beloved Terrington Marsh. Very soon it was as if he had never been away, as the hunting excursions with his friends in *Kazarka* resumed once more. Peter's mother continued to take a close interest in her son's activities and was concerned that once again, as at Cambridge, Peter was neglecting his studies. She saw the beginnings of a pattern and wondered whether he would stay the course at the Royal Academy. Peter was living at home, so she was therefore well aware of how often he was neglecting his studies to go shooting.

As in previous years, Christopher Dalgety was a regular wildfowling companion, but they were now joined by David Haig Thomas who Peter had met as an undergraduate at Cambridge. Peter and his friends had long been following the skeins of pink-footed geese as they flew inland to feed on the potato crops in the fens. They had got to know many of the farmers in the area, one of whom was a man called Will Tinsley who farmed near Holbeach, around twenty-five miles from the marsh and who was also a hunter and a passionate ornithologist. Will had a pond at his farm where he kept a number of ducks as well as some geese that he had shot but not killed and which he had nursed back to health. By this time, Peter's love of watching the wild geese in flight and at rest had become almost as important as his passion for shooting them. He was not ready to give up hunting them, not yet at least, but seeing what Will Tinsley was doing was doubtless one of the main spurs that got him thinking about keeping a few birds himself if he could. The problem was, that the only birds he ever had in his hand were ones that he had just shot. Nursing the odd injured bird back to health was one thing, but it was hardly an acceptable operating method for assembling a collection of wildfowl. How then to actually catch birds without shooting them first? Whether or not Peter expressed these thoughts to Will is unknown, but his life was about to change. On 5 March 1932, Will took Peter to meet a friend of his, Billy Williams, who ran the duck decoy at Borough Fen near Peterborough. Peter was aware of duck decoys, but he had never thought to learn how they worked, nor indeed it seems, had he ever considered their potential for catching ducks alive and keeping them for enjoyment.

The word decoy comes from the Dutch for a duck cage, *eende kooi*. The decoy itself is an ancient method of catching ducks for food. A series of water channels, each covered by a tunnel of netting, surrounds a large pool. The channels, which are called pipes, curve away from the pool and get progressively narrower along their length. Alongside each of the pipes is a series of screens behind which the decoyman can hide without being seen by the birds on the pool. Ducks on the pool are attracted into the pipes by one of three methods. The pool is so arranged that there is nowhere along the banks for ducks to rest; by creating resting areas just inside the pipe entrances, ducks will be encouraged into the mouths of the pipes. Alternatively, the resting places can be baited with food which will also attract the birds. The third and most interesting method is to lure the ducks into the pipe using a trained dog. In the wild, ducks will group together and swim towards a predator in order to keep it in sight. They will only do this if the predator is upwind, since ducks take off into the wind and feel safer facing in the direction from which it is blowing. The dog is trained to run around the screens, appearing and disappearing in front of the ducks and moving progressively further up the pipe until a group of ducks following it have entered some distance into the pipe. At this moment, the decoyman appears in the first gap between the screens where he can be seen by the ducks in the pipe but not by those on the pool. Taking fright, the ducks fly up the pipe and are caught in the net at the end.

In the eighteenth century, there were over 200 decoys operating in England, and many were serious commercial businesses. A skilled decoyman could harvest in excess of a ton of duck meat a week to send to the markets in London. In the early nineteenth century, during the winter of 1802 to 1803, over 5,000 ducks were caught at Borough Fen. One of the oldest working decoys in Britain, Borough Fen had been in operation since before 1670, during which time it had been run exclusively by the Williams family, the role of decoyman passing from father to son, down through the generations; Billy was the latest Williams to hold the post. Decoy dogs traditionally all have the same name, and at Borough Fen there are twenty-five gravestones, each engraved with the name Piper. The decoy lake at Borough Fen occupied two and a half acres set in seventeen acres of woodland; each of the eight pipes was between 150 and 180 feet in length.

Peter was fascinated by the decoy, not only because it was a means of catching ducks without shooting them first, but also because there was a great deal of skill involved in making a catch. Just as in shooting, the decoyman had to use all his cunning to outwit the quarry; once again man was pitting his wits against wild creatures, and the outcome was by no means certain. He started visiting the decoy on a regular basis and was able to stay in the adjacent farmhouse. Billy Williams was doubtless happy to have the company and assistance (unpaid) of this personable young man so welcomed having him around.

After getting to know the routines and becoming adept in the art of making a catch, Peter asked Billy for permission to create a small enclosure and keep examples of the rarer species of duck that were caught. Billy was himself a lover of wild birds, and given that Peter was assisting him at the decoy, he agreed. A pen was built and Peter, for the first time in his life (but not the last), began to keep a selection of ducks which he could enjoy. He now borrowed his mother's 16 mm cine camera and made a film about the decoy and how it operated. One frustrating aspect of working at the decoy was that there was no place from where he could have an uninterrupted view of the pool which was entirely screened off to avoid disturbing the ducks. In the early summer of 1932, Peter had his appendix removed and went to the decoy to convalesce. What a fine idea it would be, he thought, to construct a wooden observation hut which could be approached from behind screens and from which he could have an uninterrupted view of the pool without disturbing the birds. He put the idea to Billy who, probably with some reluctance, gave him permission to build the structure between the north and north-east pipes. A path was cut through thick vegetation to the lake shore where the hut was built. To avoid frightening the birds and antagonising Billy, Peter made the viewing aperture just six inches wide and half an inch deep. Thus was born the concept of the bird hide, that ubiquitous structure now found on reserves all over the world. Peter had little idea at the time what a momentous moment it was when he first stepped into the completed hide and looked out over the throngs of duck on the pool. During the following winter, there were times when in excess of 3,000 ducks would congregate together on the pool which was only 100 yards across. One reason for this was the pool's isolation among the potato fields; it was one of the few places in the local area where ducks could rest and feed.

Having filmed the duck on the pool as well as the operation of the decoy, Peter realised that the decoy and the ducks that gathered in such numbers would make an admirable subject for an illustrated talk. In November 1932, Peter showed his films and gave a talk to the Spalding Gentlemen's Society, the first of thousands of lectures and talks that he would make over his lifetime. This first occasion didn't pass without mishap. The bulb in the projector blew, and while a new bulb was located, Peter kept the audience entertained by drawing ducks and geese from memory on the blackboard. This proved extremely popular and would become a regular feature of talks in the future.

During the winter of 1932, Peter returned frequently to Borough Fen, staying in the farmhouse where he began to paint in earnest. Kathleen was concerned about the time he was spending away from the Royal Academy and was doubtless conflicted when, in January 1933, he told her that he was going back to the decoy again to paint. She reluctantly told him she would allow him to go provided he came back with eight canvases, obviously still of the view that she could tell her twenty-three-year-old son what to do. In the event, she was relieved when he returned in a cheerful frame of mind a fortnight later, with many more than eight paintings in the car.

Peter had been painting and drawing pretty much from the time when he was first able to hold a pencil. He had already painted ducks and geese in flight but had painted other subjects too; much of his early work had been in watercolour. It hadn't been until his time at

Munich that he had first attempted to use oil paints. Now, during the winter of 1932 to 1933, inspired by the birds all around him and by his vivid memories of nights and days out on the marshes, he began to paint canvas after canvas of geese and ducks in flight in all seasons and weathers, all of them with a new assurance and confidence. All his agonising about whether the horse was 'right', all his slightly gloomy thoughts that there were so many better painters than him, disappeared. Nobody could paint geese in flight like he could because nobody had spent night after night out in the wild places as he had. His considerable experience of the subject, together with his innate ability to draw and paint and his uncanny knack of freezing a moment in his mind's eye, resulted now in an avalanche of paintings of wild geese and ducks, each one fresh, new and alive. An art critic could no doubt find aspects of his style and approach to criticise, and he may not have been the best student during his time at the Royal Academy, but nobody looking at these paintings could fail to understand something of the great windswept spaces and the birds that lived free among them as he captured them that winter. Finally, he had escaped the nagging doubts about his future that had dogged him since his early days at Cambridge.

Despite his mother's concerns about his actions, Kathleen and Peter remained as close as ever. He was anxious to introduce her to his new world out in the fens so took her to Holbeach to meet Will Tinsley and some of his other friends. Kathleen wrote of the event in her diary: 'Attended a dinner party of a dozen farmers and their wives, they all dressed in velvet and fine linen, Pete and I in jerseys. Nice worthy folk with limited outlook' (*Cambridge University Library MS Kennet D/25*). At this remove, it is difficult to determine if she was aware of quite how condescending this view was. Whether anyone felt embarrassed by the disparity in dress code is not known, but what is clear is Kathleen's keen interest in everything that Peter did and her devotion to him, despite his apparent waywardness.

During the winter, working at Borough Fen and Will Tinsley's farm, he painted around forty canvases. In the spring of 1933, he submitted three of the Borough Fen canvases to the Summer Exhibition at the Royal Academy and two were selected for showing. In June, with Kathleen's help, a one-man exhibition was arranged at the gallery of Messrs Arthur Ackermann and Son in New Bond Street, London. The show was a great success and all but a handful of paintings were sold, achieving prices up to £25, quite a sum in those days. Following the exhibition, he received a number of commissions which meant that his paintings would now be seen and appreciated by even more people. At this time word of mouth was an important way of getting yourself and your work known to others. Now at least, Peter knew there was a good chance he could make a living from painting; it must have been a great relief to know that he had found a way to become financially independent. It must also have given him great pleasure to know that through his paintings he could engage and delight others with the landscapes and the birds that he so loved.

In the corner of the dining room in Peter's house at Slimbridge hangs a small watercolour painting, not of ducks and geese in flight but of a pool which is viewed from above like a map. Radiating from the pool are eight channels of water while in the top right-hand corner is a tiny drawing of a hut. The map is enclosed by a circular border, beyond which, in the four corners of the painting, there are ducks in flight in different weathers. Over the map is an arrow or pointer; the title describes the painting as a design for a wind vane at Borough Fen. No doubt the idea was that you could use such a device to tell which way the wind was blowing, knowledge that would determine which pipe would be in use that day. Peter chose to hang this tiny watercolour in a key location in the dining room of his house at Slimbridge where it would have reminded him of those days long ago, spent at the decoy. Before he went to Borough Fen he was an unknown painter with a passion for shooting. Just over a year later he had started collecting wildfowl, filmed them, given a talk about them, built his first ever bird hide, had his first one-man exhibition and made quite a lot of money in the process. Peter must have remembered Borough Fen with great affection and maybe recognised, as we do, that it was there that the Peter Scott we all remember first made his appearance.

Despite all the excitements at Borough Fen, Peter remained unable to catch and keep wild geese as they did not come to the decoy pool and were, in any case, too big to be caught in the decoy pipes. Peter continued to shoot and he still found it a thrilling experience, but we know that he was thinking about catching and keeping geese alive because he wrote about the idea in his book *Morning Flight* published a couple of years later in 1935.

One morning (in Spring 1932), two of us shot twenty-three greylags at flight. One of them was only wing-tipped, and we kept him alive, but it occurred to both of us that it would have been very much pleasanter if there had been only one dead and twenty-two alive. Instead of a load of corpses we might, had it been possible to catch them, have had as many fine live birds, which would have given us interest and enjoyment for years to come.

Once again, Will Tinsley provided the inspiration needed. He took Peter to meet a man who caught plovers using nets which were pivoted on poles and released by a rope held in tension. Peter adapted the equipment, making it more robust and able to cast a wider net. One of the problems with the original design was that the rope which was held in tension to release the poles often got in the way of the nets. Peter, ever resourceful, had sets of springs made which could be used to release the poles at speed. Nevertheless, the nets with which he experimented were tiny, covering only twenty-five square yards when spread. After several false starts, when nothing was caught, Peter finally caught his first goose in a net on 27 December 1932 on a farm in Norfolk, followed by further small catches later that winter. These birds were put onto the pond at Will Tinsley's farm. Of that first catch, Peter wrote in *Morning Flight,* 'I had one goose – a paltry bag, one might say, for so long a wait; but he was alive and well, and worth a dozen strung up by their necks.'

For Peter, at that time, the netting excursions, just like the hours spent pursuing wildfowl in his punt, were as much about the excitement of the hunt as making a catch. He had to spend endless hours setting up the nets in the dead of night and many more hours lying in a cold muddy ditch waiting for the birds to walk into the area where the net was prepared. For him it was all worth it if he could outwit even one bird and catch it alive. It was a way of continuing with the thrill of the hunt without killing or injuring the birds. Peter wrote in his diary:

Netting geese will, I believe, prove much more exciting than shooting them, and with the tremendous advantage that never a wounded bird will be lost, and that the prize will be a bag of fine live geese instead of bloody corpses.

Peter little knew how important rocket-netting would become for him in the years ahead.

4

To the Lighthouse

In summer 1933, Peter completed his studies at the Royal Academy. The course on which he had embarked lasted five years, but Peter had had enough after two years. Following his highly successful first exhibition at the Ackermann Gallery, he was convinced he could make his living by painting without needing to spend three further years studying. In *The Eye of the Wind* he wrote:

> I wanted things to happen ... For me to be happy things had to be happening, and in a curious way they seemed to happen all the time. It seems that I was serendipitous. Adventure was indispensable ...

The course of his life at that time was not simply the result of serendipity however; he was fortunate to have an indulgent mother and a supportive stepfather, while his own fierce determination to succeed in the things that most interested him also played a part. He was not at this time in immediate need of money; he had earned enough from his first exhibition to keep him going for the time being, and his parents were always willing to help out when required.

During his time at the Royal Academy he had lived with his parents at Leinster Corner while staying for weeks at a time at Will Tinsley's farm and at the house at Borough Fen. For some time he had been thinking about renting a disused lighthouse, one of two standing sentinel at the mouth of the River Nene, close to Terrington Marsh. His initial plan was to use it as a retreat during shooting excursions and as a place to store equipment. During his many days spent out on the marsh he would have seen the two small towers away in the distance. The lighthouses stood one hundred yards apart across the channel of the River Nene where it met the sea. They had never actually been used as lighthouses but were ornamental in nature, having been built at the end of the eighteenth century to commemorate the completion of the last phase of the draining of the fens.

The East Lighthouse, in which Peter expressed an interest, had been vacant for several years as it was considered too damp for occupation. It stood at the end of the sea wall where the River Nene entered the Wash and was surrounded on three sides by salt marsh. At spring tides, the building would be almost completely surrounded by water. The nearest village was Sutton Bridge, from where a road ran along the raised bank containing the river for two miles, after which one drove along the top of the grassy bank to the end where the lighthouse stood. This last section of the journey seemed somewhat perilous, particularly after heavy rain, and it is a wonder that nobody ever drove off the bank and into the river.

Peter secured a lease from the Nene Catchment Board and threw himself into making the place habitable. The lighthouse had four storeys, each one smaller than the one below, the top one containing a single room, little more than six feet in diameter. Peter repointed the brickwork to keep the damp at bay; a lean-to outside was converted into a kitchen and a small bathroom built beyond it. There was also a basement room reached by steps from outside, in which was living an itinerant vagrant called Charlie who made a living as a cockle picker and occasional handyman. Charlie continued to live on and off in the cellar, a sort of twentieth-century Caliban to Peter's Prospero.

For the first time, Peter was going to live completely independently, but, as always, he wanted to show his mother what he was doing. He therefore brought her down for the weekend to see his new project and to take her out into the marshes to watch the huge flocks of geese flying in. As ever on such excursions, Kathleen's doubts and worries about his lifestyle and prospects were dispelled by seeing him come to life in his natural surroundings. It was plain to her that he loved the world of the fens and the salt marsh, and that there he flourished and was happy. Kathleen herself possessed a lively and independent spirit, and she recognised the same restless energy in Peter. If this was what he wanted to do then she would be happy for him, whatever her reservations about his future success. In her diary she wrote of their visit:

It was fun being out with him those mornings ... He is so completely in his element there. A grand fellow. It must be right not to interfere too much with what appears to be a waste of time. It isn't work it's true, it does no good to anybody, it makes no money but – at any rate it does no harm to anybody and I think some good to yourself. Anyway I felt those nights I would not have him any other sort of boy at all! So there. (*Cambridge University Library MS Kennet D/25*)

When Peter arrived at his new home there was no fresh water available. The nearest supply was at the West Lighthouse across the river, so he simply laid pipes across the channel to connect to the supply. Large ships had occasionally sailed up the River Nene, and it was pointed out to Peter that a passing vessel would almost certainly cut through his water pipe. He was not concerned; if this happened he would simply wait for the boat to depart and then reconnect the supply.

There was a customs office at Sutton Bridge, managed by two officers. Every day at high tide, one of them would drive out to the East Lighthouse to hail any ships that might enter the river mouth. The officers had previously used the lighthouse as a shelter during the period around high tide. Now Peter was in residence, he felt obliged to allow them to sit in his living room-cum-studio on the ground floor while they waited. Eventually, a hut was built for them on the opposite bank, and Peter was left in peace. Fortunately, during Peter's time at the lighthouse, no ship of any size entered the river and his water supply remained undisturbed.

Quite soon after arriving, Peter decided to live at the lighthouse permanently and in time he added to the facilities, building himself a separate studio outside, enlarging the bathroom, building bunkhouse accommodation for guests and adding a porch and front door so that entry was no longer directly into the living room. All this cost a considerable amount of money, but Peter was unruffled. He knew something would turn up and he always had his painting to fall back on. Peter retained this attitude to money for most of his life; he was never reckless with his finances, but equally he never let the lack of funds prevent him from doing the things that he wanted to do. In addition, in later years, he proved extremely adept at persuading others with money to support the causes for which he strove.

Once the building was habitable, Peter's thoughts turned to establishing a collection of waterfowl. He had long admired Will Tinsley's geese and ducks at his farm and was also familiar with a collection held by Lord Lilford on his estate near Oundle, having been instrumental in adding specimens to it. During his university days, flight netting was still practised in England. Long panels of vertical nets were set up into which flew all manner of birds which were taken, often illegally and without permission. This was not an activity he would have wanted to engage in at the time as there was no skill involved; certainly it could not be regarded as a sport. Peter and his friends had been in the habit of releasing from the nets a variety of waders including redshank, grey plover, curlew, knot and dunlin and taking them to be introduced into Lord Lilford's aviaries. Other friends had now started keeping wildfowl, including Michael Bratby and Christopher Dalgety, and Peter was keen to do the same. The first enclosure was built just below the lighthouse, the netting enclosing a tiny area of salt marsh just a few yards across, with a permanent pool in the middle. Into the pen went the three geese that he had caught with his goose nets and which had been kept for him by Will Tinsley. Word of Peter's intentions had no doubt got about because he was offered a dozen pink-footed geese that had been caught in flight nets. These fifteen geese formed the nucleus of his first ever collection of birds.

Problems soon arose. A high spring tide swamped the netting allowing the geese to swim away across the flood. The birds had been pinioned and were therefore flightless. Peter was concerned for their safety, particularly given the prevalence of shooting in the area. Ultimately one goose returned of its own accord, and several more were brought back. Peter then built a larger, more substantial enclosure covering three acres, surrounding the lighthouse and including an area at the top of the sea wall; this began gradually to fill up with geese and ducks.

In the early days of the collection, Peter found that the geese, which formerly had been wild birds, were extremely wary of him and kept to the far side of the enclosure when he was around. Gradually however, they became used to him and eventually would come to be fed by hand. He realised that geese, like many living creatures, will adapt to circumstances over time, becoming quite tame when they realise that they are not threatened by their surroundings. This meant that the more people they saw over time, the more relaxed they would become in the presence of humans. As the collection grew, Peter took great delight in the wild birds that began to come into his enclosures, attracted by the crowd of birds around the lighthouse and the morning and afternoon feeds. The wild birds doubtless sensed that the birds in the enclosure were calm and unstressed and took this as a sign that it was a safe place to congregate. The lessons learned here would inform Peter's work after the war when the collection at the Severn Wildfowl Trust was founded. Today at Slimbridge, wild birds regularly join the collection birds in the pens, some coming to be fed with grain by the thousands of visitors who pass through the enclosures each week. Wild oystercatchers and herons, birds which outside the centre would be off at the first sign of human presence, will feed on the banks of the pools in full sight of the crowds. At the lighthouse, one particular pink-footed goose became very tame immediately upon arrival. Christened Annabel, she remained close by the lighthouse all winter then left in the spring for the northern breeding grounds. Peter assumed that was the last he would see of her so was delighted when she reappeared the following autumn and spent the following winter season in his company.

In 1935, Peter was best man at the wedding of his friend David Haig Thomas. While visiting David's home in Shropshire, Peter was shown the birds that were kept on the lake at the property; these included a pair of white-fronted geese that David had brought back several months previously from an expedition to Greenland. Peter was immediately struck by the appearance of the geese; they were much darker than the ones he was familiar with in Britain and had yellow bills rather than the usual pink. Initially he put this discrepancy down to the fact that the birds had been collected as goslings and fed an artificial diet on the ship back to England. He continued to consider the matter however, and two years later when David returned to Greenland, Peter arranged for him to send more white-fronted geese back to England. Four birds were duly delivered to the lighthouse and Peter saw at once that these birds were the same as the two in Shropshire, with their dark colouring and yellow bills. Clearly there was a chance that these birds, breeding on the west coast of Greenland, were a different race.

If they were a different race, the next question was, where did they spend the winter? Logic suggested that the birds that wintered in North America should be from the same race, given their winter feeding grounds would have to be somewhere south of west Greenland. Peter knew however that there were insufficient numbers gathering there in winter. He then recalled reading a description of white-fronted geese with yellow bills in a wildfowling book that had been published in the previous century, in Ireland. Could it be the case that the west Greenland birds wintered there? In 1939, Peter took a trip to Ireland where he managed to shoot three white-fronted geese, one of which was only wing-tipped and could be kept alive. All three had darker plumage and yellow bills. Peter contacted the well-known ornithologist H. F. Witherby and was able to demonstrate to him that the birds were clearly of a different race. Witherby included this information in *The Handbook of British Birds* which he was working on at the time.

In 1948, working with Christopher Dalgety, Peter was able to furnish the necessary scientific proof in the form of a bird shot in Ireland that had been ringed in west Greenland and which exhibited the same characteristics as the other birds, as did further live specimens. A new scientific name was assigned, and the discovery of the race was attributed to the two friends. In 1983, Christopher Dalgety donated his collection of sixty-three skins, representing nineteen European species of wildfowl, to the Wildfowl Trust; they included six skins of the Greenland white-fronted goose.

No sooner had Peter discovered the Greenland white-fronted goose than he had to take steps to protect it. Numbers declined rapidly during the 1950s, largely due to shooting both in Greenland, and in the British Isles. By the late 1970s, numbers had been reduced to 15,000, but a successful campaign by the Wildfowl Trust eventually brought almost complete protection, and numbers rose to 20,000 in 1985. No doubt Peter would be delighted to know that the occasional Greenland white-fronted goose still appears among the flocks of wild white-fronted geese at Slimbridge in some winters.

The collection at the lighthouse gradually increased, and Peter expanded the enclosure to seven acres which he surrounded with a fox-proof fence. By 1938, there were approximately 250 birds surrounding the lighthouse; driving up to Peter's door became an increasingly hazardous experience. Peter was often away so needed someone to look after the geese and ducks as they needed feeding twice a day. Initially he hired Charlie, the itinerant cockle picker, but he proved unsuitable as he was ill-disposed to the routine that was required. Peter then offered the job to a well-known local character,

Mackenzie Thorpe. Thorpe was a boxer, poacher and like Peter, a lover of wild geese. Their relationship thus far had been uneven and they had more than once crossed swords over shooting rights on Terrington Marsh. Thorpe proved a reliable employee however, and Peter felt safe leaving his precious collection in his care when he was away. Inspired by Peter's example and possibly aware of the money that Peter was making from his art, Thorpe took up painting and set up a studio in the cellar. He was sometimes able to pass himself off as 'Mr Scott' if visitors came to the lighthouse while Peter was away, and it has been said that he was not averse to signing one of his own paintings as a 'Peter Scott' and selling it to an admiring visitor.

Peter's initial intention was to keep examples of British native species only. These were the birds that he loved and which he had settled down to paint, once installed in the lighthouse. A visit to Walcot Hall in Shropshire a few years later changed all that. Brothers Ronald and Noel Stephens had gathered together the largest collection of waterfowl in England at that time, and their collection included a wide range of non-native species. At the time of his visit, Peter had recently had a successful exhibition of paintings and he decided to spend some of his money on some new non-native species of geese, returning to the lighthouse with a pair each of emperor geese and Ross's geese in his car. The birds were expensive, but Peter was able to justify the impact on his bank balance. As his art career took off, he had succeeded in having the cost of keeping his geese made tax-deductible since the birds, as models, were indispensable tools for his work as an artist. In order to include these new geese in the scheme he would need to paint them to demonstrate, if necessary, that they too were models for his work, but he took such delight in his new acquisitions that he felt it a small price to pay.

5

Racing Years

Another passion that was now reignited was Peter's love of sailing. For a number of years, Peter had joined his family on holidays in Norfolk. Here he had sailed with Stewart Morris and got to know members of the Colman family, whose famous mustard company was based nearby in Norwich. In 1933, one of the Colman sons, Alan, invited Peter to crew for him in his International Fourteen *Telemark* which had been built by up-and-coming boat designer, Uffa Fox. Peter leapt at the chance to gain further experience of this racehorse of the sailing world. His former sailing companion, Stewart Morris, had won the Prince of Wales Cup the previous year at Torquay. 'If he can do it,' thought Peter, 'why can't I?' Unfortunately, when the time came, Morris won the trophy for the second year in a row, while Alan Colman and Peter finished in twelfth place.

All was not lost however. Britain was sending three International Fourteens to the United States to compete with the Americans in a series of races to be held in the waters off Long Island. Alan's boat was chosen as one of the three, and he invited Peter to crew for him. During their time in America, Peter and a paid assistant diligently prepared the boats for racing each day and undertook all the post-race duties. The trip wasn't all sailing however. The British team members stayed with various wealthy families on Long Island and there were plenty of opportunities for socialising and entertainment. Peter stayed with the Roosevelt family and dined with the former president, Theodore Roosevelt. By the end of the trip, Peter felt he had learned a lot and was ready to own his own International Fourteen. On his return to England he commissioned Uffa Fox to build him one. Such an enterprise would have cost a great deal; his choice of boat builder indicates the confidence he now had in his ability to earn good sums of money through his painting. Since his first one-man exhibition in 1933, Peter had held exhibitions every year with the prices he could command for his work increasing steadily. Nevertheless, the commission of a sailing boat from Uffa Fox would have been a significant financial commitment. At the time, Fox was still only in his thirties but had already become the *enfant terrible* of the yachting world, a man who, because of his extraordinary design skills, could afford to ignore what he saw as some of the stuffier aspects of the upper echelons of British yachting.

Uffa Fox had his yard on a converted chain ferry moored on the River Medina near East Cowes on the Isle of Wight. Peter went down for the launch of his new boat accompanied by John Winter, a sailing acquaintance from his university days, who already owned an International Fourteen called *Lightning*. The two were destined to become firm friends.

Peter's new boat was given the name *Eastlight,* and she brought Peter a great deal of joy. Now for the first time he was skipper of one of these beautiful craft and he revelled in the excitement of sailing her. Once again he had found a pursuit which took him out into the wild places that he loved, a pursuit which, like wildfowling, required a considerable amount of skill. The play of wind against wave, the finely balanced control of the sails and the sheets and the sheer exhilaration of skimming at speed across the surface of the water all appealed to the adventurer in him. Once again, he was on the way to mastering something that not many other people could at this level of performance. As with any activity for which he developed a passion, he wanted to excel. He recognised his intensely competitive nature in *The Eye of the Wind* when he wrote:

> Inescapably I am and have always been a competitive sort of person. I cannot seem to undertake anything without sooner or later wanting to do it better than others. It is a defect which I clearly recognise, but cannot eliminate.

During the 1934 season, Peter came either first or second in half of the seventy races he sailed in *Eastlight*.

Another transatlantic competition was organised, this time a three-way contest between Britain, Canada and the United States, to be held in Toronto in Canada. Four boats were to represent Britain, and *Eastlight*, with Peter at the helm, was one of the boats selected to compete. Another selection was *Lightning,* skippered by John Winter. Stewart Morris was captain and Uffa Fox was the team manager. The British boats proved greatly superior to the American and Canadian ones, while *Eastlight* also won Canada's premier sailing dinghy competition, the Wilton Morse Trophy, making Peter the Canadian dinghy sailing champion that year. Back in England, Peter had high hopes of finally winning the Prince of Wales Cup which had now twice eluded him and which was to be held that year in Falmouth. In the event it was won by John Winter in *Lightning* and Peter came sixteenth. After the race, Peter sold *Eastlight* and bought another International Fourteen called *Whisper* which had come third in the Cup that year and whose wooden hull Peter admired. He entered *Whisper* for the Prince of Wales Cup the following year at Osborne Bay in the Isle of Wight. This time, he suffered a broken mast during the race and had to retire. It seemed that the Cup would never be his.

The following year, 1936, the Olympic Games were to be held in Germany, with the sailing events based at Kiel on the Baltic Sea. Peter decided to enter the trials for the British team, and to his amazement he won the event and was selected to represent his country with Stewart Morris as his number two. Before departing for Germany there was to be the small matter of the Prince of Wales Cup once again, which this year was to be held on the Clyde. Peter decided to sell *Whisper* to Michael Bratby and commissioned another boat from Uffa Fox, this one to be called *Daybreak*. On this occasion, Peter decided on an innovation. The International Fourteen had a centreboard made from phosphor bronze which weighed 100 pounds and kept the boat from capsizing in rough weather. Peter decided to replace it with one made from wood, but to prevent his competitors from finding out what he had done, he painted the wooden board with bronze paint. Before the race, he and his crew made a great pantomime of carrying it around as if it was made of heavy bronze. In the event he did better than he had ever done so far but still only came third behind Stewart Morris and John Winter in very heavy weather.

It is almost certain that this latest failure to win the Prince of Wales Cup spurred Peter on at Kiel. The racing was to be in a German designed sixteen-foot boat called an Olympic Monotype. Peter and the rest of the team had a brief opportunity to race with the boats in the Netherlands before the Games, but he entered the competition less prepared in this class of boat than his German competitors. In the event, he did well throughout the competition and in the final race was lying second in the silver medal position in front of the German competitor. Rounding a buoy, Peter's boat fractionally clipped the stern of the German; Peter put the mistake down to the fact that he sailed regularly in fourteen-foot boats and these were sixteen-footers. Whatever the cause, Peter immediately retired from the race without waiting for a challenge and so took the bronze medal. It was a disappointment which, at the time, was hardly assuaged by knowing that he had acted in a highly sportsman-like manner.

In 1937, undaunted, Peter planned his next campaign for winning the Prince of Wales Cup which this year was to be held at Lowestoft. He asked Uffa Fox to design another International Fourteen, the third that Uffa had built for him. This one was called *Thunder,* despite his friend John Winter pointing out that 'lightning' always came before 'thunder'. Peter came up with another ruse to try and fool the other competitors. He painted his wooden mast silver and let it be known that he had installed a new, lightweight, aluminium mast. It is doubtful whether this approach brought any psychological advantage but either way it wasn't needed for Peter finally won the Cup at his fourth attempt. He wrote of the occasion:

> The years of failure had perhaps built it up to a disproportionate significance. But even now I look back on those few minutes after the finishing gun as among the most triumphant and utterly satisfying moments of my life.

Peter wasn't satisfied to rest on his laurels however. For some time he and John Winter had been discussing racing tactics and had reached the conclusion that the best chance of success lay in dividing up the tasks on board in a different way. They decided that the crewman should be responsible for race tactics, while the skipper concentrated on making the boat go as fast as possible. They also realised that tiredness could be better kept at bay in a long race if skipper and crew switched over between race legs. Until now, Peter had been reluctant to team up with John because his friend had already won the Prince of Wales Cup and he hadn't. If he were to win the race with John he would never know if he could have done it on his own. Now, with his own victory under his belt, it was time to put their plans into action.

A new boat was commissioned from Uffa Fox. The boat, called *Thunder and Lightning,* was jointly owned though each kept his own boat in case the experiment didn't work. For this new dinghy they designed a revolutionary piece of equipment which they christened the trapeze. The crew would wear a harness attached by a wire to the masthead. In strong winds, he would stand with his feet on the side of the boat and lean out horizontal to the water, allowing the helmsman to steer much closer to the wind. A wooden centreboard would lighten the dinghy, since the extra force of the trapeze obviated the need for a heavy bronze centreboard. The boat was finished shortly before the Prince of Wales Cup at Falmouth in 1938, so they had no time to try it out or its new secret weapon, in race conditions. It says much for the confidence of the two men that they went into the most prestigious dinghy race in the British calendar without ever having experimented properly with their new invention. Worried that their competitors might cry foul after the race, they announced their use of the trapeze the night before. Most of the other crews thought they were foolish to rely on an untried gadget, but nobody tried to have the device banned. In the event, the following day, *Thunder and Lightning* swept to victory. Nobody now dared call for their disqualification, given the opportunity they had had to object the night before. The Yacht Racing Association's Dinghy Committee had other ideas however, and they decided to ban the trapeze in future races. As a past winner of the Prince of Wales Cup, Peter had been made a committee member of the Yacht Racing Association, so it seemed a little unfair to him that, following his triumphant win using the trapeze, he was instructed to write the rule that would ban its future use. The trapeze was disallowed thereafter until its reintroduction in 1955. *Thunder and Lightning,* the boat on which its use was so ably demonstrated, was subsequently donated to the National Maritime Museum in Greenwich where it remains to this day.

Shortly after his second Prince of Wales Cup win, Peter returned to Canada with a British sailing team and three International Fourteens, now as team captain. Michael Bratby was team manager, but this time things didn't go Britain's way; the Canadians had upped their game, having learned about small boat design from the British, and won the competition after a British boat was disqualified. The racing took place in the shadow of the Munich crisis in September 1938, though few who enjoyed the sailing that autumn realised that there would be no more international competitions for several years to come. Peter was to have one more opportunity to sail. In 1939, shortly before the outbreak of the Second World War, he took *Thunder and Lightning* to Fritton to compete in the local regattas on the Norfolk Broads and in the sea races at Lowestoft for one last time. Despite having won the Prince of Wales Cup twice in two years, the threat of impending war took some of the magic out of the sailing. Peter recalled being in the winning position in a race at Lowestoft and not feeling at all elated. He looked back across the sparkling sea at the colourful sails ranged behind him and felt nothing but sadness that all of this was about to come to an end.

6

New Horizons

After his move to the lighthouse at Sutton Bridge, Peter had finally found his confidence as an artist. He now painted steadily, adopting larger canvases and painting in oils. His ability to capture fine detail with accuracy was now coupled with a confidence and a new freedom of expression, which resulted in paintings with big landscapes and skies, all created with a new and flourishing assurance. Each year, there was a one-man exhibition at the Ackermann Gallery in Bond Street where he would exhibit approximately forty new paintings. The great and the good began to come to his exhibitions; on one occasion Queen Elizabeth (mother of Queen Elizabeth II) attended and bought a painting.

Once established in the lighthouse, Peter was also free to continue with his shooting, without the distraction of studying. Despite the fact that he tended a group of geese at the lighthouse with loving care, his passion for the sport remained undimmed. His friend David Haig Thomas had rented a shoot at Brogden Marsh in Westmorland, and Peter was often to be found there in the winter with David and with Christopher Dalgety. At Cambridge, Peter had tried to combine his love of shooting with his university work and his work had suffered. Now, during the winter months, Peter was free to indulge his twin passions of shooting and painting without hindrance; as before, the one continued to inform the other. In the summer months, as we have seen, sailing came to occupy much of his time.

Peter was finding other ways to make money too. In 1935, he completed his first book, *Morning Flight,* about his adventures out on the fens and marshes. It included a chapter about his time at Borough Fen and was lavishly illustrated with his paintings, many of them created during the winter he spent at the decoy in 1932. The book quickly sold out and went through several reprints; it was to remain in print right through the Second World War. A second book entitled *Wild Chorus* followed in due course and achieved similar success. Here was another way Peter could share his love of wild geese with others and make some money in the process.

In spring 1936, Peter was commissioned by *The Field* magazine to travel to Hungary as their correspondent to report on the spring migration of geese on the Hungarian Plain. He travelled with his cousin, Eric Bruce; together they flew to Budapest, then continued onwards by train to the village of Hortobágy which was a centre for wildfowling at the heart of the migration route. Even before they got off the train, they had seen flocks of white-fronted geese numbering in excess of 10,000 birds. Shooting was carried out from purpose-dug pits. On his first morning, Peter assessed that there were five flocks of approximately 5,000 birds in the immediate vicinity and possibly more than 100,000 in the area. The bags were, he felt, unnecessarily large; one gun could easily shoot over 100 geese in a morning. Birds that were wing-tipped were kept with a view to returning with them to the lighthouse. The bulk of the flocks were white-fronted geese, but among them Peter was delighted to discover small numbers of lesser white-fronted geese and red-breasted geese. This was the first time he had seen the red-breasted goose and he was thrilled at his first sighting. He desperately hoped to be able to add both species to the growing group of wing-tipped birds that he could take home with him. One lesser whitefront was obtained, but the red-breasted geese eluded him and he saw only about twenty of them during his trip. Nevertheless, he was able to bring back the lesser white-fronted goose, a bean goose and several white-fronted geese to add to his collection.

That autumn, he returned to Hortobágy under his own steam, having fallen under the spell of the red-breasted goose. None were to be found, so he travelled east to the Danube delta, on the shores of the Black Sea in Romania. Here he saw small numbers of the geese together with some lesser white-fronted geese, but the large flocks that he knew to exist somewhere in the region evaded him still. He returned to England via Hortobágy where his Hungarian friends had assembled a small group of fifteen wing-tipped geese for him, including four lesser white-fronted geese. The birds were put into three crates for his journey home by air. Fog in Germany caused Peter to be grounded in Cologne, and he barely caught the train to England with his precious cargo. The transfer to the train was so rushed that he left his luggage and his money behind, arriving back in England temporarily destitute but with the geese alive and well. These were different times. It is now unimaginable that you might travel to Eastern Europe and return by train with a collection of geese.

His search for the red-breasted goose had taken on the same mythic proportions as his quest for the Prince of Wales Cup. In the autumn of 1937 he renewed his search, travelling this time to Persia and the shores of the Caspian Sea where he had read there were large numbers of the geese. To reach his destination he flew to Lebanon then on to Damascus, from where he took the bus across the desert to Tehran and stayed for a week with the British Ambassador. From Tehran, he drove north to Pahlevi on the shores of the Caspian Sea where a large lagoon, measuring some ten by thirty miles, hosted in excess of twenty million waterfowl in the winter season. Here, as well as familiar European ducks, were new species to enjoy, including his first encounter with the white-headed duck. Alas, there were no red-breasted geese, so he journeyed east as far as the Russian frontier, encountering thousands more birds, including pelicans and flamingos, but again, no red-breasted geese. It was a wonderful trip, and Peter hugely enjoyed this new-found experience of travel, something else to which he would frequently return in future years.

Back in England, he gave a number of lectures about his travels. His quest came to the notice of the Duke of Bedford who had a flock of around forty red-breasted geese, bred from a pair given to him some years previously. Peter was invited to stay at Woburn Abbey where discussion turned to the plight of Père David's deer, a species native to China which had become extinct in the wild but which had been preserved by the Duke in a herd at the Abbey. He had originally gathered together eight animals from various zoos and from them had built up a herd of over 200 deer. Peter was most impressed and it is probable that the idea of saving animal species from extinction by captive breeding was seeded in his mind during the visit. The following day, he was shown the flock of red-breasted geese; here in a park in England were more individuals of the species than he had seen throughout his travels in Europe and the Near East. As he was leaving, the Duchess offered to give him a pair, and Peter was overjoyed. They duly arrived at the lighthouse but failed to breed as both were females; this would not be the last time that Peter's plans were scuppered in this way. Having got this far, Peter was not to be thwarted. At the time, pairs of the geese cost £50, a not inconsiderable sum. Peter went for broke and found a source willing to sell him twenty-five pairs for £350. Of these, he duly sold seven pairs at the full price, ending up with thirty-six geese for free to add to the two he had been given at Woburn.

From humble beginnings at the Spalding Gentlemen's Society, Peter's confidence at public speaking had grown. He began to give talks about birds, particularly geese, and these developed as he had more to say. His activities came to the attention of producers at the BBC who thought he would be a good candidate to present radio talks. Thus it was that in August 1936, he gave two fifteen-minute talks, one about dinghy racing and the other about his life at the lighthouse and his recent travels in Hungary. An early outside broadcast took place in St James's Park from where the ducks and geese were heard by the listeners at home while Peter talked about the birds with the keeper, Thomas Hinton. Peter had an easy, fluent speaking style and his subject matter was of interest to many. His appearances on radio would continue, and increase, from here.

It was in 1936 that Peter's stepfather, Edward Hilton Young, retired from the government and went to the House of Lords as Lord Kennet of the Dene. He had been, until recently, Minister of Health in Stanley Baldwin's government and was tipped to be Chancellor of the Exchequer, but the call never came. At this time too, the family rented a summer home in Norfolk. Peter's stepfather reasoned that they spent so much time there that they might as well have a more permanent base for their holidays. The house, Fritton Hythe, was on Fritton Lake near Great Yarmouth. The family were to enjoy holidays there for a number of years thereafter. The house had once been owned by Francis Palgrave who, while living in the house in 1861, had compiled a compendium of poetry called *Palgrave's Golden Treasury,* a volume which found its way into many households in Britain over the following century. Philippa Scott had possessed a copy long before she knew Peter. Her copy can now be found in the small but eclectic library of books in the downstairs loo at their house in Slimbridge.

Peter's Canadian sailing trip in 1938, mentioned in the previous chapter, was different from his two earlier North American visits. This time, in addition to the sailing races, he had a number of other matters to attend to as well. First, there was the completion of his second book, *Wild Chorus,* for which the publication date was looming. Peter took the manuscript with him to America, finishing it while cruising with friends on Lake Ontario. Then there was to be his first American one-man exhibition in New York which would open in November. For this, Peter had taken with him a number of paintings, and he had agreed to undertake more works with American subjects prior to opening.

Peter returned to the United States in November 1938 for the opening of his exhibition but first made a trip to Canada to observe greater snow geese on their annual migration. One of their key staging posts was at a place called Cap Tourmente on the St Lawrence Seaway. Here there was a gun club which combined both sporting and conservation activities in a way unknown at home in England. Peter was very impressed by the way the two activities were successfully dovetailed in the one location. He had never lost his love for the sport but by this time was giving some thought to ways in which shooting could become sustainable, ensuring that large bags of birds did not lead to dangerous declines in numbers, as was thought to be the case with pink-footed geese in England. At the time, it was estimated that 80 per cent of the pinkfeet wintering in Britain were shot. Here, at Cap Tourmente, membership numbers were limited, and each member was allowed no more than five geese per day, with a maximum of fifty in any one season.

After going out to view the birds in the morning, Peter returned to the clubhouse and found himself sitting down to lunch in front of an enormous window, immediately beyond which was a flock of more than 700 greater snow geese, all within thirty yards of where he was sitting. The total number of geese in the immediate surroundings was over 5,000; this represented almost the entire world population of the species. Peter was astonished at how close the birds were to the window, feeding, completely unconcerned, just beyond the glass. He must also have thought ruefully of the bird hide he had built six years before at Borough Fen where the viewing aperture was just half an inch high to avoid frightening the birds. That day, at Cap Tourmente, he promised himself that one day he would build a house with a giant window just like the one in front of him at the gun club. Peter took numerous photographs and was able to obtain two wing-tipped specimens to take back with him to England.

Back in New York, the exhibition did not go as well as he had hoped. He suspected that one reason for this was the absence of his mother's organisational skills and contacts which had proved extremely useful at his earlier exhibitions in London. Nevertheless, a number of paintings were sold, and he hung on in New York for a couple of weeks, staying with an old friend of his mother's, Frank Chapman, who was head of the Bird Department at the American Museum of Natural History; during his time in New York Peter gave a talk to a packed Explorers' Club.

Next, Peter set out across the country on a trip to see as many wildfowl as he could. In Connecticut he encountered hooded mergansers and buffleheads for the first time and saw many other species of duck, some more familiar than others. At Barnegat Bay in New Jersey, he was taken to see flocks of Atlantic brant geese and black duck. He flew on to California, excited because the state hosted eight different species of goose, six of which he had never seen before. In California he saw lots of waterfowl including his first ruddy ducks and lesser snow geese as well as cackling geese, lesser Canada geese and whistling swans, close relatives of the European Bewick's swan. At a place called Gridley were huge congregations of waterfowl, exceeding in number even the flocks he had seen in Hungary and Persia. He was horrified by the extent of weekend shooting however. On the Sunday he was there, the sound of gunfire was almost continuous; the geese and ducks were no longer frightened by the noise and simply stayed put on the ground. He read that on the opening day of shooting in the Sacramento Valley, 14,000 pheasants were shot, and he frequently came across dead and decomposing ducks on the ground. The need for wildlife refuges like the one at Cap Tourmente was clear. Peter compared the spectacle he saw with those in Hungary and Persia and felt they were equal, though the remoteness of the reserves in those countries lent them an additional appeal that was lacking in a country with a filling station every five miles, paved roads and supermarkets. California had its advantages though, with easy travel and plenty of experts on hand to fill in the gaps in his knowledge. Peter was also very aware that he was getting more enjoyment out of photographing the birds than shooting them.

From California, Peter flew back to Washington, then on to Cape Hatteras. From here, he was flown in a private plane to Charlotte, North Carolina, a trip during which bad weather forced the pilot to make a crash landing in a field, from which everyone escaped unhurt. Reaching Louisiana, he spent some time watching vast flocks of blue geese and finished up at a duck ringing station in the Mississippi delta as the guest of businessman Ned McIlhenny, who, among other enterprises, held the monopoly on the manufacture of Tabasco sauce. Finally, back in New York, Peter gave three lectures in two days before heading for home. Peter left New York for England in the company of forty geese, thirty-two ducks and four baby alligators. Quite a trip.

Peter's excursions overseas were occasionally the cause of renewed tension with his mother. She was concerned once again about what she saw as his laissez-faire attitude. In her diary she wrote of an incident in 1936:

Arriving home very tired I found a telegram from my elder son to say that a crate of his wild geese was arriving at Croydon by Imperial Airways, and would I fetch them, with seven pounds to pay. After much cajolery the airways consented to take a cheque. After endless enquiries I found my son on the telephone, in Westmorland. Finally I went to bed and was very sick. All night the geese bloomped about in the water-tank in the back garden under my window. Yet I am fond of my sons.

Prior to his departure for Persia in autumn 1937, Peter stayed with his mother at Leinster Corner. On the morning he was due to depart she found him painting in his pyjamas at ten o'clock; the boat train left at eleven o'clock, but Peter evidently had no sense of what time it was. In 1938 while Peter was away in North America, she found herself once again having to deal with a multitude of his affairs. She wrote:

Today alone I have had hours of work releasing your snow geese from Liverpool because they hadn't got a certificate, pacifying the income tax, hearing Grimwood's groans, writing to Kenzie, answering a letter from a magazine ... This sort of thing happens often. I think you should come home. (*Cambridge University Library MS Scott (Peter) A.436*)

She was also worried about his spending and could see that his bank account was constantly in the red. 'Was that £200 for expenses?' she wrote, 'or are you – oh I do hope you aren't buying birds again?' (Ibid.). Peter's stepfather was also worried about his spending and urged him to cut back and maintain a working balance at the bank.

Back home at the lighthouse, Peter returned to his old routines. The new birds from America settled in, and Peter resumed his painting. The lighthouse by this time was an extremely comfortable home. The wife of a local farm worker brought his mail every morning, cooked breakfast and laid out a cold lunch, before returning in the evening to cook his supper. He also had a part-time secretary who came in for a couple of hours each morning, and of course, Mackenzie Thorpe was on hand to feed the birds; by October 1938, there were 250 waterfowl in the collection at the lighthouse. Word had spread about Peter's domain. The number of visitors gradually increased, including, on one occasion in 1939, Prince Bernhard of the Netherlands. A regular visitor to the lighthouse during these years was the chairman of Vickers, Archie Jamieson, who had purchased a number of Peter's paintings, some of which hung in the wardrooms of aircraft carriers constructed by his company.

In 1939, Peter was invited to give a talk and show his slides of his Caspian trip at an event called the Duke of York's Camp which was held for boys every year at Balmoral. Peter stayed in the castle and dined with the royal family. He had not seen the king since he had come to his home at Leinster Corner some years before to sit for two busts. Now Peter sat next to him at supper and no doubt told him something of his recent travels. Peter had, at last, begun to make something of his life. An established painter, writer and broadcaster with a comfortable home, many friends and enough money to allow him to do the things he wanted to. It had taken him a long time to get his life just the way he wanted it. What a great pity it was then, that international events were about to tear apart the world that he had so carefully created for himself.

7

For Those in Peril

For some time, Peter had been thinking what he would do if, as seemed increasingly likely, war broke out. Initially he was attracted to the RAF, but his father's experience in the Royal Navy drew him ultimately in that direction. An additional spur was the fact that his sailing experience was likely to give him a better chance of joining the ranks of officers in what was known as the Senior Service. He therefore added his name to the reserve list for the Royal Naval Volunteer Supplementary Reserve. Nothing happened immediately, and he was staying with John Winter at his home in Stafford on 3 September 1939, the day that war was declared.

Peter had sufficient time to make arrangements at the lighthouse. The most valuable birds, the red-breasted geese, were sent to Walcot Hall in Shropshire, while the others were divided between the collections of Will Tinsley and David Haig Thomas. While staying at Stafford, Peter had time to develop a camouflage scheme for the roof of the factory where John Winter worked. He was later proud to report that during the war, the factory remained unscathed, despite the damage inflicted in the surrounding area.

War suited Peter. Action was called for, and he had always loved action above inaction. There were rules to be followed it is true, but the cause was a great one and offered opportunities for adventure and excitement that were lacking in peacetime. Peter rose readily to the challenges the coming conflict presented and slipped easily into naval life. He wrote:

The prospect of war and change was exciting and unsettling. For the adventurous there was no particular merit in the comfortable security of my present existence, but I bitterly resented the prospect of its interruption.

Eventually, Peter was called up, given the rank of Temporary-Acting-Sub-Lieutenant and sent to HMS *King Alfred*, a land-based training establishment at Hove in Sussex. Here, with a group of fellow civilians, mostly yachtsmen, he went through a ten-day training course which included basic navigation and Morse code. Like so many of his fellow trainees, one of his main concerns was that the war would be over before he finished training. Early on during his course he applied to serve on a destroyer. He was accepted but required specialist training which would not be available for a further three weeks. He was therefore given a temporary liaison post, helping to introduce new waves of recruits to life at HMS *King Alfred*. His post required him to organise weekly concerts to boost morale; these included appearances by Stanley Holloway, Ludovic Kennedy and Elsie and Doris Waters.

The first specialist course was on anti-submarine warfare at HMS *Osprey* at Portland, another shore-based establishment, from where he went on to Torpedo Control School at HMS *Defiance* at Plymouth. Here, he learned that he was to be assigned to the destroyer HMS *Acasta* which was currently in port at Devonport, so Peter went along next day to pay his compliments to the captain and meet the officers with whom he would serve. He was delighted with the ship but next day came down with a heavy cold and was unable to finish the torpedo course. Since he could not go to sea without completing it, his posting was rescinded, and HMS *Acasta* sailed without him. Downcast as he was, it turned out to be a very lucky break indeed. A few weeks later, HMS *Acasta* was sunk in an engagement off Norway and went down with her entire crew, apart from one survivor.

Having recovered, Peter completed his course and was assigned as a Lieutenant to HMS *Broke*, an older destroyer dating from 1926. Peter was soon in action, escorting convoys around the British Isles. He hugely admired his captain, Bryan Scurfield, but did not get on so well with some of the other men on board, most of whom were professional sailors in the regular Royal Navy, who, Peter felt, had little time for newcomers from outside the service. Nevertheless, HMS *Broke* was soon in action, and then there was little time to worry about such things; the common threat rapidly bound all the men into a unified fighting force.

One problem Peter had to overcome was seasickness, something that had never troubled him when sailing dinghies. Conditions at sea in a destroyer were different however, and Peter succumbed easily. On deck it was less of a problem, but he found it difficult to read a nautical chart without feeling ill. In the wardroom, if the seas were rough, the smell of fuel oil seeped in and made him feel unwell. The captain kept a bucket on the bridge, and Peter had to accept there were some things he simply couldn't control. Eventually things got better, and he only felt ill for the first day or so after leaving port. Not long after joining HMS *Broke*, Peter fell ill with a heavy cold again and was confined to the sick bay. Unable to shake it off, the illness developed into jaundice, whereupon he was given three weeks' sick leave to recover.

He spent his leave during Easter, 1940, at Fritton Hythe with the family. There, he met Jane Howard, an intriguing sixteen-year-old girl who, with her brother, had been invited to spend the holidays in Norfolk to provide company for Peter's half-brother, Wayland. Though Peter was feeling unwell and depressed, he couldn't help being attracted to Jane who he described as:

Lanky and young with steady grey eyes, a mouth which turned up at the corners and a dimple in her chin. She was inventive and adventurous, full of original ideas and unexpected turns of phrase.

The day after they were introduced, he asked if he could draw her and seems to have been very attracted by her appearance. He later recalled that they sailed boats, played running games on the lawn, talked about music, painting, acting and writing and laughed a great deal. He also reported that they began to fall in love. Jane described her first sighting of Peter as a stocky man, wearing a thick jumper and painting at an easel. Her childhood had not been a happy one; she had been brought up in a family with a strong puritan streak where praise for one's achievements was muted or non-existent. Now she found herself surrounded by a throng of confident, happy, successful people. To a young, inexperienced girl, the family gathered at Fritton Hythe seemed glamorous and sophisticated, chatting about the doings of cabinet ministers and other well-known figures, sailing, playing games and generally having a thoroughly good time. She and her brother Robin were not neglected in all this and quickly came to feel part of the glittering circle. Jane's description of the holiday provides a fascinating insight into the Kennet/Scott family at home. Through her eyes we see, at least on the surface, a confident, assured, well-adjusted family, thoroughly enjoying their holiday together. It is possible to imagine the family's vitality and bravura, described by Jane, as the impetus for Peter's self-confidence, his easy manner with all sorts of people and his conviction that he could succeed in whichever endeavours he chose.

Jane noticed that Peter could do nothing wrong in the eyes of his mother, who hung on his every idea and thought. To her he was a paragon, the only son of Robert Falcon Scott and the reason why she had been forced to overcome her grief at her husband's loss and to forge a new life for her and her son. Dropped into this golden circle of happy, confident people, it is easy to see how Jane would fall for the handsome naval lieutenant at the heart of the family. There is no doubt that Jane was enthralled by the attention of this glamorous naval officer, though she also recorded that when she left Fritton Hythe her head had been turned but her heart remained untouched.

In his autobiography *The Eye of the Wind*, there is very little mention of women in Peter's life before he met Jane. It might be thought he was too busy with his wildfowling, painting and sailing to think about girls, but there is clear evidence that he was no stranger to romance as a young man – it just didn't interest him to write about it much. In St Moritz, at Christmas 1927, he had encountered a dark-haired Canadian girl called Elizabeth who later visited him at Cambridge and subsequently poured her heart out to Peter's mother before returning to Canada. In Germany there had been 'Mouse', the daughter of the house where he stayed. At that time too there was a Swedish ice dancer who Peter regretted was too good a skater for him to partner. Later there was Dinah, the daughter of friends of his parents, who was very much in love with him but unsure of what his intentions towards her were. Then there was Brenda, who Peter met while sailing in Norfolk, and who he hinted that he hoped to marry. For some reason, when writing about her in *The Eye of the Wind*, he gave her the pseudonym 'Deirdre'; Jane recalled him talking about a beautiful woman with whom he'd had a long affair but who he'd decided he didn't want to marry. According to Jane, Peter's mother was given to mentioning that he had broken a lot of hearts in his time.

Back on HMS *Broke*, Peter was soon in the thick of the action. In June 1940, the British Expeditionary Force (BEF) fell back to the beaches of France. In the aftermath of Dunkirk, there remained in France the remnants of the BEF which were rapidly being surrounded by advancing German forces. HMS *Broke* was dispatched to Le Havre where she came under air attack and narrowly missed a direct hit from a cluster of bombs. She was then ordered to proceed to St Valery to affect a rescue of some wounded British soldiers. Peter was dispatched into the harbour with a small rescue party, unsure whether the town was still occupied by Allied troops or had been overrun by the Germans. He performed his duties remarkably coolly under pressure. His small party landed in the early hours under cover of darkness. By the time he had found the men who were to be evacuated and arranged to get them to the ship it was already light, and they were under growing threat of attack by German aircraft at any moment. In the end he had time to evacuate 120 men of whom ninety-five were wounded, and HMS *Broke* returned to Portsmouth unharmed.

A few days later, HMS *Broke* was steaming into the harbour at Brest in Brittany to embark troops and to demolish as much of the port's infrastructure as possible ahead of the advancing German troops. Once again, Peter was in the thick of things, making six trips ashore in the one of the ship's motorboats to round up stragglers and to assist the demolition team by delivering the explosives and charges and embarking the team afterwards. Thousands of troops from several nations were evacuated, and HMS *Broke* left harbour as explosions rocked the port and a pall of black smoke covered the scene. She returned to Plymouth with 300 people on board including 200 Polish troops. Despite having been on the go for twenty-seven hours, Peter wasn't too tired to identify a Dartford warbler among gorse bushes on a headland during the final stages of the campaign.

Peter wrote frequently to his mother during the war. The letter describing his exploits at Brest had a profound effect upon her. She wrote:

> My sweet, what an adventure – it's breath taking – I rush round with you, I demolish, I ignite, I embark, I signal, and most of all I stride out, dead tired along the gorse covered cliff. What a life, what marvellous service, how grateful we are to you. Your letter has gone to be copied. (*Cambridge University Library MS Scott (Peter) A.439*)

And copied it was, to all her friends. Whatever previous doubts Kathleen may have had about her son's approach to life were now completely dispelled by his courage in action and his exploits in battle.

As 1940 wore on, and England awaited the anticipated German invasion, HMS *Broke* moved to Plymouth to assist with convoy duties in the English Channel. Support for the convoys bringing food and supplies across the Atlantic was urgently needed; the first convoy they joined had lost nine ships out of thirty-six on the previous day. As Anti-Submarine Control Officer on HMS *Broke*, Peter was kept busy hunting for and attempting to destroy the marauding U-boats. It was at this time that Peter invented a new kind of night camouflage for warships. He was aware that even light-coloured boats would appear as black silhouettes on the horizon at night so came up with a new version of the so-called 'dazzle' camouflage, in which flat planes and surfaces were disguised by the colours and shapes painted on the hull. HMS *Broke* was painted with his design which turned out to be particularly effective during night patrols but also equally useful at both dawn and dusk.

During his Channel patrols, Peter had plenty of time to think about Jane Howard, and while he was on leave they began dating. She was attending drama school in London. He would call for her, and they would drive out to Kew or Richmond. On other nights he took her to the theatre where on one occasion they went backstage to meet an actress that Peter knew. It was Jane's first time behind the scenes at a professional theatre and she was suitably impressed. Peter also took her to the Ackermann Gallery in Bond Street to show her his pictures. He gave her an original drawing of a nightingale, one of the illustrations from his stepfather's book; she was thrilled to become the owner of her first original artwork. The impact of all this on a young girl is not hard to imagine. Just started at drama school, taken to the theatre and art galleries and courted by a handsome naval officer in his thirties, her world had suddenly been transformed in the most thrilling way imaginable. She recorded that Peter's mother telephoned hers to warn her not to let Peter break her daughter's heart, adding that he had broken many hearts before. It's possible that Kathleen thought this now seventeen-year-old girl was unsuitable for Peter and, knowing that a direct approach to him would not succeed, thought to try a more indirect method.

In late 1940, HMS *Broke* moved to a new base at Londonderry in Northern Ireland and was assigned to work on the North Atlantic convoys. At the same time, Peter was promoted to First Lieutenant, the first RNVR officer ever to reach this rank in the Royal Navy. The engagements on the North Atlantic convoys became known as the Battle of the Atlantic and were, in Peter's words, tough and bloody. Convoys of merchant ships heading for North America would be escorted several hundred miles out into the ocean until they were out of range of the ever-threatening U-boats which hunted among the convoys in packs. The submarines always attacked at night, while during the day, shipping would regularly come under attack from German aircraft. To add to the difficulties, the Atlantic Ocean was a very different environment from the English Channel. There were frequent storms and violent seas, with waves up to fifty feet in height sweeping the decks from end to end, while in winter, severe cold was a constant problem.

Given the harshness of the conditions under which they laboured, the moments of shore leave that could be snatched became hugely important. Peter had friends, Guy and Grace Goodliffe, who lived twenty miles away over the border in the Republic of Ireland. Guy was a passionate snipe shooter, so Peter grabbed every moment he could to go shooting with him. To get back into the wild, away from the hardships of the North Atlantic, made his life just about bearable. He found desperately needed moments of peace and tranquillity during his visits to the Goodliffes. In December 1940, HMS *Broke* was in port for a refit which would take a couple of weeks, so Peter was able to join Michael Bratby and John Winter for a few days' punt-gunning in Morecambe Bay.

At around this time, Peter was offered command of a flotilla of motor launches as part of Coastal Forces. He was briefly tempted, before turning the offer down. His reasons for doing so provide a clear insight into his thinking at the time. Obviously, service in a destroyer was more glamorous and exciting, and Peter was hoping that within a year he might get his own destroyer to command. But command wasn't the be all and end all, as he wrote to Michael Bratby, claiming that he would rather have an exciting and interesting subordinate job than a dull command. He also felt that his months of hard-gained experience on the convoys could be used most effectively by continuing to serve where he was.

Once back at sea, HMS *Broke* was soon in the thick of things once again. Summoned to assist a stricken ship, Peter and his captain faced an unenviable task. HMS *Comorin* was a 15,000 ton ex-P&O liner converted to an armed merchant cruiser. An accident had created a blaze in her boiler room which had prevented the crew from using the fire main to put out the flames. The ship was disabled in storm conditions, with fifty-foot-high waves running from stem to stern. Two other ships were in attendance and had managed to run lines to HMS *Comorin,* by means of which life rafts could be used to evacuate the crew of the stricken ship, a few at a time. The fire was growing however, and it seemed that not all the crew could be taken off in time. Added to this, the pitching of both HMS *Comorin* and the other ships risked the life rafts being flipped over and the men in them thrown into the water.

As night fell, a decision was made to try and bring HMS *Broke* close up under the stern of the liner where the remaining crew had gathered. As the two ships rose and fell, the men would step or leap from one to the other. This was easier said than done. The size of the waves and the motion of the two ships meant that HMS *Broke* could only make contact with HMS *Comorin* for a few seconds at a time, during which the men would have to judge the timing of their leap within a split second; it would be like leaping from a fast-moving lift onto a hard deck, with a drop which would change in a moment from a couple of feet to fifty or more. Peter was put in charge of the jumping zone; the decks were padded with cushions and hammocks, and the work began. Each time HMS *Broke* moved in under the stern of HMS *Comorin*, a few men jumped. Some landed safely, others were injured in the fall. HMS *Broke* could only hold position for a few seconds or they risked being crushed under the descending stern above them. Time and time again, they drew in under the stern of the other ship and more and more men were saved. By now, HMS *Broke* was suffering damage from the repeated battering against HMS *Comorin* and water was flooding into various parts of the ship.

After working all night, and never knowing quite if HMS *Broke* could continue to withstand the strain being put upon her, the last crew members and finally the captain, were taken off. HMS *Broke* rescued 180 men that night, most of whom survived, and the ship limped back to Greenock with her passengers. The return voyage took two and a half days, and they had to bail water continuously during that time. The passage in *The Eye of the Wind* that describes this incident is vivid and gripping and gives a clear indication of the ordeal for everyone involved. While Peter's war memoirs can sometimes seem a little too full of detail, when it came to the big events he could grip and enthral the reader as well as any other war writer and better than most. After this event, his captain, Bryan Scurfield, got the DSO, and Peter received his first mention in dispatches.

In the summer of 1941, HMS *Broke* transferred her base to Liverpool, and Bryan Scurfield was moved on to command a new, bigger destroyer, much to Peter's dismay. He liked and admired Scurfield and initially found it hard to get on with his replacement, Walter Couchman. The two men bonded eventually over an incident on a convoy, 200 miles out in the Atlantic. HMS *Broke* was one of the naval vessels on escort duty when it collided with another of the escort destroyers, HMS *Verity*. The incident happened at dawn when Peter was in command of HMS *Broke*. He had thought the other ship, which was on a zigzag course behind the convoy, was moving away from him when instead it suddenly turned towards his own ship. The Officer of the Watch on board HMS *Verity* claimed later that he did not see HMS *Broke;* this is very likely true as she was painted with Peter's camouflage design which rendered her extremely difficult to see in the dawn light. Damage to both ships was moderate but enough to put them in port for repairs for several weeks, something the Admiralty could ill afford at such a critical time. Walter Couchman, as captain, necessarily took a share of the blame, even though he had been below decks when it became obvious that a collision was likely. Peter spent an anxious few weeks before the enquiry into the incident and found his new captain extremely supportive. In the event, it was determined that, though the Officer of the Watch of HMS *Verity* was marginally more to blame, both he and Peter should be declared jointly responsible and given cautions. Peter doubtless felt it unwise to point out that his camouflage design had contributed significantly to the event.

For some time, Peter had wanted to experience an RAF night bombing raid over Germany. He wrote of his admiration for the RAF and in particular the bomber crews who, he felt, were taking the war to Germany at a time when most other military activity was defensive in nature. During the summer, HMS *Broke* was docked at Newcastle for boiler repairs, so Peter had some time on his hands. On a visit to the summer exhibition at the Royal Academy he encountered Air Commodore Sir Victor Goddard and asked for permission to join a raid, giving as his main reason the fostering of inter-services relationships. In reality of course, he was looking for some excitement; as always, inaction was anathema to him. His plan was not without risk as Bomber Command was losing aircraft on raids over Germany on a weekly basis.

Permission was granted, and he was assigned to 15 Squadron which was flying Stirling bombers from Wyton Aerodrome near Huntingdon. His first mission was aborted, but on his second visit he was successful, joining an aircrew on a night flight to bomb Kiel in northern Germany, a somewhat ironic destination for Peter as it was at Kiel, five years previously, that he had been beaten to an Olympic silver medal by a German competitor. His account of the night is, as usual, full of detail. During the afternoon before the flight he had chatted to the second pilot whose previous sortie had ended in a crash landing which wrecked the aircraft. This must certainly have given Peter pause for thought, and he recorded that at supper he would have been extremely grateful for any reasonable excuse not to go. Nevertheless, go he did, and the raid was a complete success despite a slightly worrying moment prior to landing when an engine failure nearly resulted in them having to bail out and abandon the aircraft. From Wyton, Peter was flown to Norwich en route to Fritton Hythe where he was due to take a week's leave. The flight took them directly over the house, so Peter got the pilot to circle round while he took some photographs.

Jane came to spend a few days at Fritton Hythe where they went sailing. Peter had an afternoon's shooting before he went to London for meetings at the Admiralty about the possibility of promotion to captain and about his camouflage designs which were now being used on more and more warships. There followed a few days' leave at Jane's family home in Sussex, where it became clear to both of them that their relationship was becoming more serious. Peter declared his love for her; she was less sure what she felt – this was, after all, her first real romance. By this time, Jane's career as an actress had begun. She was about to leave for Stratford to join the Royal Shakespeare Company. At the end of the week, the family drove Peter to Lympne in Kent where he was collected by a Stirling bomber, prior to taking part in another night raid over Germany. This time Cologne was the target, and the ground defences were much more volatile and threatening than on the previous occasion over Kiel. Jane listened to the news of the bombing raids that evening full of apprehension, realising that she would be devastated if Peter didn't return.

Peter's designs for camouflage had been adopted on other navy ships, and the Commander-in-Chief Western Approaches, Admiral Dunbar-Nasmith, asked Peter to write a report about his scheme for the Admiralty. The report was considered with some favour in light of the growing number of sinkings, but there were still concerns about the possibility of collision between vessels. HMS *Broke* and HMS *Verity* had not been the only ships to collide as a result of effective camouflage. In the end, the benefits of the scheme outweighed the risks, and Peter was asked to draw up designs for a range of different types of warships; these were then widely used throughout the rest of the war. Peter subsequently received the MBE for this work.

Back on HMS *Broke,* the convoys resumed; another long winter in the North Atlantic beckoned. The weather this season was, if anything, worse than the last as gale followed gale with weather of the utmost severity. By this time, Peter had come to admire his captain, Walter Couchman, who he saw as an extremely able captain and leader, his only fault in Peter's eyes being an inclination to be sometimes more critical of others than necessary. It is possible that Peter's discovery that his captain was a keen wildfowler may also have had some influence on his opinion of the man. A change in convoy routes meant that HMS *Broke* sometimes refuelled in Reykjavik in Iceland where his friend Michael Bratby was stationed as an army intelligence officer, and the two friends were able to meet from time to time, however briefly. In the early months of 1942, HMS *Broke* came near to foundering in stormy weather as she was heading for Loch Ewe on the west coast of Scotland to refuel. With almost empty tanks, the ship was riding high out of the water when an unnaturally large wave caused her to heel over until she was virtually on her side. Fortunately, she was eventually righted, though two seamen were lost overboard, and some of the crew lacked trust in their ship after the incident. A few weeks later, she sailed to Portsmouth for a refit before reassignment to the Mediterranean. Peter, along with his shipmates, was decommissioned; very few returned when HMS *Broke* was ready to sail once more. Peter had served in her for almost exactly two years.

8

Fortunes of War

Upon leaving HMS *Broke*, no other destroyer was in need of a captain in the foreseeable future, so Peter was given command of a steam gunboat, which was currently under construction at J. Samuel White's shipyard at Cowes on the Isle of Wight. The Admiralty assured him that the commission would not interfere with his ambition to command a destroyer. Peter now had some breathing space and would be able to take a few weeks' leave. Since the previous summer, theatre work had dried up, and Jane was now taking a secretarial course in London, sharing a flat with a friend, Dosia Cropper. The two were clearly having a fine time in London and shared a similar sense of humour. They called their home *Mon Debris* and invented a butler called Chortle who was always inexplicably absent when people came to visit. Shortly before Peter's leave began, they held a dinner party at which they pretended Peter was Jane's deaf uncle who was visiting them, telling their guests that they would have to shout at him to make themselves heard. A friend of Dosia's called Kit Dodds, brought to the party his girlfriend, Philippa Talbot-Ponsonby, who spent the first part of the evening bellowing at Peter, little realising that this was the man with whom she would, eventually, spend most of the rest of her life.

In *The Eye of the Wind*, Peter wrote that at this point he and Jane had been engaged for a while and that he saw his extended leave as an opportunity to get married. Philippa, in her first autobiography *Lucky Me*, also described the dinner party, mentioning that Peter and Jane were engaged. According to Jane however, it was on the night of the party, after everyone left, that Peter suggested to her that they get married. People's recollections of events often differ, particularly after time has passed, but it is curious that the matter of an engagement could be so confused. Jane recalled Peter telling her that he had three weeks' leave coming up and thought that it would be a good time to get married. Jane wrote later that she was astonished and flattered but added that she hadn't had any thoughts about marriage. This assertion runs counter to previous correspondence between the two in which the possibility of marriage had been mentioned, though it seems that nothing had been decided between them. It is likely that Peter assumed they would eventually be married and imagined that Jane thought the same so therefore considered himself already engaged. This version of the story is supported by events described in Elspeth Huxley's biography, *Peter Scott, Painter and Naturalist*. According to Huxley, before the dinner party, Peter asked his mother if she approved of the idea and she, despite some reservations about Jane's age, said she would support Peter if that's what he chose to do. Peter then wrote to Jane, saying that the family approved of him marrying her but went on to pour out his concerns about their relationship, wondering if the long weeks at sea and time slipping by were influencing him unduly, while on her side he thought she might be accepting second best because of the lack of available young men; he then continued the letter by wholeheartedly declaring his love for her. It therefore seems likely that, on the night of the dinner party, Peter was simply confirming what he thought had been agreed between them, while Jane had not, until then, understood that he was intent on marrying her.

Whatever the truth of the matter, after the events at the dinner party, the families were told and preparations rapidly made. Jane later wrote of having doubts about marrying Peter. She had not thought about marrying anyone before now; was this really what she wanted? But she was also flattered that this handsome older man, a naval officer, wanted to marry her. At nineteen she was desperate to be grown up; she thought she loved Peter, and marriage to him would seem to resolve many of her problems. The only doubt in Peter's mind was her age, but Jane assured him that wasn't a problem. He clearly loved her and wanted her to be his wife. Before the wedding, Jane and Peter went to Fritton Hythe where Lord Kennet, Peter's stepfather, gave Jane a gold watch, and Peter's mother gave him a turquoise and diamond ring to give to Jane. Jane recalled being disappointed that Peter hadn't picked out a ring himself.

The couple were married on 28 April 1942 at St Mary's Church in Lancaster Gate, followed by a reception at Claridge's hotel for 400 guests who included Joyce Grenfell and Malcolm Sargent. The honeymoon was spent at Lord Kennet's cottage, The Lacket, near Marlborough. They walked and rode on the downs and visited the stone circle at Avebury. To Peter, after the grim winter in the North Atlantic, it must have seemed like bliss indeed, and he wrote of his feeling that the beauty of the woods and hills of the Wiltshire countryside reinforced in him the realisation of what he was fighting for, a sentiment that was shared by many of his comrades in arms throughout the war. Jane recalled Peter saying that his lighthouse would be too small for them when they had a family. She had replied that their home would have to be in London. Peter, in the first flush of marriage, said that it could be wherever she liked.

Peter was going to have to spend most of the coming weeks on the Isle of Wight where his steam gunboat was under construction, so the couple took up residence in the Gloster Hotel in Cowes. Jane had only stayed in a hotel for one night before and that had been with her mother on the eve of her wedding. Now, suddenly, she was on her own in a strange hotel. On the first morning she had to ask Peter how she would be able to get lunch; it is clear in hindsight that she was ill-prepared for the new life in which she found herself and that Peter imagined she was more mature than she actually was. Understandably, Peter was now focused almost exclusively on his new command and assumed Jane would be able to manage for herself. In the event, he still had plenty of time to spend with her while they were based in Cowes, and he made several pen portraits of her during their stay.

The steam gunboat was a new class of ship, built to serve as part of the forces of Coastal Command in the English Channel. She was bigger than the existing fleet of motor torpedo boats and motor gun boats and had a steel hull. One of a flotilla of seven steam gunboats, SGB 9 was launched by Peter's mother at Cowes and undertook her sea trials in the Solent before moving to Weymouth for her final fitting out. Peter immersed himself in the work of getting the ship and her crew of forty into shape; he was pleased that three of them had served under him on HMS *Broke*. Meanwhile Jane, who had come to Weymouth with Peter, found herself living again in a hotel with no friends around and nothing to do during the day when Peter was working. She recorded that she felt bored and lonely.

Finally, all preparations were complete, and Peter received instructions to sail his new command to Portsmouth where he would receive his orders on 16 August. It seemed SGB 9 was to be thrown in at the deep end. His orders revealed that he was to take part in a raid on Dieppe, a major offensive with the aim of establishing a beachhead on French soil. Four SGBs were to take part. Peter's ship would be protecting landing craft on the flank of the invasion. They departed Portsmouth on a calm summer evening, part of a considerable fleet of infantry assault ships, destroyers and gunboats together with a large number of smaller vessels. Arriving before dawn off the French coast, a ship in the fleet encountered a German convoy and the alarm was raised. A fierce fire fight erupted between the ships and the coastal batteries. At dawn, German aircraft arrived, and SGB 9 nearly ended her career almost before it had begun when a bomb narrowly missed her but temporarily disabled her steering. SGB 9 spent the rest of the day during the abortive raid attacking enemy aircraft and assisting in covering the retreat from Dieppe. She was one of the last ships behind the returning convoy, turning back on more than one occasion to pick up British airmen who had ditched in the sea. For his part in the raid Peter was, once again, mentioned in dispatches.

Looking back on the day's events, Peter could be happy that his new ship and her crew had acquitted themselves well. The Dieppe raid had, however, revealed a shortcoming in the design of the new steam gunboats. Having only one boiler and fuel pump, the ships were at risk of being disabled and unable to move and therefore become an easy target to be picked off by enemy aircraft. While the engine design could not be significantly altered it was felt that they should be fitted with more robust armour plating. A programme was put in place to carry this out, and the SGB fleet was consigned to coastal convoy work until the work was complete.

Peter and Jane took a house temporarily at Seaford to be near the fleet's home port at Newhaven. Jane was pleased to be settled at last in a house they could call their own though her pleasure was short-lived, since after six weeks Peter told her that they were moving on once again. By this time, Jane was pregnant. Peter was delighted at the prospect of becoming a father, but Jane had reservations; she had not wanted to start a family straight away. Peter's mother wanted a grandson however and had apparently made this very clear to her during a visit to Fritton Hythe shortly after their marriage. Jane had a difficult relationship with her mother-in-law, a forbidding figure whose devotion to her son seemed at times to Jane to be all-consuming. She recalled later an event that occurred when she was staying at his mother's house on her own. She came down to breakfast to find that a letter to her from Peter had been torn open and read, clearly by Kathleen. Jane was furious and upset but felt unable to confront her mother-in-law. When she told Peter later, he said that his mother always liked reading his letters, and he didn't mind that she had opened and read it.

At the end of 1942, SGB 9 went in for her refit at Southampton, and Peter and Jane moved to a house in St John's Wood in London that had previously been owned by her grandfather. Peter spent much of his time away in Southampton, Portsmouth or Newhaven and made frequent visits to the Admiralty in London, campaigning for improved artillery in the SGB fleet. At this time, he was promoted to Lieutenant Commander and put in command of the SGB flotilla. On 2 February 1943, Peter and Jane's daughter Nicola was born, and Peter, consumed with feelings in the same way as any first-time parent, began to think seriously about his own mortality. In the early stages of the war it had almost been a game, and he hadn't given much thought to the risks he was taking. Now he had a wife and child to support and questioned his right to have a family at a time when his life was seriously at risk.

The first ship in the gunboat flotilla to complete the refit of the new armour was SGB 6. Peter took temporary command of her in April 1943 and began offensive operations in the Channel once again. A few days later, he found himself in sustained action off the mouth of the River Seine. With her rudder disabled, Peter ordered that his ship be converted to manual steering then went in pursuit of a group of enemy armed trawlers, engaging them in close combat until his ammunition ran out. Shortly afterwards they took a direct hit on the bridge from an incendiary shell which started a fire. On the way back, two of the motor gunboats in his group collided, and one was badly holed. As dawn broke, the small group of ships limped back across the Channel at a speed of four knots, expecting at any time to come under attack from enemy aircraft. Despite some criticism of tactics from the Admiralty, Peter's bravery under fire was recognised, and he subsequently received the DSC for this action.

Peter campaigned to allow the steam gunboats to have names rather than numbers; he felt it would be good for morale amongst the crew and give the flotilla an extra sense of shared unity. At the time there was a rule that ships under 130 feet in length were not allowed to be given names. With an overall length of 150 feet there was clearly no impediment to having his fleet of SGBs named, but it took a while for the permission to come through. Peter had been experimenting with ideas, needing six names for the whole flotilla which had to be linked in some way. Of course, geese came to mind, and he wanted to call his own boat *Grey Goose,* but others in the flotilla were unhappy about having their ships named after geese. So 'Grey' became the common link, with the other ships named *Grey Seal, Grey Fox, Grey Owl, Grey Shark* and *Grey Wolf.* Peter had got his way on the issue of armaments as well. The refitted ships had considerably more fire power than before, though this increase and the added armour, reduced their speed considerably.

In June 1943, *Grey Goose* completed her refit and went to Weymouth to be made ready for action, before joining her sister ships at Newhaven. For the first time, the SGB flotilla was complete and could engage the enemy as a single unit. At the end of July, four of the flotilla were involved in a fierce battle off Cherbourg when they encountered a fleet of at least ten German ships including three armed trawlers and some smaller gun boats. Peter led his flotilla in line past the German ships, engaging them in heavy gunfire. An ammunition locker at the stern was set alight, and soon fires were blazing fore and aft, with the first lieutenant and several other crew members injured. *Grey Shark,* coming to the rescue of *Grey Goose,* which looked in worse condition than she actually was, came under heavy fire and was immobilised. In the ensuing melee, the other two SGBs collided with each other, causing considerable damage. Withdrawing from the engagement, *Grey Shark* had to be taken in tow. Peter in *Grey Goose,* with her fires extinguished, laid smoke to conceal the crippled ship thereby attracting once again the full attention of the German fire. In this action, the flotilla lost seven men with a good number injured. Peter felt responsible for the deaths and would subsequently re-run the engagement in his head to see what he could have done differently. The Admiralty had no such reservations. Peter was awarded a bar to his DSC for his bravery in the thick of battle.

In a subsequent action, later in the summer, the flotilla once again came under heavy fire. *Grey Goose* was badly holed in two places and lost her rudder and internal communication systems. She returned to

Dover where she was temporarily stationed, steering by means of her two engines which, by operating at different speeds, could be made to control the ship's direction. Arriving in the port they were offered a tow which Peter declined, a decision he was to regret ten minutes later when, manoeuvring into position at their dock, the difficulty of steering by this method caused him to reverse into a Norwegian warship. This was bad enough but made worse by the fact that various members of the naval top brass had lined the dock to welcome the flotilla back into port, word having spread about their latest action in the Channel.

Towards the end of 1943, the SGB force was moved under the umbrella of Combined Operations. Peter by this time had been in the flotilla for nearly two years and was beginning to feel the effects of continued close action with the enemy forces. He asked once again about the possibility of commanding a destroyer and was told that he was first required to undertake a period as an instructor, providing training to new recruits at HMS *Bee*, which had been moved from Weymouth to Holyhead. To Peter this seemed like a welcome opportunity to spend some time away from the front line with his young family.

The weeks at Holyhead provided a welcome respite, and Peter enjoyed explaining to the recruits some of the ideas he had developed during his previous four years at sea. Nicola was staying with grandparents, so Jane was able to indulge her love of theatre, mounting an amateur production of *The Importance of Being Earnest*, for which Peter was stage manager; as always he was extremely supportive of her artistic endeavours. Things were not going well between Peter and Jane however. She, it seems, felt left behind in the marriage, an appendage to Peter, having to wait while he pursued his war with vigour, determination and total commitment. He clearly loved her deeply but had taken her love and support for him for granted, assuming she understood that he had to focus everything on the war effort.

Spring of 1944 saw Peter refreshed and ready for action once again. Surely now he would get the command he so desperately wanted. The war in Europe was coming to a head, and he thought there must soon be another attempt to gain a foothold on the continent. Once again his hopes were dashed, as he was sent to a new post at Coastal Forces, Channel, based in Portsmouth. Christopher Dreyer was a regular naval officer who had previously commanded a flotilla of motor torpedo boats based in Newhaven. He and Peter had worked together successfully in the past. In his new role as Staff Officer Operations to the Captain, Coastal Forces, Dreyer needed a second-in-command, and Peter was duly appointed Staff Officer Operations (2). Peter liked and admired his new boss; the opportunity to work with him made up, in part, for the pass on the destroyer.

Peter moved base to Portsmouth where he and his commanding officer had offices in Fort Southwick, on top of Portsdown Hill behind the city. Later, they moved into new accommodation in tunnels dug deep beneath the hill. Together they were responsible for day-to-day operations of the ships of Coastal Forces based in Portsmouth. The galleries dug under Portsdown Hill housed the Portsmouth Combined HQ and included the naval plotting room where ship movements in the central English Channel were constantly monitored. Approximately 100 people worked in the complex.

With day-to-day Coastal Forces operations continuing as usual, Peter had to get used to being behind a desk, planning operations rather than taking part in them. In April however, things got much more interesting when, with Christopher Dreyer, he was briefed on the plans for D-Day. The pair would be co-ordinating the protection of the huge convoys of ships that would be crossing the Channel when a beachhead had been established on the French coast. Once they were party to the information, they were forbidden to take part in any operations for fear they might be captured. The intention was that ships of the Coastal Forces, which had previously been patrolling the sea lanes, would now be mainly concerned with protecting the supply ships in the wide seaway created across the Channel, particularly at night when air cover by the RAF was not possible.

One problem to be overcome was that of communications. Operations in the northern half of the Channel were based on information provided by the radar station on top of St Boniface Down at Ventnor on the Isle of Wight. The radar could capture information on ship movements most of the way across the Channel, but the area covered by radar did not extend to the French coast. In order to have up to the minute information on enemy ship movements along the whole of the D-Day supply route it would be necessary to have reliable radar cover for the whole of the Channel between the English and French coasts. Dreyer and Peter came up with a plan to station controlling officers on board ships off the French coast, each equipped with a radar set providing up to the minute information which would allow them to direct defensive operations on the spot.

The two of them presented their plans to the top brass and were delighted when they were offered the use of four frigates equipped with radar sets and the use of the radar set on the destroyer HMS *Scylla* which would be based in the British assault area off the French coast. Radar operators and control officers were trained, and the plan was made ready. As D-Day neared, Peter recalled looking out from Portsdown Hill at the extraordinary fleet of ships being assembled in Portsmouth Harbour and regretting that he was not going to be part of the biggest naval invasion in history. Once things got under way on the evening of 5 June however, nobody had any time for further reflection.

In the event, the scheme worked perfectly, and from D-Day plus one, the control officers from the four frigates returned to Portsmouth each morning to provide reports on the previous night's activity. Dreyer or Peter would then prepare the plans for the next night's operations which had to be agreed by their commanding officer. In the afternoon, one or both of them would attend a briefing at HMS *Dolphin* in Portsmouth Harbour, where the controlling officers and the frigates' commanding officers with their navigating officers all assembled before setting off back to France for the next night's operations.

At this time, Peter was saddened to hear of the death of his old friend David Haig Thomas at whose wedding he had been best man and who had brought back from Greenland the geese which set Peter on the trail of the Greenland white-fronted goose. David had been part of No. 4 Commando, dropped behind enemy lines on the morning of D-Day. Shortly after landing, his party had run into a German patrol and he had been shot.

Once the invasion had taken place, it was quickly realised that it would be beneficial to have one or more radar stations on high ground, close to the landing beaches in Normandy. Peter was instructed to go to France to make the arrangements; if a command HQ could be established in Normandy it would obviate the need for the crews of the frigates to make the daily journey from French waters to Portsmouth and back. On 15 June, D-Day plus nine, Peter crossed the Channel. Within days, a new command centre was established in a dug-out close to Sword Beach, with a plotting table similar to the one in Portsmouth. Signals were received each night from several temporary radar positions established along the nearby coast and from the radar sets on board the frigates positioned offshore. The positions of enemy ships could then be transferred to the plotting table. New instructions or changes to operations could be relayed by radio directly from the command centre to the motor torpedo boats on patrol off the coast. Peter, as Staff Officer Operations (2), Coastal Forces, was responsible for planning these coastal operations and ensuring that the flow of information was used to best effect during the operations themselves. Before leaving England, he had created a map of the coast overlaid with a coded grid. He made two copies, gave one to Christopher Dreyer in Portsmouth and kept the other himself. In this way, he could make situation reports by radio to Portsmouth without giving away Allied shipping positions. On occasion, Peter was required to relieve one of the four controllers on board the frigates offshore if one of them needed some time out or needed to return briefly to England.

Peter was often free in the afternoons and with other officers went off by jeep into the surrounding countryside to watch the progress of the invasion force as the Germans were pushed back and then overrun. Often, there was a stated purpose for these excursions, to inspect the damage inflicted by naval shelling or to investigate a shipyard as a potential new HQ for operations. In addition, it was felt useful for the commanding officers of ships in the area to be taken to see the fighting on the front line a few miles inland. From the descriptions of the trips, the impression that they were enjoying the excitement of the moment is inescapable, coming as they did under light enemy sniper and mortar fire on a number of occasions, and one is left to wonder if all the excursions were strictly necessary. It is hard to be critical. They had fought for four long hard years, and now the enemy was on the run. At last, the Allies were taking the battle to the Germans, and Peter and his fellow officers had the opportunity to see this extraordinary operation as it happened. First-hand experience of the successful advance would certainly be an excellent boost to morale for all concerned. On one occasion, Peter and his group got too close to the front line however and came under a more sustained attack. They managed to escape back to their jeep and to safety, but the event increased Peter's respect for the fighting soldiers who had to live from day to day under continual attack.

The last months of the war were, for Peter, a chequerboard of short assignments. After serving for some time at the Coastal Forces

Command HQ in Normandy, he was assigned to set up a similar operation with American naval forces at Cherbourg. The Americans were using PT boats, their equivalent of motor torpedo boats, to attack German convoys that were still operating in the area. Once established at Cherbourg, he was given further orders to set up an operation to harass German convoys in the Channel Islands. He was given the use of an American warship, the USS *Maloy,* which was similar in size to a British frigate. Peter set up his control on the *Maloy* using her radar equipment to direct night operations. Though the war was coming to an end, the Germans still held control of the Channel Islands and surrounding waters, and some of the encounters in the autumn of 1944 were particularly fiercely fought.

Peter was then ordered to return to his original base at Portsmouth, where Christopher Dreyer was still in command. His role now was to assist in the completion of the official report on the actions of Coastal Forces during the D-Day invasions. He had, for some time, been writing what was to be an official book on operations in the Channel during the war and offered the manuscript as part of his record. The Admiralty however agreed that the book, once censored, could be issued independently and so *The Battle of the Narrow Seas* was published in 1945. In negotiation with the publishers, Peter agreed to reduce his royalty for the book from 17.5 per cent to 10 per cent. Peter's mother was dismayed over what she saw as his lack of business acumen and approached the publishers herself to try and influence matters but got nowhere in her negotiations which was perhaps just as well. It was at this time that Peter started taking flying lessons at Gosport, taught by a squadron leader from Coastal Command.

Peter was now reassigned once again, this time to Great Yarmouth to join the division of Coastal Forces operating off the Dutch coast, where German evacuation convoys were in progress. Because he spoke some German and had extensive experience of fighting in small boats in the Channel, Peter was asked to interview a captured German officer. Karl Muller was the senior officer of a flotilla of boats similar to the one Peter had commanded, and he and Peter had fought each other directly on more than one occasion. Captain Muller had been captured after an engagement off the Dutch coast when three E-boats had been sunk by British forces. The purpose of the interviews was to learn more about technical issues concerning E-boats; the German captain agreed to cooperate on the understanding that he would not reveal anything which might put German lives at risk.

The two interviews gave Peter much pause for thought. Until now, the enemy had been faceless and had been engaged without any thought of what the people they were attempting to kill might think or feel. Peter now found himself in conversation with a polite, intelligent man, who had experienced very similar circumstances and conditions to Peter during the last four years. Peter imagined that but for the circumstances of birth, he could have found himself fighting on the other side. Clearly, there was no question that the war had to be fought with total and unrelenting determination, but he was now reminded that not all Germans were ruthless barbarians. This attitude caused Peter some difficulties when, in May 1945, he was given permission to be among the party of officers that took the surrender of two German E-boats at Felixstowe. The officers sailed out to meet the enemy ships in a fleet of motor torpedo boats. Because he spoke German, Peter was selected to go aboard one of the E-boats to help bring it in to port. His request that the crews should be allowed to round up their possessions before leaving the ships was felt by some of the British there that day to be close to fraternisation, and there was a worry that, if given any time alone on board, the Germans might attempt to scuttle the vessels. Peter was therefore charged with accompanying a German officer as he rounded up the crew's personal belongings.

Just as the war came to an end, Peter was offered command of a new frigate, HMS *Cardigan Bay*. She wasn't the destroyer he had craved, but he was thrilled at the opportunity and threw himself into preparations, visiting sister ships at the shipbuilders and taking the courses he would require before he assumed command. The war might be over in Europe, but the war against Japan in the Pacific went on, and Peter felt it might continue for years to come. However, he now found himself presented with a dilemma. His new command would take him away from home for months, and his marriage to Jane was in difficulty. She was now pursuing her own interests with a job at the BBC and a novel was under way. The strains that had begun to appear would only be increased by Peter's prolonged absence.

9

The Birth of the Trust

The war in Europe was over. Peter had thrived on the challenges it had offered, and his talents had equipped him well to respond to the demands it had made on him and his comrades. If he declined the new commission with HMS *Cardigan Bay*, he would be forced to face a new life in which the routines and certainties of military existence were stripped away and re-establish his former career in a new and uncertain world. If he accepted the commission, he felt that his marriage would almost certainly be at an end. Around this time, Peter and Jane left her grandparents' former house in St John's Wood and moved into a new house in Edwardes Square, London.

It was shortly after this that Peter was approached by the Conservative Party to ask if he would be interested in standing as a member of parliament. He discussed the proposition with Jane who felt strongly that he should accept. He applied initially to stand for the Rugby constituency but was not chosen to contest the seat. Shortly afterwards, he was selected to represent the Conservatives in the Wembley North constituency, and at the election in 1945 he was defeated. Peter was downhearted at this reversal of fortune but remained as prospective candidate for Wembley North until 1948 when, with all his energies and interest now channelled elsewhere, he stood down. He later wrote to a friend: 'I have frequently had occasion since those days to thank my lucky stars that I never became a member of parliament.' He knew well enough that, had he succeeded in becoming an MP, his life would have taken a very different course. His political life wasn't quite at an end though. In 1953, Peter was invited to stand as the Conservative candidate for the Gloucester constituency and turned the offer down. He continued to support the Conservative Party however, and in the 1955 General Election went out on the campaign trail in support of Frances Vale, the candidate for the Aston Division in Birmingham, on whose behalf he made thirty-six street corner speeches in the course of a single day.

It is clear that after Peter's failure to be elected in 1945, matters between Jane and Peter became more strained. It is also clear that their subsequent memories of this time were different, certainly in matters of detail. Jane wrote in her autobiography that Peter had been offered a destroyer, not a frigate. She maintained that with the sudden end of the war in Japan the offer of a command was withdrawn; it wasn't. Peter recalled that he had made a decision to swap naval life for a career in politics and after the election never considered returning to the navy. Their autobiographies even record different figures for the number of votes by which Peter lost in the election, 435 versus 225. Peter discussed his marriage with his mother; Kathleen was convinced that Peter should end it but he was not ready to do so. Their sharp disagreement over the matter was the nearest they ever came to a rift between them.

Peter was invited at this time to illustrate the English edition of *The Snow Goose,* by Paul Gallico. This story about a painter who lives in a lighthouse and is brought an injured snow goose by a village girl was obviously based, in part, on Peter's life before the war. Peter had met Gallico and told him something of his life in the lighthouse though he had not been consulted before the book was published. Now, at an exhibition of Peter's paintings in London, Gallico saw a portrait of Jane and asked Peter to make her 'Fritha' in the illustrations. There was to be another exhibition of Peter's work in the United States. He and Jane sailed together to New York, Peter working on the illustrations for *The Snow Goose* during the crossing. The exhibition was rather more successful than the previous one, this time in a different gallery. Jane met the head of Random House Publishing who asked to see the manuscript of her first, unfinished, novel, and both she and Peter made some radio broadcasts. There was an endless round of parties in a city that seemed untouched by the war, with all kinds of food readily available and the streets lit up as if the past five years of hardship, loss and turmoil hadn't happened. Peter visited the Bronx Zoo, run by his old friend Jean Delacour, and they were given snakes, alligators and turtles to ship home on the *Queen Mary*, to be distributed round British zoos. Jane went on a shopping spree and admitted spending nearly all the money Peter had made from selling paintings at the exhibition, though he seemed only to be glad to see her happy again. On their return to England, Peter's mother met them at Southampton with Nicola and her nanny. Kathleen made it very clear how she felt when she invited Peter to drive back to London with her and told the others that they would have to go by train as there was no room for anyone else in the car.

During the all-consuming effort of military action, Peter had never lost his love of wild places and the birds that inhabit them. He had taken every opportunity during his periods of leave to escape briefly to shoot with his friends, times during which the marshes and fens he so loved seemed more precious to him than ever. Now, another prospect came to the fore. As he wrote later, he had for some time been developing the idea of establishing a research station for the study and protection of wildfowl. It seemed likely that the population of some wildfowl species had declined during the war years, making the need for their study and protection a matter of some urgency. He might well have returned to the lighthouse at Sutton Bridge, but during the war the salt marsh around the lighthouse had been reclaimed for farming and the building now stood over a mile from the sea, surrounded by farmland. It was no longer the wild and beautiful place that he had once fallen in love with.

While thinking about where such a research station might be established, Peter received two letters which were to change his life fundamentally and for ever. The first letter came from Howard Davis, a leading member of Bristol Naturalists' Society and later, in 1951, its president. He sent Peter a paper he had written on the flocks of white-fronted geese that wintered each year on the Severn Estuary and invited him to join him on a visit to the marshes near the village of Slimbridge in Gloucestershire where the geese could be observed. Peter had been to Slimbridge once before, in February 1937. On that occasion, he had given a talk to Bristol Naturalists' Society and stayed overnight with a birdwatching friend, Harold Savory, who, with Howard Davis, took him to Slimbridge to see the wild geese the following day. Photographs taken that day show a youthful-looking Peter in a long greatcoat and highly polished shoes, appearing for all the world like he was setting out for a walk down Oxford Street rather than a tramp across a marsh. As it was late in the season, only thirty or so geese remained on the feeding grounds.

Now, in 1945, Peter was wondering whether to accept this new invitation, when the arrival of the second letter settled the matter. This was from his old friend Will Tinsley in Lincolnshire who had received some of Peter's collection of wildfowl when he had to leave the lighthouse at the start of the war. Among these birds were a pair of lesser white-fronted geese which Peter had collected during his trip to Hungary in 1936. Will now wrote to say that in 1943, a wild lesser white-fronted goose had landed next to the pen containing the captive birds and had stayed for several days. The goose was at this time virtually unknown in Britain, the only previous sighting being a bird that was shot in 1886. Peter was convinced that if Will said it was a lesser whitefront then that's what it was, and he began to wonder whether more of the geese might be found in winter among the huge flocks of visiting white-fronted geese, their presence unrecognised because of their similarity to the other species. Perhaps, on reflection, it would be nice to visit Slimbridge again, see the duck decoy in the little wood and observe the huge flocks of geese. And, who knew, might there be, hidden among the flocks, an example of this rarest of British geese? There was only one way to find out.

On 15 December, the party assembled, Howard Davis, Peter and John Winter among them and walked down the track past the decoyman's cottage to the sea wall overlooking the Dumbles, an area of salt marsh bordering the River Severn. A happy day was spent observing the flock of over 4,000 geese, but there was no sign of the elusive lesser white-fronted goose. That night, Peter stayed with Howard at his home at Little Stoke Farm and the next morning decided to tell the other members of his party about his theory. To illustrate the difference between the two species, he made a sketch of the lesser white-fronted goose showing the key identifying features. Back on the sea wall, they had been watching for only forty-five minutes when Howard asked Peter to take a look at a particular bird; and there it was, right in front of him, a lesser white-fronted goose, only the third ever seen in Britain. It was a heart-stopping moment for Peter, a moment which would shape his entire future. That afternoon, a second lesser whitefront was discovered among the flocks. Apart from the white-fronted and lesser white-fronted geese observed that day, another five species of wild goose had been seen. As they walked happily back up the lane, the thought crystallised in Peter's mind – this was the place he had been looking for, this was where he would set up his research station. In an account of the visit written the following day, Peter wrote, 'Yesterday, Sunday December 16th was the best day's goose watching that ever I had.'

The New Grounds was an area of grassland reclaimed from the River Severn which, together with the salt marsh known as the Dumbles beyond the sea wall, was owned by the Berkeley family who had hunted across the land for generations. One of the reasons why the area was such a magnet for wild birds in winter was that the Berkeleys had maintained the land in a manner to make it attractive to wildfowl and waders. The shooting had always been carefully managed to ensure that the large flocks of geese continued to arrive each winter from northern Russia. Other factors made the New Grounds a good location for the new centre. The sea wall provided an opportunity to view the birds at close quarters without being seen, and the presence of a number of Second World War pillboxes which overlooked the marsh meant that observers could stay dry, without disturbing the birds. In addition, there was the duck decoy in the wood, the Berkeley New Decoy, built in 1843. By the time Peter visited in 1945 it was disused and somewhat run down, but he could see that with some repair it could be brought back into use and he would be able to catch ducks to ring and examine them. Finally, there was a cottage, a bungalow and some dilapidated old farm buildings on-site. The Berkeleys had retained three keepers here in winter to manage the shooting grounds and the decoy. On this remote, bleak, isolated spot Peter was to build something quite extraordinary.

Peter began negotiations with Captain Robert Berkeley for an area of land for his project. In 1946, he was able to secure a lease which included the cottage, the bungalow, the farm buildings and twenty-three acres of land. The Berkeley family reserved the right to shoot over the land on up to eight days a year. Across the road was a house occupied by a Mr and Mrs Bowditch. Mr Bowditch worked for the local farmer, and as an indication of the relative isolation of the place even in 1945, Philippa Scott later noted that Mrs Bowditch had only once left the New Grounds and that was to travel to Gloucester by canal boat.

Work now quickly began in earnest. Peter continued to live at his house in Edwardes Square in London but spent most weekends down in Gloucestershire, staying in the cottage and working on his new project. German prisoners of war were brought in to build a fox-proof fence surrounding seventeen acres of the site and to construct a number of simple wooden observation huts on the sea wall. Peter designed these, just as he had designed his first hide at Borough Fen before the war. This time, the viewing aperture was adjustable and could be made narrower or wider depending on how close the geese were. They were also provided with foot rests for additional comfort. Ponds were dug, paths laid out and individual pens fenced off. The decoy in the wood was repaired by Peter and made ready for the first catch of wild ducks, becoming one of only eight decoys still operating in the United Kingdom at that time. Mains water and telephone lines had to be laid under the canal. There was no electricity, and there would be no supply until the new house was built in 1953. There was no bathroom or toilet in the cottage; for water, everyone had to make use of a single tap in the stable yard. Heating in the cottage came from the Rayburn stove and it was possible to have an open fire in the room that became Peter's studio. Lighting was by paraffin lamps. Conditions in the early days were extremely primitive, something that was remarked upon by many of the people who helped to develop the site.

The first member of staff, ornithologist John Yealland, had previously worked for the Duke of Bedford so would have had experience with the Duke's flock of red-breasted geese. Peter and John Yealland made plans to receive the first group of birds, which came from a number of sources. From Will Tinsley came the pair of lesser white-fronted geese that Peter had kept at the lighthouse before the war. Another small group of ten birds from that original collection included a pair of Peter's beloved red-breasted geese which had been kept by another of Peter's friends in Lincolnshire, Rick Pilcher. The bulk of the new collection however came from Gavin Maxwell, the author of *Ring of Bright Water*. Maxwell had a collection of around fifty birds in Scotland which he was happy to make available to Peter, and these became the nucleus of the collection at Slimbridge. Driven down from Scotland on 19 September 1946, the birds arrived slightly ahead of schedule and had to be corralled in the bungalow overnight, until they could be introduced into the Rushy Pen the following morning.

Towards the end of 1946, with the collection properly established, Peter felt the need to provide the operation with a name and with some sort of official status and so the Severn Wildfowl Trust was formed. A group of people met at the Patch Bridge guest house by the canal bridge half a mile up the lane on Sunday, 10 November and after some discussion passed the following resolution: 'That a Society be formed with the name of "The Severn Wildfowl Trust" and that the draft rules produced to the meeting be adopted as the rules of the Trust'. Attendees at the meeting, apart from Peter, included his old friend, the actor James Robertson Justice, Michael Bratby, Captain Robert Berkeley and Howard Davis. The Trust required a president, someone with authority, energy and a passion for birds. Peter was fortunate to secure the services of Field-Marshal Viscount Alanbrooke who had been Winston Churchill's Chief of the Imperial General Staff during the war. The Trust also required a treasurer, so Peter approached Sir Archibald Jamieson, who had recently retired as chairman of Vickers Ltd and who had bought some of Peter's paintings before the war to hang in the wardrooms of the aircraft carriers his company had built. Peter himself became director. Members of the public were invited to become members at a cost of one guinea per annum.

Peter later wrote to Howard Davis:

You will be delighted to hear that Lord Alanbrooke has accepted the Presidency of our Trust, and also that Bernard Tucker is prepared to serve on our Council. I have also done well, I think, in getting Sir Archibald Jamieson, the Chairman of Vickers, and a very 'big noise' in the city, to agree to be our Treasurer. I have two good candidates for Secretary, both so excellent, that I did not know which we should select. I am bringing my wife down to see the geese this weekend; I wonder if you would be there.

Lord Alanbrooke proved to be an excellent choice and would attend every council meeting for the next fourteen years, except when he was ill, working tirelessly in support of the Trust in matters great and small. Peter wrote of him in *The Eye of the Wind*:

His acceptance of the Presidency turned out to be one of the most important factors in its success, and it demonstrated once more how really great men can and do find time to go into the detail of quite small things when they are interested.

Peter could quite easily have been talking about himself of course, though his innate modesty would have prevented him from saying so, even if he had thought it.

The secretary of the Severn Wildfowl Trust was to be Michael Bratby, and in addition to him, Lord Alanbrooke and Sir Archibald Jamieson, members of council for the new organisation included Max Nicholson, who would shortly become head of the Nature Conservancy Council, Captain Berkeley, Howard Davis, James Robertson Justice, Phyllis Barclay-Smith, secretary of the British Ornithological Union and Bernard Tucker, editor of *British Birds*. It is hard to imagine a better suited group of people to get the Trust up and running.

The aims of the Trust were stated as follows:

To promote the study of wildfowl and to undertake any activity which, in the opinion of the Council, is calculated to promote knowledge of and interest in wildfowl and in particular to establish and maintain a wildfowl and research observatory at the New Grounds on the estuary of the River Severn which will provide facilities for:

1) A close study of the winter flocks of wild geese and other birds.
2) The ringing of wild ducks in the decoy pools and of wild geese on the marshes for the further study of migration.
3) The study of a comparative collection of live wildfowl.

Considering the role the Trust was ultimately to play in the conservation of species and wetlands around the globe, these aims and objectives seem remarkably modest, but then of course, in those early days, Peter could have had no idea of the impact his new organisation was going to have in future years. Nor could he have envisaged that less than fifteen years later, he would be a co-founder and chairman of the world's most well-known conservation body, the World Wildlife Fund.

Peter was now firmly established in what had become an all-consuming enterprise; there was to be no turning back. To save his marriage, he had turned down a promising career in the Royal Navy. During his negotiations with the Berkeley family in early 1946 he had wanted to show Jane what he was planning and to share with her his excitement and hopes about the future. At Peter's urging, Jane had come down to Slimbridge. She was not at all interested in wild geese and saw only a flat, desolate landscape of soggy fields and drainage ditches with a clump of trees and a couple of run-down cottages in a spot which seemed to be miles from anywhere and even more remote from the bustle and excitement of London. She felt ill and unhappy. She went with Peter to Berkeley Castle and listened to the discussions about the possibility of leasing the land and the cottages and was clearly filled with unease. Whether she made her feelings known to Peter at the time is not known. What is clear, is that this was the beginning of the end. As wife of an MP, based in London, Jane could perhaps have happily pursued the kind of life she wanted to live, but the idea of being marooned amid bleak and muddy fields in the middle of nowhere, clearly caused her considerable disquiet. She was to return for a further visit in early December 1946 but the progress that had been made in the development of the site clearly did nothing to change her opinion. In August 1947, Jane left the house at Edwardes Square, and the marriage was over.

It was not simply the prospect of living at Slimbridge that caused the break-up of the marriage, though it might have been the last straw for Jane. There is no doubt that they had once loved each other, but they were different in many ways, in age, in temperament and in their aspirations. Jane was young, uncertain and desperate to be loved. Peter did indeed love her but was unable to give her the attention she craved, distracted as he was by the constant demands of wartime. When he met her, Peter clearly thought her more mature than she was and had no sense of the difficulties she would face, living alone for prolonged periods. But then how could he have known? Jane had made every effort to appear mature and grown-up, anxious as she was to distance herself from a less than happy childhood and join the world of adults. Things might have been different had there been no war to divert Peter's attention, but it seems likely that they were too different for the marriage to have survived in the long term, war or no war. To the credit of both of them, there were no recriminations, and they both openly acknowledged their own contribution to the breakdown. They were to remain friends, and Jane and Philippa, Peter's second wife, were also to establish a good relationship. Some years later, Jane edited the manuscript of Peter's autobiography *The Eye of the Wind*, helping him to whittle it down to a publishable length. Her signature appears regularly in the Scotts' visitors book in their house at Slimbridge in the months leading up to publication. In 1962, when Jane was the Director of the Cheltenham Literature Festival, Peter agreed to be a key speaker, giving a lecture on whales.

Peter dealt with the unhappiness of their separation by throwing himself into his work and his painting. He continued to make frequent visits to Slimbridge, driving down at weekends to review progress in the building of fences and pens. He would sometimes paint two or three landscapes in the cottage and leave them to dry for a week before adding flying ducks the following weekend. These could be sold for modest sums, augmenting the Trust's very limited funds. In the early days the team always worked hand-to-mouth, and Peter would sometimes make purchases then cancel them again because there wasn't enough money to pay for things.

During the first year of the Trust, expenditure amounted to a little over £5,500 while income fell short of this by £2,800. An appeal for £5,000 in 1947 brought in just over £600. At the time of the first annual report, income included fees from 1,100 members at one guinea per head and gate money of a little less than £20 – members of the public were allowed into the grounds for one shilling per head, but they were not allowed to visit the hides and see the wild geese on the Dumbles. This privilege was reserved for Trust members who were escorted down to the hides by a warden. By April 1948, Peter was able to report that the Trust had had 2,500 visitors in the previous year. Because one of the primary aims of the Trust was education, they were at least relieved of the burden of paying income tax, and as the collection was open to the public Peter was able to apply for an allocation of ration coupons for feed for the birds.

With no regular income, Peter was forced to rely on help from friends, who were more than happy to descend on Slimbridge for the weekend. Among the frequent visitors were Michael Bratby, Keith Shackleton, Gavin Maxwell and Lord Alanbrooke, who was a keen ornithologist. Friends were encouraged to help with the ongoing work in the collection area, digging ponds, building fences and laying paths. It seems that Gavin Maxwell sometimes brought a bit of excitement to the proceedings at the New Grounds. In April 1955, Peter's second wife Philippa wrote in a letter to Maxwell's uncle, Lord William Percy:

Your nephew Gavin drove me in his new racing car at 108 m.p.h. on the lane between the canal and this house – a distance of exactly half a mile! On the main road it went 120 and I was rather frightened! He says it will go 140.

One can only hope that the grounds weren't open at the time.

The naturalist Gerald Durrell came down to Slimbridge to meet John Yealland who was to accompany him on a trip to Africa to collect animals. Gerald was to write later of the visit:

> John and I were planning a collecting trip to West Africa, but at the same time I wanted to see what Peter was up to as it sounded suspiciously like an idea I was formulating to found my Wildlife Preservation Trust in Jersey. Peter showed me round with great ebullience, pointing out soggy field after soggy field and describing in glowing terms what he intended to do with them. Privately, I vouchsafed my view to John Yealland that I thought Peter was mad. The idea of the Trust was an excellent one, but the place I thought impossible. Who, I wanted to know, was going to go to the back of beyond to stand up to their ankles in freezing water? No one. Well, fortunately I was wrong, for most of the British Isles, to say nothing of people all over the world, apparently were just waiting for the chance to do just that and Slimbridge today is the huge success it deserves to be.

Another regular visitor to Slimbridge in the early days was Philippa Talbot-Ponsonby, who had been appointed Peter's personal secretary and Assistant Secretary to the Trust. Her salary was paid out of Peter's own pocket. At the time, she could have little imagined the contribution she would make to the Trust in the years to come.

The winter of 1946 to 1947 was extremely harsh. The tap froze, as did the water in the new ponds, and conditions were extremely difficult. The allocation of corn for the birds allowed by the Department of Agriculture was insufficient to feed the growing collection, and Peter was forced to scrounge odds and ends of corn leftovers from nearby farmers. It is a testament to Peter's determination and leadership and the dedication of his small band of helpers that they managed to survive at all. Five years later in 1952, the problem of providing enough feed for the birds was resolved when Peter arranged a sponsorship deal with Blue Cross Poultry Foods under which the company provided the Trust with twelve tons of feed each year.

The Trust was always short of money in the early days; a series of 'wanted' requests in the Trust's bulletins in the early 1950s give a flavour of the kinds of things that were in short supply. Over the years, the requests included, among other things: garden seats, bulbs, gardening equipment, a scythe, a garden roller, a wheelbarrow, a saw bench, carpenters' tools, a pressure spray, a bath chair, a microscope, a small square-ended punt, an old dry-stone wall and advice from a hydraulic engineer.

Peter's mother came down for a visit, and her reaction could not have been different from Jane's. Of her visit she wrote in her diary:

> I had a lovely week-end with my son at his wild-goose resort [on the Severn]. Oh dear, I do love going off for such a lovely weekend. The geese were terrific, so was the cold; but I wouldn't have minded if it had been ten times colder. We sat in hides behind the sea-wall for hours, but the movement of the geese was enthralling. And then the evenings back at the inn, very snug with a big wood fire; and then up early in the frost and back to the marsh.

Peter can only have wished that Jane had been equally enthusiastic.

One of Peter's early problems was how to build up numbers of waterfowl. From the start, he was determined to establish as large a collection as possible, but with limited funds and a scarcity of available birds, he faced a considerable challenge. During the war, many collections of waterfowl had been dispersed; nobody had time for the indulgence of keeping ducks and swans on their properties. Furthermore, during times of food rationing, it is probable that many ornamental waterfowl found their way onto the dinner table. When the first birds arrived from Will Tinsley, Gavin Maxwell and one or two others, Peter found himself in possession of fifty-four waterfowl representing a handful of species. Clearly, if the grounds at Slimbridge were to be opened to the public he would need more species and many more birds. But how to achieve this?

In late 1946, under the auspices of the Avicultural Society, Peter compiled a document he called the Waterfowl Registry. Letters were sent to everyone in the country who had kept, or might have kept, waterfowl before the war. This included zoos, stately homes and other private individuals who he knew either directly or through third parties. Each owner was asked to confirm what species they held and how many of each sex. Many individuals and organisations replied, and Peter compiled all the data into a loose-leaf binder. The Waterfowl Registry includes his own entry for Slimbridge and from it we can see that in January 1947, just after the Trust had been formed, he possessed 231 individual birds representing sixty species. The exercise was repeated on each of the two following years, and this time people were invited to indicate which species they were trying to obtain and which they had available for sale or exchange. As a result of the survey, Peter was able to augment his own collection and help others to improve theirs.

Breeding had also commenced, though the numbers were small to start with. In 1949, forty-nine goslings and 223 ducklings were reared in the collection. The sale of surplus birds was another way of raising vital cash. In the early days, birds that had been sold were crated up and taken to the nearby railway station by horse and cart. In 1948, Peter made an extended visit to North America, visiting wildlife reserves in both the United States and Canada. He took with him seventy birds for sale or exchange and subsequently shipped back to England 150 ducks geese and swans. A valuation list from 1952 shows the value of 737 birds, representing 121 species and sub-species. The total value is £6,068.00 with the most expensive species being three nene geese from Hawaii which were valued at £150 each. Not all species were available for sale; the 1953 sales prospectus shows thirty-one species with prices for each by the pair. Three species headed the list at £30 a pair: lesser white-fronted goose, Ross's snow goose and Orinoco goose. The cheapest species was the mallard at £2 a pair.

Other birds came from a variety of sources. Winston Churchill lent Peter a male black swan that was causing problems among his flock at his home at Chartwell. The swan lived happily at Slimbridge for many years and was the parent of many broods of cygnets. At the other end of the scale, in 1953 a Mrs Burnett wrote from Bideford and asked if the Trust would be able to take a single mallard off her hands. Peter agreed, and the duck was put on the train from Bideford and collected at nearby Cam station. Some birds were apparently acquired by slightly less orthodox means. One such case was described by Keith Shackleton, a lifelong friend of Peter's and a fellow artist of some distinction. Keith Shackleton was involved with the Trust from early on; the two friends had first met during the Second World War when Peter was punt-gunning on the Ribble Estuary. Keith was visiting Peter at his home in Edwardes Square in London when he suggested to him that they needed some diving ducks for the growing collection at Slimbridge, adding that there were plenty of tufted ducks in nearby St James's Park. A plan was hatched, and the two unlikely outlaws sneaked into the park at dead of night armed with a bag of breadcrumbs; the resulting catch of a pair of plump tufted ducks was put in the bath at Edwardes Square.

Whether or not Peter ever felt guilty is unknown; he had after all stolen the birds from a Royal Park. It seems that amends were made however. In 1953, Peter received a letter from Thomas Hinton, who had retired as bird keeper in the Central Royal Parks. Born in 1879, Thomas had held the post for fifty-two years and five months and had served under every monarch from Victoria to Queen Elizabeth II, becoming the last person to serve in this historic role. It was with Thomas Hinton that Peter had made an outside broadcast for the BBC from St James's Park in 1936. Thomas now wrote that he hoped to visit Slimbridge at some point and went on:

> It will always be a mystery to me how the 8 Pinkfooted you presented to St James's Pk left the water and got to the Serpentine, I was never able to contact anyone who had seen them cross Hyde Park Corner which of course they would have to do.

Peter wrote on the bottom of his letter, 'So nice to hear from him. Hope he will come here sometime as would love to show him the birds.' It's nice to imagine Peter and Thomas wandering around the grounds and stopping to admire a particularly fine pair of tufted ducks.

10

Philippa

It is a well-known saying that behind every great man stands a great woman. In Peter's case it is fair to say that for the rest of his life after the war, a great woman stood not behind him but right at his side, sharing with him the trials and tribulations but also the successes and formidable achievements of the Severn Wildfowl Trust. Peter was later to write of her:

> The part that my wife Philippa, plays in my life is central. She is my principal adviser. She manages my business and financial affairs. She cooks my food and looks after me and the house. Although both of us have Scottish ancestry, she seems to have inherited more of the proverbial thrift of the Scots than I have, which at least to some extent counteracts my own tendencies to gross extravagance. Without her I'd be lost – and bankrupt.

In a tribute to Peter written in 1989, long-time friend and colleague Max Nicholson echoed the same sentiment when he wrote:

> I cannot forbear to quote from the Trust's first Annual Report the two line note, 'Miss Philippa Talbot-Ponsonby is now Assistant Secretary and has picked up the rather complicated threads of the Trust's activities with great efficiency.' No appreciation of Peter Scott can fail to echo very loudly this modest tribute to Lady Scott, not only to the Trust but to the conservation of Peter himself.

Philippa Talbot-Ponsonby was born in 1918 in Bloemfontein in South Africa. Her father's family came from the village of Langrish in Hampshire. A naval commander during the First World War, he was invalided out due to ill-health when he contracted tuberculosis. As a result of his illness, he retired to South Africa and took up breeding bulls. Philippa grew up in South Africa but travelled to England every year as a child, making the sea journey from Cape Town to Southampton on the famous lavender-coloured Union Castle steamers. She confessed in her autobiography that over the years of travelling to and fro, she assembled a collection of cups, spoons and table napkin rings, all carrying the Union Castle crest. Of this collection, one teaspoon, with the badge of the steamship *Arundel Castle* at the end of the handle, remains in a drawer in her house at Slimbridge. Philippa made the three-week journey fifteen times, until in 1931, the family moved back to England after her father's death. Philippa was twelve at the time.

During the 1930s, Philippa developed a passion for mountain climbing and walking and had several entertaining trips to the Alps, which included ascents of the Mönch and the Wetterhorn in Switzerland. Of her ascent of the Mönch she was to write, 'It was an exhilarating climb – even though, rather shamefully, we took the mountain railway up as far as the Jungfraujoch.' There was no shame here; the Mönch is one of Europe's biggest mountains and a tough ascent wherever you start from. In the house at Slimbridge that she shared with Peter for over thirty-five years, there are two photographs of the same mountain scene. In the foreground is the railway station at Kleine Scheidegg in Switzerland, where passengers who have ascended on the funicular railway from Grindelwald change to the mountain railway that runs through the face of the Eiger and up to the Jungfraujoch station, the highest in Europe. Behind the station, in the photographs, are ranged in magnificent array the high peaks of the Bernese Oberland: the Eiger, Mönch and Jungfrau. One of the pictures is on the back of the door to the drinks cabinet in Philippa's study, and it's not hard to imagine her gazing with fond memory at the mountains of her youth as she poured Peter's Sunday lunchtime sherry. The house is full of memories, not all of them Peter's.

When the war started, she worked first as a Land Girl near her home at Droxford in Hampshire. In 1943, she went to work at Bletchley Park where Alan Turing decoded the German Enigma codes. As previously noted, Philippa first met Peter in 1942 at the dinner party where he pretended to be Jane's deaf uncle. It might be thought that such a prank might put a young girl off a man forever, nevertheless she would eventually marry him. Not at first though, for they each went their separate ways without ever imagining that their paths would cross again. Immediately after the war, Philippa secured a posting to work at the British Embassy in Belgrade. She remembered with some fondness a walking holiday in Yugoslavia in 1937 and relished the prospect of returning. Her year there, during which the British Mission became an embassy, gave her further opportunities for walking and climbing adventures, so it was with mixed feelings that she returned to England at the end of 1946.

Back in England, she spent the best part of a year looking for a job. She particularly wanted to work abroad and would have applied to work at the Foreign Office, but the lack of a degree made this impossible. Philippa was therefore somewhat in the doldrums when, in November 1947, Anthony Part, an old Cambridge friend of her brother Evelyn, rang her up and asked if she would like to work for Peter Scott. It seems Philippa didn't remember the 'mad uncle' and had to be reminded that he was the man who painted ducks and geese. His secretary, Elizabeth Adams, was leaving to marry his half-brother Wayland and he needed a replacement. No doubt happy at the thought of any job to be going on with, Philippa applied for the post and was interviewed by Elizabeth Adams in a tea shop in Sloane Street. Not long afterwards, she was invited to a further interview with Peter. The second interview took place at Peter's house at Edwardes Square. As Philippa remembered, it was more of a general chat and he never asked to see her references. She remembers the meeting as being very casual: 'We sat at the long refectory dining-room table and talked of this and that.' Peter remembers interviewing 'a shy, quiet girl who sat before me looking small and neat and serious'. What appears slightly strange is that at the time, neither seems to have remembered their previous encounter in 1942, or if they did, neither mentioned it. During the conversation it became apparent to her that the job was hers if she wanted it. She did, and it was arranged that she would start work in a fortnight.

Her job was to be Peter's personal secretary and Honorary Assistant Secretary to the Severn Wildfowl Trust, based at his house in Edwardes Square in London. At that time, a year after the founding of the Trust, there were just 500 members and very little money, so her salary was paid directly by Peter. Philippa started work on 10 December 1947. Also employed by the Trust at the time was Douglas Eccleston who did much of Peter's typing; like Philippa, he had previously worked at Bletchley Park. Shortly after Philippa started work, Ray Aickman came on board to manage the Trust's accounts and to help generally, working two days a week. Also living in the house was Peter's five-year-old daughter Nicola and her nanny. Peter's wife, Jane, had left earlier that year.

From the very beginning, working as Peter's personal secretary meant that Philippa became closely involved with many aspects of his life. Peter's approach to work was organic in nature. If something needed doing then he would get someone to do it, without letting roles, duties or job descriptions get in the way. A less charismatic person might soon run into difficulties working this way, but just about everybody who ever worked for or with him mentioned the way in which his energy, enthusiasm and kindness swept you along and made you think that anything was possible and that you were just the person to get it done. Very early on, Philippa found herself looking after Peter's daughter Nicola on days when it was Nanny's day off, and Jane couldn't have her. Philippa was surprised that she managed to keep her job in the early days. She had no secretarial experience and could type only with two fingers, but Douglas Eccleston, who was already working for Peter, knew shorthand and was a skilled typist.

Peter's manner warmed her to him and she must have felt some sympathy for him as he had separated from his wife and lost his mother in the same year. Ray Aickman managed the Trust's accounts but Philippa and Douglas had to look after Peter's personal finances, and she recalled being summoned with Douglas by Peter's stepfather, Lord Kennet, to go over the books, an experience they found quite daunting. Philippa got to know many of Peter's friends and acquaintances who were frequent visitors to the house. Among these were Keith Shackleton, the actor James Robertson Justice and Michael Bratby who had become the first secretary of the Severn Wildfowl Trust.

In those early days, it seems that where Peter went, Philippa went too. Though the headquarters of the Trust were still at Edwardes Square, frequent trips were made to Slimbridge, and Philippa made an effort to try and identify the different species in the ever-growing collection of waterfowl and among the wild geese on the marsh. She recalled that

Keith Shackleton told her that if she saw a lesser white-fronted goose she would get a medal. Peter was learning to fly and would stop off for lessons at Kidlington Airport en route to Gloucestershire. He offered to pay for Philippa to learn too. On one occasion, Peter offered to fly her to Slimbridge in a Tiger Moth and looped the loop over the New Grounds. There were presumably no complaints from the Trust, but Philippa later revealed that in the village, the vicar complained that they had been flying dangerously over the church, though how he knew it was Peter in the plane remains a mystery.

Peter was at Cowes Week for the sailing in 1948, and Philippa, Nicola and Nanny went too. At this remove, it is hard to disentangle Peter's flamboyant approach to employment from what was clearly a growing affinity between the two; whatever the truth of it, they clearly enjoyed each other's company. Peter certainly had no complaints about how Philippa carried out her duties; when he went to America in the autumn of 1948 he left her in charge of the Trust. Then there is the matter of the rather beautiful portrait drawing of Philippa which Peter made. Looking at it now, one might assume that it was created after they started going out together, both from the look in Philippa's eyes and the care and attention devoted to the work by Peter. The portrait was made in 1948, less than a year after Philippa became his secretary.

By late 1948, it was clear that Peter could not continue to live at Edwardes Square and manage the Trust in Gloucestershire. Apart from the logistical problems involved, there was virtually no money available to continue to run the Trust, so on the advice of Peter's stepfather, Lord Kennet, the house in London was sold and Peter and his staff moved to Slimbridge. It was a complex operation. Philippa remained in London before the move to pack all the files and clear the cellar. On moving day itself, 14 January 1949, things did not go entirely to plan. A barge on the canal had collided with the bridge at Shepherd's Patch which meant the lorry was stranded on the other side of the canal. The driver insisted on returning to London with the vehicle and its contents, and it was not until three days later that the move could be completed. Peter was away in America again at the time, and Philippa recalled writing to him that she felt like 'a broody hen sitting on a lot of explosive eggs'. Both Peter and Philippa were now based full time at Slimbridge.

11

Canal Boats and Rockets

Once the Trust was based completely at Slimbridge, money was found to begin to recruit a few additional members of staff. In 1949, John Yealland took leave of absence from his post as curator to accompany Gerald Durrell on an expedition to Cameroon and was replaced by Eunice Overend. On his return from Africa, he resumed the post of curator and moved in to live with Mr and Mrs Bowditch in the house across the road from Peter's cottage. Assisting John Yealland now as warden was Tommy Johnstone who, with his wife Diana, lived in a cottage in Slimbridge village about half a mile from the New Grounds. Philippa was later to recall that Tommy 'became one of the staff without Peter really noticing', another example of Peter's fluid approach to employment. Tommy would later become curator himself, after John Yealland left in 1950 to become Curator of Birds at London Zoo. Tommy was to serve as curator until his retirement in 1973, while his wife Diana ran the gatehouse and the shop for the Trust. Mr Cameron arrived to take up the post of keeper; he and his wife and their two daughters moved into the bungalow which had been vacant from the start. Before Peter moved from London in 1949, Mrs Cameron, known as 'Chammy' by Peter and Philippa, had helped out by cooking and generally looking after the cottage when he was in residence. After the move, she became full-time housekeeper-cum-cook at the cottage. Peter and Philippa already occupied two of the rooms, and in 1949 they were joined by Hugh Boyd who had been appointed resident biologist. He was to remain with the Trust for over seventeen years. E. A. Scholes was recruited on a part-time basis as the membership secretary, although he carried out a great deal of other administrative work as well.

By all accounts, they were a happy group of people working together under difficult conditions, in pursuit of a common objective. Credit for the cohesion and hard work of the team must go to Peter who invariably had a direct and open manner about him. Tommy Johnstone remarked on his kindness, adding that he was always unaffected and natural with everyone with whom he came into contact. In those early days there was no television of course, but they did have a radio in the cottage. Philippa recalled John Yealland coming over on summer evenings to listen to the Promenade Concerts that were broadcast live from the Royal Albert Hall. Peter would certainly have been present on many of these occasions as he had a deep love of classical music. In *The Eye of the Wind,* he remembers playing a pianola (a form of piano, which plays automatically when operated by foot-pedals) when he was a small child at home. He wrote:

> I am easily and deeply moved by music – perhaps the more so because I do not understand its mechanisms. There are parts of the Brahms Violin Concerto, and of Sibelius's First Symphony and of Beethoven's Ninth and of the very end of Rosenkavalier, which, quite apart from their spiritual uplift, give me a purely physical sensation which can be compared on level terms with any other extreme of sensuality.

Peter had a habit of linking passages of music to significant events in his life. His last term at Cambridge he called his bolero term, because he had been listening intently to Ravel's *Bolero* at the time. While at university, he and a friend discovered the nest of a pair of garganey at Fulbourn Fen, the first nesting record for this species of duck in Cambridgeshire. The same evening, in a friend's rooms in Cambridge, he heard for the first time Mozart's *Symphony No. 40* which he referred to thereafter as the Garganic Symphony. Recalling in *The Eye of the Wind* the moment when he first set eyes on a lesser white-fronted goose at Slimbridge he wrote, 'I realised that it was a Lesser Whitefront. My spine tingled delightfully as it does in the slow movement of Sibelius's *Violin Concerto*.'

Elsewhere in *The Eye of the Wind* Peter wrote, 'The nightingale and the blackcap and the curlew are nature's soloists, but the geese are her chorus, as rousing, over the high sand, as the "Sanctus" of Bach's *B minor Mass*.' Philippa picked up the habit. Writing of John Yealland, she described him as a delightful person, very good company, with a deliciously dry sense of humour, adding that his favourite piece of music was Schubert's *Ninth Symphony*. She went on, 'I cannot hear it without thinking of him. Music is as evocative of people and places as are smells.'

With the cottage full and the bungalow occupied, there was a desperate need for accommodation, particularly for visiting ornithologists and other interested people who were beginning to descend on Slimbridge as news spread of Peter's activities. A solution was found in the purchase of an old canal narrowboat called *Beatrice* which was converted into a floating hostel moored by the bridge at Shepherd's Patch, half a mile from the cottage. Peter was encouraged in this scheme by Ray Aickman's husband, Robert, who in early 1946 had founded the Inland Waterways Association with the aim of preserving Britain's disappearing canal system for leisure purposes. Peter was an enthusiastic supporter and became a vice-president of the Inland Waterways Association shortly after it was formed, a post he held until 1986, when a dispute over recreational use of the River Derwent in Yorkshire, a river with important wildlife habitats, created a conflict of interest that he could not avoid.

Conditions on *Beatrice* were somewhat primitive. Eleven guests could be accommodated in six cabins. Four people slept on settee bunks in the main saloon, while two smaller cabins contained three bunks each. Full board cost twelve shillings and sixpence, while bed and breakfast was ten shillings. Visitors had to bring their own towels, sheets and ration cards and had to state their height in advance 'as some of the bunks are shorter than others'. In 1952, *Beatrice* was sold to a new owner in London, and for a while there was no accommodation available for visitors, who were now directed to the Patch Bridge guest house near the bridge. Subsequently the old stables behind the cottage were converted into a hostel for visitors and part-time workers. This accommodation remained in use for temporary staff members until 2016 when the hostel was converted into offices.

Word was getting around about Peter's plans and the founding of the Severn Wildfowl Trust, and various ornithologists and lovers of birds began to descend on this remote corner of Gloucestershire. Konrad Lorenz, Austrian ornithologist and ethologist and author of *King Solomon's Ring*, was an early visitor to Slimbridge and came down to stay on a number of occasions. In 1953, he gave a series of lectures at Bristol University and spent much of his spare time at the cottage. At the time, he was engaged in his work on imprinting, the process whereby young birds become attached to their parents or a surrogate, something he was able to demonstrate with geese and goslings. Lorenz took films at Slimbridge which he showed to a scientific conference in Oxford in 1953. During this visit he presented to Peter a copy of *King Solomon's Ring,* his famous work on animal behaviour in which he wrote an inscription thanking Peter for the opportunity to work alongside him at the Severn Wildfowl Trust. Peter recalled that when he visited Konrad in Bavaria to see his collection of birds, Konrad told him, 'I feel exactly like a small boy who is going to show his new toy railway to his best friend.' Another visitor in the early days was Ludwig Koch, a pioneer in the recording of bird song. He came to Slimbridge to record the calls of white-fronted geese. His equipment was so heavy that a team of people was required to carry it round for him. He stayed in the cottage while Peter was away and fell heavily down the narrow staircase, causing Philippa some concern as he was by that time in his seventies. Fortunately, he survived the ordeal.

The Trust also received its first royal visits at this time. Prince Philip, Duke of Edinburgh, came with James Robertson Justice and had lunch in the kitchen of the cottage. As Peter did not know how to carve a chicken, the task was left to Philip; carving meat was a skill Peter never mastered, and it was Philippa who carved the Sunday roast throughout their marriage. In early March, 1950, Princess Elizabeth made a formal visit to view the flocks of white-fronted geese on the Dumbles. The viewing was marred somewhat when the geese were scared off by a girl who walked across the reserve to get a view of the princess. Elizabeth didn't seem to mind and enjoyed lunch cooked for twelve people, served once again in the cottage kitchen.

Once the collection of wildfowl was up and running, Peter was able to turn his mind to other matters. Most pressing for him was the issue of the scientific study of wild ducks and geese in which he wished to engage. As soon as the Berkeley New Decoy was repaired, Peter began to use it to catch and ring ducks as part of a scheme called the National Wildfowl Count which had been established in 1947 by the International Wildfowl Inquiry, part of the British Section of the International Committee for Bird Preservation. Catches were small at first, indeed in the first year he caught only six mallard, but it was a start, and numbers began to increase each season. On Peter's birthday, in September 1950, he and Philippa secured 145 ducks in a single catch. The record catch for the decoy came in the winter of 1957 to 1958 when 2,237 ducks were caught and ringed. This was an excellent performance considering the Berkeley New Decoy has only four pipes, a circumstance which limits the number of days when the wind is in the right direction for a catch to be made. There was a further problem with the decoy however. As visitor numbers started to build at Slimbridge, the disturbance caused by people near the decoy reduced the numbers of ducks caught; other means of catching ducks needed to be found if a meaningful quantity of data were to be gathered. One obvious way to do this was to gain access to one or more of the other decoys still in operation in England. By extending operations elsewhere in the country, he would also have a better geographical spread of catches which could only improve the data he was collecting. Back in the eighteenth century, over 200 decoys were in operation. By 1886, this number had shrunk to forty-four and to nineteen by 1918. At the time Peter began looking at alternative decoys, there were just eight left operating in England.

The obvious place to start was at Borough Fen, of which Peter had such fond memories. The decoy was still operating and Billy Williams was still the decoyman. From 1949, the Trust paid the market price for ducks other than mallard to be ringed and released, rather than killed. From 1954, mallards were included in the scheme, and from that point no ducks were killed after capture. Billy Williams was very happy to switch from killing the birds to ringing them. He had always been punctilious in dealing with his catches and had learned to dispatch the ducks quickly, making death instantaneous. A buyer once told him that his ducks were always in demand with his customers as they looked as if they had died in their sleep. Now he was releasing the birds after ringing and was always delighted when he caught a bird he had ringed previously or received news of a ringed bird turning up somewhere else. On one occasion he caught a heron in the pipe, his first ever. Not having a suitable ring he applied a mallard leg ring, checked that it seemed comfortable, released the bird and recorded it. He duly came in for some criticism from the British Museum where records were kept, as it was thought the ring must be too small and might cause the bird distress. The following year, to Billy's surprise, the same heron turned up in the same pipe and he was able to inspect the ring. He was pleased to find that it still fitted properly without any indication of rubbing. He subsequently reported to the British

Museum that the bird had attended for its annual inspection and had proceeded on its way without need for maintenance. Perhaps Billy's favourite ring recovery story was the tale of a mallard leg ring which turned up in a pork pie served in a London restaurant and was sent to the British Museum for identification.

In 1956, the Trust took a lease at Borough Fen and thereafter it was run as a scientific resource, each bird caught being weighed, measured and ringed before release. The activities at Borough Fen were regularly reported in the Trust's bulletins and attracted considerable interest from Trust members and others, so arrangements were made for visits to the decoy by Trust members from time to time.

Another famous decoy was at Nacton, near Ipswich. Built in 1835, the decoy had been run by the Skelton family; the Williams and the Skeltons were the two most well-known decoy families in the nineteenth century. Nacton's peak season had been in 1925 to 1926 when 9,303 ducks were caught. The decoy ceased commercial operations in 1966. The following year, aided by a grant from the Nature Conservancy, the Trust leased the decoy from the Orwell Park Estate and ran operations for fifteen years until August 1982. As at Borough Fen, access was provided for Trust members at various times of the year.

At Abberton Reservoir, south of Colchester, was a duck catching station which consisted of a series of trapping cages rather different in design from a traditional decoy. Built by Major General Wainwright on his retirement from the army in 1949, the ringing facility took advantage of the large number of waterfowl that congregate on the reservoir in winter. The Trust developed close links with the operation in 1954, and with the support of the owners, the Essex Water Company, were instrumental in helping to obtain permanent protection for the reservoir's wildlife. Once again, valuable ringing data were made available to the Trust over a period of years. By 1986, approximately 200,000 ducks had been ringed across the sites from which the Trust was gathering data.

One way of raising additional funds from the ringing programme was the creation of a duck adoption scheme. For five shillings, members of the public could adopt a ringed bird and would receive news if the bird was captured again elsewhere. Bulletin number sixteen published in October 1954 explained:

The chances of recapture or recovery are rather better than ten per cent. And there is a great thrill in hearing news of a bird, perhaps from Greenland or Siberia, which may be the year's long distance winner. When adopting a duck for someone else you receive a special token. What about it for Christmas!

Three months later, as a result of this feature and a mention in *The Sunday Times*, 1,500 ducks and geese had been adopted.

Peter was also keen to start ringing geese as well as ducks so that their migration patterns could be determined in more detail and better assessments of populations established. Back in 1932, he had first discovered the joys of catching ducks at Borough Fen and had then turned his mind to the problem of catching geese as well. At the time it had been all about the thrill of the chase and catching a few geese for his collection at the lighthouse at Sutton Bridge. Now he wanted to catch geese to ring them but this time in significant numbers. He wasn't sure if the system he had developed in 1932, based on the fairly primitive equipment used in the fens to catch lapwing, would be adequate for his purposes.

There is some confusion over who first discussed with Peter the idea of using rockets to propel the nets. It might have been Christopher Dreyer, Peter's commanding officer in the run up to D-Day, or his friend James Robertson Justice. Whatever the truth of it, all three men had wartime naval experience and would have remembered the rockets that were fired by pistols to shoot a line from one vessel to another. The question was, would it be possible to create something based on that principle? Peter knew there was only one way to find out. He contacted the manufacturer of the pistols used by the Royal Navy, Messrs Schermuly Brothers and was invited to visit their testing ground at Newdigate. Peter went down to Surrey with James Robertson Justice and another friend who was passionate about wildfowl, Lord Geoffrey Percy, brother to the Duke of Northumberland. The company were delighted to assist in this entirely new application for their technology and Mr Schermuly came down to Slimbridge in February 1948, to attend the first attempts at what became known as 'rocket-netting'. A photographer from *Country Life* was also invited to record the event. The work involved in preparation was considerable, and they were by no means certain of success. However, on the morning of the first attempt, the system worked perfectly and thirty white-fronted geese and one pink-footed goose were caught. Fifteen of the white-fronted geese were kept for the collection and the rest of the birds were ringed and released. The system was a success! At a subsequent catch in February 1950, seventy-one white-fronted geese were caught.

In March 1950, the netting system was taken north to Scotland to catch pink-footed geese, an expedition which became a regular event over the next few years. By 1955, the team had made over seventy-five catches in twenty-one different areas where the geese congregated in winter. Peter was particularly anxious to study the distribution of pink-footed geese. At that time, it was known that they wintered in Britain in considerable numbers but were also shot in large numbers too, and there was a concern that the geese might be in decline. Records showed that on the River Severn years before, thousands of pink-footed geese had overwintered. By the time Peter started studying them, the numbers had dropped to around 100 each year. (In 2019, The Trust were delighted when a flock of just eight birds decided to winter on the reserve.) In addition, though it was known that the geese bred in Iceland, nobody knew exactly where. By ringing geese in different locations round the country over a number of years it was hoped to build up a clear idea of their numbers and distribution, and also to determine if shooting was causing any significant decline in their numbers.

The nets with which Peter was working were significantly larger than the ones he had used before. They were set out in pairs, each net measuring sixty by twenty yards, so the area covered, when fired, was 2,400 square yards, compared with twenty-five square yards back in the 1930s. As the team became more experienced, the numbers of netted birds grew. The record single catch was 490 pink-footed geese, and in later years they were regularly catching 3,000 per month. Peter was particularly pleased when they began to catch geese that had been ringed previously; eventually, they were catching an average of twenty ringed geese for every 300 birds netted. By 1954, Peter was confidently able to assert that some 46,000 pink-footed geese were wintering in Britain of which, he was fairly confident, between 12,000 and 15,000 were shot each year. As time progressed, the equipment and the nets were refined and refined again as their experience grew. The mesh of the nets became finer, flaps were added around the edges to stop geese from escaping from under the net, and more powerful rockets introduced. Various members of the Slimbridge team accompanied Peter on these trips and in the early days, Philippa was a constant companion while Lord Geoffrey Percy also took a keen interest.

Peter wrote about his netting activities more than once in *Country Life* and later made a television programme about the pink-footed geese and his method of catching them. The general public were highly interested, and it would seem that others started to emulate his methods, because in December 1954 the government made it illegal to use rocket nets to catch geese without a licence. Peter received a good number of letters from members of the public who wanted to join him on netting trips. The publicity attracted other enquiries as well. A Mr Higgs wrote in to say how much he had enjoyed the television programme but wondered whether any of the geese ever got hit by the rockets? Peter replied:

> ... it is true that they do sometimes hit the geese but the proportion is so small in comparison with the numbers which we are able to preserve as a result of the study that we feel it is justified, distressing though it may be at the time. It is rather like Sir Winston's 'few' being sacrificed for the 'many' in the bird world.

Peter's military analogy is telling. For him it was a campaign – he was still pitting himself against the quarry – the geese – even if he was no longer deliberately killing them. Years after he first experimented with nets to catch geese the thrill of outwitting and catching the birds was as strong as ever. Writing in *Country Life* in 1955 he explained:

> ... this continues to be the most exciting occupation I know; combining the satisfactions of successful scientific research with the thrills of a new and unusually difficult kind of wildfowling. It calls for an even greater knowledge of the thoughts and actions of the quarry than ordinary wildfowl shooting.

The end purpose may have shifted from collecting geese to scientific endeavour but the excitement of the chase remained undimmed. Over the years, the rocket-netting programme continued to provide valuable data on the distribution of various goose species, and by 1962 when rocket-netting of pink-footed geese had ceased, around 12,000 individuals had been netted and ringed, in addition to the 9,800 birds rounded up while flightless in Iceland. Rocket-netting had become an instrument for serious scientific research.

12

Mr and Mrs Scott

It is not easy to pin down the exact moment when the relationship between Peter and Philippa moved from one between employer and secretary, to something more personal. From early on in their relationship it was clear that they liked each other, and Philippa felt sorry for Peter, who seemed lonely after the break-up of his marriage and the loss of his mother, who had died of cancer in 1947. Peter's somewhat cavalier approach to their working relationship and her duties as his secretary certainly brought them closer together, and she took to watching geese like a duck to water – if the pun can be excused.

In 1949, Peter joined an expedition to the Perry River region in the Canadian Arctic to study the rare Ross's goose on its breeding grounds. While he was away, Philippa was once again left in charge of the Trust. Clearly they were thinking of each other, perhaps Philippa more than Peter. In her first autobiography *Lucky Me* she wrote:

> From the long letters that I wrote to him during his absence that summer, it is evident that I was already falling under his spell. Events at Slimbridge, the breeding success of the birds, new arrivals, the problem of the proposed bombing range – all were reported in great detail, and also the fact that I missed him.

Whether Peter missed Philippa as much, is hard to tell. He was totally absorbed in his first major expedition, with all the excitement that involved. We do know however, that Philippa had not been banished entirely from his thoughts. In the manner of all great explorers, when called upon to find a name for a previously undiscovered topographical feature, Peter named a hitherto unrecorded lake 'Philippa Lake'. One can't help feeling it might have sounded a little grander had it been 'Lake Philippa', but it shows at least that she was in his thoughts.

During the expedition, Peter and his team experienced severe weather with snowstorms and freezing conditions unusual in the Arctic for that time of year. Peter bore the discomfort with fortitude and reflected on the conditions that his father had to endure in his last days. For the first time perhaps, he gained an insight into his father's thoughts at the end; Peter wrote:

> These tuppeny-ha'penny adventures of ours and this dash of bad weather cannot help but cast new light, for me, on the story with which I grew up. And if I am enjoying the minor discomforts and difficulties – as indeed I am! – then it serves to remind me particularly of one phrase in my father's diary, which says: 'How much better this has been than lounging in too great comfort at home'. It was good to be able to say that, when death was imminent and inevitable. But in much lighter vein the phrase still applies to our days, beside this Arctic river. However inclement the weather, I'm still glad we came.

There is a sense of resolution in these words. His father's story had been ever present as he grew up. Exploration was something that Peter had felt compelled to avoid for fear of comparison with his father's achievements. Now, he was embarked on an expedition on his own terms, engaged in his own field of expertise; now he could enjoy such experiences for himself, his father's shadow no longer a hindrance but a comfort.

The International Ornithological Union held a congress every four years, and in 1950 it was to take place in Uppsala in Sweden, the first such event since the founding of the Severn Wildfowl Trust. For Peter, this was an opportunity to present the Trust on an international stage, and he was keen to bring the results of his studies of the population and migration of pink-footed geese to a wider audience.

Philippa persuaded Peter to let her accompany him on the trip. Once at Uppsala, Peter stayed in the university while Philippa lodged with a family in the town. She found the conference sessions rather dull, despite her burgeoning interest in ornithology, but she loved the various excursions that were organised around the main event. The first trip took them to Handöl on Lake Ann, close to the Norwegian border in central Sweden, where they went out on a boat and saw large numbers of water birds, including long-tailed ducks, phalaropes, divers and terns. On a subsequent excursion, she remembered being told off for talking by the leader, David Lack. A leading ornithologist of the day, Lack was famous for his studies of robins and would later be a regular visitor at Slimbridge. Philippa recalled that she was always a little bit scared of him after this slightly unfortunate first encounter. Later on the trip, Peter and Philippa split off from the rest of the group and with two other delegates, spent some time catching and ringing lesser white-fronted geese, three of which were brought back to Slimbridge. One of the two other delegates who accompanied them was Finnur Gudmundsson, the director of the Natural History Museum in Reykjavik, Iceland, who took the opportunity to discuss with Peter the possibility of mounting an expedition to central Iceland the following year, to look for the breeding grounds of the pink-footed goose. Peter and Philippa found time to get away alone and walk amongst the beautiful scenery of northern Sweden. In Peter's account of the trip we get a hint of what he was now feeling:

> My companion on the trip was the Trust's secretary, Philippa Talbot-Ponsonby. We visited a Lapp camp, caught a lemming which ate its way through my coat pocket, found the nests of Velvet Scoters and Buffon's Skuas, rode in leaky boats and were devoured by mosquitos; but above all we walked and walked over the fells and through the birch woods. I was happier than I had been for years.

Peter and Philippa may have thought that they were being fairly discreet; after all, Peter was still a married man and Philippa was his secretary and indeed was nine years younger than him. Clearly however, what the two of them were feeling for each other must have been evident to those around them, because two years later Philippa received a letter from a lady who had been with them on the excursion to Handöl. She introduced herself, saying she had been in the same boat as Philippa and Peter, adding that Philippa might remember her because she was 'lame and rather fat!!' She went on to say how well-suited she had thought Peter and Philippa were at the time and was delighted later to have read in the paper about their subsequent marriage. Philippa certainly did remember the lady. In her first autobiography, *Lucky Me*, she wrote of the occasion:

> The bog was the quaking variety and we had a slight problem with an elderly, stout, female bird-watcher who started to sink in. Peter pulled her out while she remained remarkably cheerful throughout.

Clearly though, it must have been obvious to everyone on the trip that Peter and Philippa were in love. Matters were finally settled on 28 March 1951 at the Annual Dinner of the Severn Wildfowl Trust in London, when Peter asked Philippa to marry him. Philippa wrote afterwards:

> What an exhilarating shock and how difficult to keep it secret! Three years had been a long time to wait, and there had been occasions when I had thought of quitting, but I was too involved with the creation of the Wildfowl Trust to tear myself away and venture into the unknown again.

Philippa's comment about waiting for three years suggests that something had indeed blossomed between them in 1948, around the time that Peter had created Philippa's portrait. The wedding would not be possible yet however, because Peter was still married to Jane. The divorce case was heard a couple of months later, and Peter got his decree nisi, though the decree absolute would have to wait and the engagement remain a secret.

During the IOU Congress at Uppsala in 1950, Finnur Gudmundsson, Peter and Philippa's companion on the goose-ringing trip, had clearly been busy. Not only had he discussed an expedition to central Iceland with Peter, he had clearly also broached the subject with James Fisher. James was perhaps the most eminent and best-known ornithologist in Britain at the time. His father had been headmaster of Oundle School when Peter was a pupil there. He was now a scientist, writer, editor and broadcaster on the subject of birds and bird behaviour. He had appeared with Peter on a BBC radio series called *Nature Parliament*, and at William Collins, the publishers, was the founding editor of the influential *New Naturalist* series of books. An apocryphal story relates that during a chance meeting with the publisher, Billy Collins, in a bomb shelter during an air raid in 1942, James had commented, 'What this country needs is a good series of books on natural history to take people's minds off this carnage.' That series of books was subsequently launched under the title of *New Naturalist,* with James as its editor. The series continues to this day to be the most comprehensive and influential series of popular natural history books ever published in Britain.

In August 1950, James wrote to Finnur Gudmundsson, reminding him of their discussion about a possible expedition to central Iceland to find the breeding grounds of the pink-footed goose. James offered to put together a small expedition with the Oxford University Exploration Club. He invited Finnur Gudmundsson to become guide and joint leader and suggested Finnur send him a map of Iceland with the route for the expedition marked on it, together with a short memorandum and a set of objectives. The original of this letter, signed by James, found its way to Peter at Slimbridge, probably sent to him by Finnur. It is possible that James had found it difficult to raise funds for the expedition, or Finnur might have thought that the Oxford University Exploration Club would lack the scientific rigour that he wanted to bring to the enterprise. In addition, James was asking Finnur to set out the agenda, work out the route into the interior of the country and write the memorandum that he would then submit to potential supporters, something which the Icelander might have been reluctant to do. Whatever the case, by the spring of 1951, plans were afoot for a trip to Iceland organised by the Severn Wildfowl Trust; members would include Peter, Philippa, James, Finnur and Lord Geoffrey Percy. The draft memorandum for the trip, written by Peter, made matters of organisation and personnel clear. This was to be the 'Severn Wildfowl Trust Expedition to central Iceland'. The party would be led by Peter Scott and would be six strong. This would be a great opportunity for Peter to continue his research into pink-footed geese at an international level.

Peter was quite happy to write a draft memorandum and to engage in extensive planning. It so happened that the British Minister in Iceland, Jack Greenway, was an old friend of his who had once visited him in the lighthouse at Sutton Bridge. Peter wrote to him, explaining what he was planning and asking advice about ways of getting the equipment to Iceland and means of access to the remote interior of the country, which had not yet been connected by road. Needing to save as much money as possible, Peter thought that the equipment might be sent on one of the many fishing trawlers that in those days commuted regularly between Scotland and Iceland. He also wanted to know where in Iceland he could acquire jeeps for the expedition. Jack Greenway consulted Finnur Gudmundsson and together they came up with the idea of using a truck and then ponies to reach the interior of the country. Jack also suggested that it might be possible for luggage to be dropped over their base camp by the US Air Force.

No doubt Finnur was delighted with his choice of leader, as Peter vigorously set about planning how many ponies they would need, how many days it would take to get to the area where they thought the geese were nesting, making long lists of stores and supplies and writing to people to try and raise funds. Peter managed to get a grant of £500 from the Royal Society and, in an attempt to save funds, he asked Lord Alanbrooke to write to the Head of Army Stores to ask if they were currently experimenting with any new types of ration pack. If so, the expedition would be happy to take part in the trials and would not, of course, charge the army for their services. The offer was not taken up though they did get a deal under which any unused rations could be returned and refunded. Tents and camping supplies were bought, including equipment for Finnur in Iceland. As he was almost seven feet tall, a special sleeping bag had to be made for him in England.

It had been originally planned that Lord Geoffrey Percy would accompany the equipment to Iceland on a trawler. Lord Percy dropped out however, so James Fisher went by sea in his place. Perhaps fortunately for James, it became impractical to go by trawler and he eventually travelled on the more comfortable MV *Hekla* which made fortnightly trips between Glasgow and Reykjavik. It is likely that he welcomed the chance to go by sea because he held a fascination for that most watchable of seabirds, the fulmar. He would have ample opportunity to study them as MV *Hekla* ploughed her way north. James's book, *The Fulmar*, was published the following year to great acclaim in the *New Naturalist* series and included, as its frontispiece, a splendid painting of a fulmar by Peter.

When Peter and Philippa arrived in Reykjavik, they stayed with Jack Greenway for a few days while the expedition was assembled. Jack told them that he was due to retire soon and happened to mention that as British minister he was licensed to marry people but nobody had ever asked him to do so. Sensing an opportunity, Peter asked him if he would be willing to marry him and Philippa provided the decree absolute came through in time. With Jack's agreement in the bag, Peter sent word to his solicitor that in the event the decree absolute should be issued while he was in Iceland, it should be sent directly to Reykjavik. At the same time, just in case, Philippa contacted Mrs Cameron in Slimbridge and asked her to send up a white broderie anglaise dress of hers. The possibility of an Icelandic wedding no doubt added a frisson to the proceedings as they boarded the lorry which was to take them to the farm where they would pick up the ponies.

From a scientific point of view, the expedition was a complete success. Camping in the remote interior, close to the edge of the icecap, they discovered the breeding grounds of the pink-footed goose. At that time of year, the geese are in moult and therefore unable to fly, so could be rounded up using the ponies and driven into circles of netting. The team discovered the remains of stone compounds which had once been used by the local people who would round up the geese just as sheep are herded into a sheepfold. Then of course, the purpose was to kill them for food, now Peter was using the same technique for ringing them. They were able to make an assessment of the breeding population in the area and hoped that when they went goose-netting in Scotland that winter, some of the birds caught might bear rings that they had fitted in Iceland.

By all accounts, they were a happy party. Peter and Philippa in particular, with the long wait for Peter's divorce nearly over and the opportunity to be by themselves, clearly had the most wonderful time. The party slept in tents and had a larger main tent which served as office and recreational area. Philippa had been allowed to join the expedition on the basis that she would cook and clean for the others which of course she did, but Peter relied on her for other skills too. She was adept at handling geese before they were ringed, and her riding skills were superior to the men's. She had been hunting at her home in Droxford in Hampshire for years and was completely at home on a pony, unlike Peter who found the ponies a trial at times. Finnur was a most genial team member and highly knowledgeable about all aspects of Icelandic natural history. All three men seemed to have got on well and their skills complemented each other's perfectly. Apart from his main diary, Peter kept a series of small notebooks in which he jotted down things as they came to mind. On one page is a list of the flowers they saw with translations in Icelandic, on another, sketch maps showing where geese had been located. In the back is a diagram of the radio transmitter indicating where all the leads were to be connected, together with a list of radio frequencies and call times. Nothing was left to chance. A curious addition in one of the notebooks is a set of measurements for a lady's dress, quite possibly in anticipation of Philippa's need for something to wear on her honeymoon, should the necessary papers arrive on time.

As the weeks passed, the ringing continued, and Peter realised he was running low on cine film and leg rings, so he radioed Reykjavik to ask if more supplies could be dropped by plane. Nothing was heard for some days, and Peter was resigned to having to do without, when a plane was sighted in the distance. At first it appeared to be heading in a different direction but then turned and flew directly over the camp, dropping two bags. In one of the bags were letters, four of them written recently by Jack Greenway. In the letters he mentioned that he had included some tinned fruit and foie gras in the air drop 'to add a little levity to your diet' but regretted not including a salmon or champagne, fearful that they might not survive the impact. Clearly, his idea of expedition rations was somewhat different than Peter's. He also indicated that he had received confirmation from London that he would be able to marry Peter and Philippa on their return provided that the Icelandic authorities agreed, which they had. Also in one of the bags was Peter's decree absolute. In his usual laconic style Peter later wrote of the occasion:

> The packages contained the much needed films – twenty cine magazines – our mail, with very important items, cans of fruit juice, pate de foie gras (coals perhaps to Newcastle) and newspapers up to 20th July (Icelandic ones later). This was a very exciting affair for us all.

In setting out their objectives, Peter had felt the expedition could be judged a complete success if they ringed 500 geese. In the event the number was 1,150. Peter returned to Reykjavik confident that they had indeed found the main breeding area and that the large number of birds they had ringed would greatly enhance future studies when, as seemed probable, birds ringed in Iceland were caught again during the winter rocket-netting excursions in Scotland.

Now there was another matter to attend to. On 7 August, 1951, the pair were married by Jack Greenway at the British Embassy in Reykjavik. Peter had managed to find a suit, and Philippa wore the dress sent from Slimbridge by Mrs Cameron. The couple look very happy in the photograph that Peter was later to include in his autobiography, *The Eye of the Wind*. Their brief honeymoon was spent at Akureyri, and we should not be at all surprised that they spent their first evening together as man and wife, studying a collection of stuffed birds and animals at the invitation of the local taxidermist.

Back home at Slimbridge at last, after the unpacking and congratulations, Peter was submerged in a deluge of work. There was a great deal of Trust business to catch up on, a report on the Iceland trip to be prepared for the Royal Society and the accounts for the expedition needed to be wrapped up. The colour film that he had taken on the trip was rather successful. Peter decided to show the films to the public and prepared a talk on the expedition. But where to present it? Most people would have settled on a medium-sized hall in London, of which there were plenty available. Peter, however, decided to book the Royal Festival Hall which, with a seating capacity of 2,500 people, might seem to be something of a risk. Doubtless many of his friends and colleagues thought he was taking a pretty big chance, and it's possible he thought so too. He need not have worried. The event, entitled *Wild Goose Chase,* was held on 13 January 1953 and was a huge success, with over 300 people turned away at the door. Peter obtained some tickets for his friend, ornithologist Eric Hosking, who had contacted the Festival Hall to try and buy tickets and had been unable to get any. Eric wrote to Peter on 7 January 1953:

> It really is most thrilling to know that all the tickets were sold and that the show is going to be such a success. When I 'phoned the box office at the Royal Festival Hall last Wednesday I was told that they were having calls almost every minute of the day and that they could have filled the hall two or three times over.

Peter's friend Robert Aickman congratulated him afterwards, remarking that such an audience for a non-political event had probably not been assembled in London since Charles Dickens drew enormous crowds in the previous century. Another friend wrote:

> You will get hundreds of these sorts of letters, but I do want to tell you too, how much I enjoyed last night. I simply adored every minute

of it. To me it is quite extraordinary that one person can completely hold hundreds of people's attention for two hours without a break.

An even more effusive (and stranger) letter came from yet another friend:

It was a tremendous success. The audience was marvellous, the arrangements very good; and you were magnificent. The dinner was most agreeable too. There was a flapper sitting just behind us at the lecture who was in an ecstasy. When things were going well for you in the story she screamed with glee. When ill she moaned 'Oh poor Peter, poor Peter.'

Clearly Peter was able to move hearts and minds in more ways than one.

In hindsight, it isn't perhaps so surprising that Peter was able to fill the Royal Festival Hall. In 1953, relatively few people had a television set and even fewer travelled abroad for their holidays. In the aftermath of the war there was a shortage of excitement in the lives of ordinary people. Here was a handsome ex-naval captain, son of a national hero, travelling to remote parts of the world and taking films of the birds and animals that lived there. Peter was already well known through his work on radio and was on his way to becoming a household name. Who wouldn't want to forget the humdrum of everyday life for a couple of hours and be enthralled by tales of adventures in far-off places? (Though perhaps the reactions of the 'flapper' were a little extreme.)

This was not the last that was heard of the 1951 Iceland expedition, for Peter and James Fisher went on to write a book about the trip and about the scientific findings that resulted from it. *A Thousand Geese*, published by William Collins, where James Fisher worked as an editor, is dedicated to Finnur Gudmundsson. Beneath his name Peter added, 'may his shadow never grow less'. On the back of the dust jacket is an advertisement for another book recently published by Collins: *The Fulmar* by James Fisher.

13

The Rarest Goose in the World

While Peter had been pursuing the pink-footed geese in Scotland and Iceland, another goose had never been far from his mind. The nene or Hawaiian goose was perhaps the rarest goose in the world and it was in trouble. Never very numerous, (it's thought that the world population at its height was never more than 25,000), the goose had gone into moderate decline when humans arrived on the Hawaiian Islands around 500 CE, but it was with the arrival of Europeans in the footsteps of James Cook, who visited in 1778, that the numbers went into freefall as a result of predation by humans as well as by the dogs and rats that arrived with them.

When the nene goose first came to Peter's attention in the 1930s, the numbers were down to around fifty individual birds. A few were known to still exist in the wild in Hawaii, but most of the remaining birds were in the collection of a Hawaiian businessman called Herbert Shipman. Before the war, Peter had asked Shipman to let him have a pair of the birds at the lighthouse to see if he could establish a breeding flock but the war had intervened and the chance had gone.

In 1949, the Severn Wildfowl Trust was invited to assist with a project set up in Hawaii to try and save the nene from extinction. The first edition of the Bulletin of the Severn Wildfowl Trust, published in September 1950, reported that only twenty-four nene geese were known to exist at that time. Peter had already written to the government of the Territory of Hawaii urging them to take action, so he was delighted to be asked to help. John Yealland was sent to Hawaii in January 1950 to provide advice on a new breeding programme, with the aim of getting the maximum number of young birds from each breeding female, a process with which the Trust had already had considerable success at Slimbridge with other species. Before he left Hawaii, John Yealland went to see Herbert Shipman, the man who had promised Peter two nene geese before the war and who had provided the initial four birds for the Hawaiian breeding programme. Would he still be willing to let the Trust have a pair? He would, and John returned triumphantly to Slimbridge in May 1950 with a pair of these beautiful little geese. The pair settled well into their new home at Slimbridge, and in early 1951 Peter and his team waited anxiously as the breeding season approached. It soon became apparent however that the Trust was facing a most formidable barrier to a successful breeding programme; both the birds laid eggs – they were both female.

Peter, ever resourceful, was undaunted. He did three things. First of all he blew the eggs and kept them. At that time it is thought that there were no nene eggs in any museum collection anywhere, so as empty shells they still had considerable value. Secondly, he made an omelette. There were nine eggs, and at a time of rationing it would clearly have been a shame to see them go to waste. He said he enjoyed this rarest of omelettes though he would probably never have another. Thirdly, of course, he wrote to Herbert Shipman, explained the problem and asked if he might be able to spare a gander for his breeding programme. Shipman readily agreed, and a gander arrived at Slimbridge just one week later. The gander quickly became attached to one of the females, and more eggs were laid, but these also proved to be infertile. It was now too late in the season, so Peter had to wait until the following year when, early in 1952, the gander mated successfully with the two females and nine goslings were produced. At that moment, Slimbridge held 20 per cent of the world population of this rarest of geese.

Looking back, it seems that it must have been a fairly straightforward process and, in conservation terms, a fairly easy matter to arrange when compared with the complex nature of many modern conservation programmes. Nothing was certain however and we can see from Peter's comments at the time that he was far from sure that he would succeed. In a letter written shortly after the first eggs hatched, he wrote:

> We're feeling very pleased with ourselves because 2 baby Hawaiian geese hatched 2 weeks ago & 3 more hatched today. In addition we have two more clutches of 5 eggs being incubated – all this from one male &

two females, three of the 28 specimens which are all that are known to remain alive in the world. If only we can raise them successfully!

If only we can raise them successfully. In light of what we now know, it is hard to imagine that Peter could ever have doubted that his plan would work. But work it did. The error made in 1950 gave the Trust a significant advantage because there were now two females to breed from, and the gene pool was increased significantly. In 1953, four more goslings were successfully reared, and a new survey revealed that there were now sixty-eight nene geese alive – thirty-three in the wild, nineteen with Herbert Shipman and sixteen at Slimbridge. Thereafter, the numbers of geese slowly increased; four more ganders were brought from Hawaii to keep the bloodlines healthy, and by November 1960 the flock at Slimbridge had increased to over 100 birds. In 1962, with the support of the World Wildlife Fund, Peter was able to return thirty-five geese to their native islands for release, followed by a further twenty birds in 1963 and another 145 birds in the years up to 1969. By 1973 the world population had risen to 1,000 and nineteen geese were laying or incubating at Slimbridge; the following year, fifty-eight goslings were added to the flock. Today, there are over 3,250 nene geese in the world. Early in 2020, the bird was declared no longer endangered and was downgraded to the level of 'threatened', something that would have pleased Peter enormously.

Peter's success was not only good for the nene geese it was also good for the Trust. Though the breeding programme had been challenging, it was easy to understand and to explain to others. It isn't difficult to grasp the principle. You take two geese and get five more, then another five, then ten and so on. Peter was able to use the success with the nenes to show people that birds and other creatures need not become extinct, even when their numbers are reduced almost to zero. People who heard the story were encouraged, and those who were sufficiently interested in the work and had money to invest were now more ready to help save other species having seen, and understood, what could be done.

The nene goslings were not the only arrival of rare birds at Slimbridge in those early years. While on a royal tour of the Dominion of Canada in 1951, Princess Elizabeth was presented with a gift of six trumpeter swans. This, the largest of all seven species of swan in the world, is also perhaps the most impressive with a large wingspan and a long straight neck. It was also, by this time, becoming extremely rare, occurring only in the United States and Canada. In 1935, the US population had been down to only sixty individuals but numbers had increased slightly, so now, in 1952, there were 451 birds in the US and about 1,000 in Canada. Peter was delighted when the princess asked him to look after her gift of this rare and beautiful swan and five of the birds duly arrived, one having escaped while being prepared for its journey in Canada. The princess visited again shortly afterwards to admire her new swans.

The swans came to the fore in the Trust's Bulletin number twelve, issued on 4 June 1953:

> The Council feels confident that all our Members will wish to be associated with the following telegram which was sent to Her Majesty The Queen, our Patron, on Coronation Day. The President, Council and Members of the Severn Wildfowl Trust beg Your Majesty to accept their homage and loyal devotion on this joyous day. Our good wishes for a glorious and peaceful reign are accompanied by a Coronation Fanfare from Your Majesty's own Trumpeter Swans.

Twenty-five years later, two of the original five trumpeter swans were still alive and mentioned again in the telegram sent to Her Majesty the Queen on the occasion of her Silver Jubilee. In June 1953, Peter had a coronation fanfare of his own when he received the CBE for his work with the Trust in the Coronation honours list.

If you had asked Peter in 1952 what he was most excited about, the nenes or the trumpeters, he would surely have said neither, because another exciting event was heralded. Philippa was pregnant, and in June of that year their daughter Dafila was born. She was christened on board her grandfather's ship *Discovery* which was moored in London at the time, and the ship's bell was used as the font. Dafila's godfathers were Keith Shackleton and Michael Bratby.

At this time Peter was extremely busy, having embarked on what would be his largest book illustration project. He had been invited to paint the colour plates for a new book by French ornithologist Jean Delacour who Peter had visited in New York when Delacour was director of the Bronx Zoo. The book, *Wildfowl of the World*, was a massive undertaking, describing every species of swan, goose and duck in the world and running to four large volumes. In 1952 he completed the plates for volume one in-between all his other work, running the Trust, travelling round the country to give lectures, working tirelessly to raise funds and engaging in his ever-growing radio work.

14

The House that Peter Built

As if life were not busy enough, Peter and Philippa were now looking after a baby in a small cottage which was both home, artist's studio, office (with two secretaries during the day) and the place where visitors were entertained; there was a live-in nanny too and the stairs were steep and narrow. Both Peter and Philippa realised that something had to be done, so the decision was made to build a house that would fulfil their seemingly ever-expanding needs. In the early days after the war it was not easy to get planning permission to build new homes, partly because of the scarcity of new materials. Plans were submitted to the authorities, and on the day the inspectors were due, Peter and Philippa made sure the cottage was absolutely at bursting point, with people at work crammed round the kitchen table and every available space taken up with furniture and belongings, while somewhere a small child was doubtless making itself heard. The surveyors got the point, and the Scotts got permission. Theirs was one of only fifteen successful applications out a total of 100 that the local authority were considering at that time.

The Scotts had very little available money to spend on the project, but a legacy from Philippa's mother provided funds to build the house and enabled them to lend enough money to the Trust to convert the cowshed next door into staff accommodation. Peter drew up initial plans for their new home which he described as a private house with an attached studio. He thoroughly enjoyed the process of designing the house and its internal features and wrote later in *The Eye of the Wind* that if he were to have the opportunity of building the house again there was very little that he would change. In the cottage he had hung a sheet of plate glass over his bed behind which he would slip papers, sketches or drawings of anything he was considering at the time so that he could think deeply about them as he lay in bed in the morning. One of the drawings behind the glass at this time was a sketch for a mechanism by which an identical pane of glass could be hung over the bed in his new bedroom.

The architect for the design was Peter Bicknell who had been at school and then at Cambridge with Peter. A site was selected on the edge of the Rushy Pen. A pool had already been excavated when the Trust was first formed, but now it was extended so that all the rooms at the rear of the house would look out over the lake. For his studio, Peter designed a large window based on the one he had seen at Cap Tourmente in Canada before the war. To fit into the shape of the Rushy Pen the house was built on a curve. The house had four bedrooms with the main bedroom and the guest bedroom both equipped with en suite facilities, something that was extremely unusual at the time. Word apparently got round the village about this, and it was assumed that the facilities in the guest room had been put there for when the Queen came to stay. For this reason the room became known as the Queen's bedroom. Prince Philip and Prince Charles stayed at the house at different times, but the Queen never did, and she was apparently amused to be told about 'her' bedroom during a later visit.

Construction started on the house in January 1953, and an infant Dafila laid the foundation stone on 27 January. Peter and Philippa had hoped to move in later that year, but construction was delayed, and it was not until 9 February 1954 that they were able to take possession. By this time, Philippa was pregnant with her second child, and she became ill during the move from the cottage. As a consequence, she had to spend several weeks sitting up in bed, enjoying the birds on the lake outside. Tommy Johnstone moved into the cottage on 16 February, and the new hostel accommodation, converted from the cowshed, was occupied from 1 March. Peter was very excited about the project, writing to a friend in November 1953:

> Come and see us down here one day. We've just built a new house with a pond right up to the windows and birds swimming and flying all round it. It's really rather nice.

In January 1954 he wrote to another friend:

> We have just built ourselves a new house with the ducks swimming about just outside the studio window which is rather fun and we are

scheduled to move in early next month. It has been a long time in the making, so we are longing to get settled as you can imagine.

And one year later, with the move behind him, he wrote to an old school friend:

We've just built a new house up to the windows of which our ducks swim in the most engaging manner. Most of today there have been 20 perfectly wild wigeon displaying within 5 yards of me as I sit at this desk. Our waterfowl are a bit of a cult here, but they are intended to be enjoyed as much by the non-specialist as the ornitholog. So do come and see them.

Peter Bicknell was clearly happy with the result. Three months after the Scott family moved in, he sought Peter's permission to bring seventeen members of staff on an outing to view the finished house. In a follow-up letter to Philippa, Bicknell said that Peter had told him she would not be at all bothered by the 'invasion'. What Philippa actually thought about seventeen architects tramping through her house is unrecorded.

Though the house was modest in size and structure it was fitted out extremely comfortably. The kitchen was well equipped with all modern conveniences including an Aga stove and a dishwasher. The cupboards and drawers lining the wall at one end were constructed so they could be opened from both the kitchen and the dining room, while one of the cupboards doubled as a serving hatch. The dining room was equipped with two tables, one for visitors and special occasions and one for everyday use which was placed in the bay window overlooking the lake. This arrangement presented the family with a dilemma during their first few years in the house. The Rushy Pen was, at that time, part of the wildfowl collection area and thus open to the public. The Scott family therefore found themselves having lunch in the full gaze of the public just across the lake. As a result of his broadcasting activities, by the mid-1950s Peter was a well-known figure, and visitors would take photographs of the family at lunch or, even worse, observe them through their binoculars. The children thought this was fun and used to make binocular faces back, but it must have been a relief to Peter and Philippa when, in the 1960s, the Rushy Pen was closed to the public, initially during the winter months and finally, altogether.

From the upstairs windows, Peter had an uninterrupted view across the wet meadows to the sea wall and was now able to observe his beloved geese every day in winter without leaving the house, should he be so inclined. Though they were rarely seen, more lesser white-fronted geese turned up from time to time. On 6 March 1952, Peter wrote to a friend that they had just had two more sightings, bringing the British records to nineteen.

Peter's studio was and remains a most beautiful room, with pleasing proportions and always well-lit through the big picture window. There was space for him to set up his easel and a large desk for him to work from. One end of the room had bookshelves from floor to ceiling with a door into a storeroom where he could keep all his canvases. At the other end of the room was space for his extensive collection of classical music records and the equipment to play them on. On the side away from the lake, a small door opened into a conservatory where Peter continued to keep hawk moth caterpillars, lizards and chameleons. One famous example of the latter was collected from a bush in Nairobi National Park and brought back to live in the conservatory. It was subsequently introduced to Prince Charles who was invited to hand feed it with flies. The chameleon was eventually released at the same location where it had been found in Kenya, no doubt with a few tall tales to tell to the folks back home.

The house was (and still is) connected by a corridor to the offices of the Trust, allowing Peter to maintain direct contact with his colleagues without having to go outside. The front of the house looks quite plain; it is the rear of the house, viewed across the lake that is most familiar to visitors, though one of its most recognisable features, the observation tower was not constructed until the 1970s. Once again, Peter drew detailed plans of what he wanted before handing them over on a long roll of paper to the architect. Another feature added in the 1970s was the swimming pool which both Peter and Philippa felt would offer Peter a good way to keep to a healthy weight. Philippa was always anxious that Peter should get his daily exercise, so he swam twenty lengths of the pool every day that he was at home, though being extremely busy he sometimes failed to find the time. To avoid worrying Philippa, he would apparently give his trunks and towel to his secretary and ask her to dip them in the pool for him in case Philippa noticed they had not been used. The pool was useful in other ways too, as Philippa was able to learn to scuba dive and take her qualifications in it.

15

In Search of the Cuckoo Duck

The waterfowl collection at Slimbridge had grown substantially since 1946, and Peter was keen to see as many of his collection birds as possible in the wild. In 1953 therefore, he and Philippa set out on an extended trip to South America. For the first part of their visit they had been invited to team up with an expedition mounted by Cleveland Natural History Museum in Ohio. The invitation came from the expedition leader, a man called Byron (Biff) Goss who Peter and Philippa had met in Iceland in 1951 and who had subsequently visited Slimbridge. Peter and Philippa flew first to the United States to stay with Goss on his plantation in Georgia where they all went quail hunting on horseback. Byron Goss seems to have been a bit of a disciplinarian who ordered his meals by blowing a whistle and dictated who could shoot at which birds and in what order. By 1953 Peter had pretty much lost the urge to shoot, and it may have been with some reluctance that he borrowed the gun of Goss's wife Dixie.

In South America, matters got worse. Peter and Philippa were there to observe and film the wildfowl they saw. Byron Goss was there to shoot them, to add specimens of skins to the museum in Cleveland. The two aims were obviously incompatible, and tempers frayed as the two different groups continually frustrated each other's efforts. Matters came to a head in Tierra del Fuego when they found a party of kelp geese, some of which were nesting. Goss walked up to a pair of geese on the nest and shot the female at close quarters then shot the male as it continued to stand by its dead partner. Philippa was dismayed, and wrote later of the event:

I was very much disgusted at this ignorant carnage perpetrated on the flimsy excuse that Kelp Geese were needed by the Cleveland Museum. (We later heard from Rendall Rhodes that the museum had several skins.) In the car proceeding from here to the picnic site I was rash enough to ask Biff whether he had enjoyed walking up to the geese and knocking them over on the ground. The result was a certain coolness during the rest of the day.

Peter and Philippa were much relieved when the two groups parted company and went their separate ways. Despite this uncomfortable interlude, the trip overall was a great success and Peter managed to find the three species of duck in which he was particularly interested. In Chile they found the curious black-headed duck which, like the cuckoo, lays its eggs in the nests of other birds, in particular those of coots and night herons. In Tierra del Fuego, Peter found bronze-winged ducks which he very much wanted to film. The birds were initially too far away, but as Peter stood by the lake, the ducks spotted him and swam some way towards him then stopped. Realising that they were behaving like ducks attracted to a decoy dog, he waved a handkerchief and the ducks swam forward again into camera range.

Flying north to the jungles of Bolivia, Peter located the duck he most wanted to see, the elusive torrent duck. Living in tropical jungle at altitudes over 8,000 feet, the birds are wonderfully adept at walking and swimming in fast mountain rivers, hence their name. Peter managed to film them under difficult conditions, and the sequence caused quite a stir when, in January 1954, Peter again hired the Royal Festival Hall to show his film called *The High Andes* and give a talk about his South American trip.

In 1954, the naturalist Gerald Durrell made a collecting trip to South America and sought advice from Peter about travel conditions and possible contacts that might be helpful. Peter wrote some letters on his behalf, including to the ambassadors in London for Argentina and Chile, as a result of which Gerald's party were offered 'Distinguished Visitors' visas. The two friends came to an agreement whereby the Severn Wildfowl Trust would provide some funding, in return for which Gerald would catch specimens of wildfowl for the Trust's collection. At a meeting at Slimbridge they discussed which species Peter wished to acquire. It became evident that the duck Peter was most keen to obtain was the torrent duck. Gerald's account of the conversation is Gerald Durrell at his funniest and worth repeating in full:

Over lunch he talked at great length about Torrent Ducks and it was obvious that he would not be satisfied until he possessed some. He waxed lyrical about their beauty and extraordinary habits and said I must get him some at all costs. Philippa had remained silent during this panegyric about Torrent Ducks, but now she felt constrained to speak: 'But Peter, that's all very well but where are we going to keep them?' she asked, sensibly enough. Peter looked at her in amazement: 'Why build a torrent for them, of course,' he said, surprised that Philippa should not have thought of this simple solution for herself. 'But where's the money coming from?' persisted Philippa. 'Money?' said Peter, as if his wife had uttered an unladylike expletive. 'Money? Oh, we'll soon get money for a torrent.' He said it with such conviction that I had a vivid mental picture of huge queues of millionaires forming, chequebooks at the ready, panting to invest in a torrent. We need a lot more of this sort of positive thinking in conservation.

During his subsequent expedition, Gerald experienced considerable travel difficulties, finding himself marooned in Buenos Aires, unable to get to Chile or to Tierra del Fuego as planned. This meant that he was unable to obtain either torrent ducks or bronze-winged ducks, the two species that Peter was particularly keen to add to his collection. Having failed to travel south, Gerald decided to go to Paraguay instead, but luck continued to evade him. Revolution broke out and, unable to depart by river steamer, he was forced to charter a light aircraft to fly out of the country which meant that most of the specimens he had collected, including some for Peter, had to be released. Peter subsequently wrote to Gerald:

It was disappointing that you couldn't get any ducks for us. I wonder how the trip went from your point of view. I imagine the revolution in Paraguay will have provided some good copy for your next book.

Gerald replied:

I'm afraid the whole trip was a dead loss from my point of view; as we have no bullet wounds to show the revolution is not such a good story as I had hoped. Still I hope to be able to hash up something sufficiently blood-curdling for the British public.

Gerald's expedition and the consequences of the revolution for his collecting activities is described in his book *The Drunken Forest*. There never was a torrent in the grounds at Slimbridge, though Peter did build a more modest waterfall in the hope of eventually being able to keep torrent ducks.

In the summer of 1953, Peter returned once more to Iceland to catch and ring more pink-footed geese. Finnur Gudmundsson and James Fisher were on an expedition in the Bering Sea, so this time Peter's companions included Hugh Boyd and Peter's friend, the ornithologist Bill Sladen. Philippa stayed at home to look after Dafila, though the two of them flew out to join Peter at the end of the expedition and stayed in Iceland for a fortnight. Peter's fame was obviously spreading; a number of people wrote to him and asked if they could accompany the 1953 expedition. When Philippa wrote to the company from which they purchased and hired all their expedition equipment to hire a two-man tent for the latest expedition, the company offered it free of charge on the condition that Peter would send them a photograph of the tent *in situ* and a short review of its performance. Naturally Peter agreed to this.

The expedition was a huge success, and they were able to ring 8,700 pink-footed geese. The total catch was over 12,000 as some birds were caught more than once. Some catches were so large that it took over twelve hours to empty the nets and ring the birds; Peter recorded that they sometimes finished ringing operations at 2 a.m. This time he had enough film for the trip but ran out of leg rings, so additional supplies were flown in by a light aircraft which landed near the camp. Writing to an acquaintance in South America in January 1954, Peter confirmed that the Trust had ringed 14,000 pink-footed geese in the previous four years. By 1962, the total had risen to more than 21,000, a truly astonishing number. From all the data collected, it was estimated that the world population of pink-footed geese fluctuated over a ten-year period between 40,000 and 70,000 birds.

Back in England in 1953, Peter involved himself in an entirely different campaign. In January he received a letter from Sir Miles Clifford, then Governor of the Falkland Islands, who wished to discuss with Peter the matter of the *Discovery* which was in danger of being broken up. *Discovery* was the ship in which Peter's father had made his first expedition to Antarctica and was also the last traditional wooden three-masted ship to be built in England. Since being taken out of service, she had been used by the Boy Scouts Association as a training ship for Sea Scouts and as accommodation for Scouts visiting from abroad. Maintenance was costly however, and there had been a proposal that the Admiralty should take her over. Various suggestions for her use were floated, including storage of files, and from Miles Clifford's letter it was clear that there were rumours, at least, that she might be broken up.

Peter had a strong interest in *Discovery*. It was a link to the father he had never known, and his daughters, Nicola and Dafila, had been christened on board with the ship's bell used as the font. Peter decided to form a committee to consider the various proposals, recruiting an extraordinarily strong team whose members included Lord Cunningham, the First Sea Lord, the Bishop of Portsmouth, Sir Edmund Hillary and Lord Alanbrooke. A plan was established to raise £100,000 to secure the ship's future, and Peter found himself beset by worries as indicated in a letter to his friend Arthur Mansfield, written in March 1954:

> I am so sorry not to have answered your letter before and even now it will have to be a short one as I have a desperate amount on my plate just at the moment, what with trying to raise £100,000 for my father's old ship the Discovery, and moving house, and having Phil ill at the same time. However she is getting along much better now and I think all will be well. Her baby threatened to arrive a long time too soon.

In the event, both emergencies passed, and as far as the *Discovery* was concerned the committee had little work to do, as the Admiralty came up with a plan to use her as a drill ship for the Royal Naval Volunteer Reserve and the Royal Naval Auxiliary Service and as a training ship for the Westminster Sea Cadet Corps. It seems likely that Peter's involvement and his recruitment of the First Sea Lord to the debate had some influence on the decision, and Peter would have been delighted with the new connection with RNVR. It must have been with relief on all counts that he was able to have his son Falcon christened on board, later that year.

16

The Gun Behind the Door

While the arguments about the fate of the *Discovery* swirled around, Peter found himself embroiled in a new controversy, one which was to call upon all his powers of tact and persuasion. The sport of wildfowling became a topic of heated debate in England in 1953 and Peter found himself caught in the crossfire. As someone who had at one time been a passionate advocate for the sport but whose recent work with pink-footed geese had highlighted the dangers of over-shooting, Peter found he had become the target for various individuals on both sides of the argument, while others simultaneously tried to recruit him for their different causes. By this time, through his writing and broadcasting, he had become a well-known public figure, and it would not be easy for him, or the Severn Wildfowl Trust, to simply ignore the issue.

Peter's conversion over the years from passionate wildfowler to ardent conservationist was a gradual and sometimes hesitant process; there was no single lightbulb moment which made Peter hang up his guns for good. As already described, in the 1920s and early 1930s, he saw no conflict between his passion for shooting and his love of the birds themselves. With the establishment of his collection at the lighthouse, he started to question the ethics of shooting, particularly the indiscriminate and careless wounding and killing of large numbers of birds. He never regretted his own shooting in the past and always maintained, probably correctly, that had he not taken up wildfowling in the first place, his love for the birds and the wild places they inhabit would never have been kindled.

During the Second World War, he found solace in shooting in the rare times he could get away from his duties. The pleasure he felt had doubtless much to do with the escape from the unpleasantness and difficulties of daily life at sea that these brief forays afforded.

After the war, his views gradually began to change further, and one particular incident in 1946 caused him some disquiet. Peter had been on a hunting trip with a group of friends when, early one morning, a goose had been hit and landed on mudflats which were inaccessible to the party. The goose was injured and sat with its head raised, unable to fly away. Later that day, Peter noticed that the bird was still there and still alive. Because it was a neap tide, the sea did not cover the mudflats. To Peter's disquiet he discovered that the goose was still lying on the mudflats the following morning – and it was still alive. He wrote of the incident in *The Eye of the Wind*:

> What right, I said to myself, have we men to do this to a bird for our fun – to impose that kind of suffering? I should not want this for a sworn enemy, and that goose was not my enemy when I shot at him, although I was his.

He wrote elsewhere in *The Eye of the Wind*:

> But there comes a time for some men when their first reaction even to the traditional quarry is no longer to kill. (Thoreau writes of leaving the gun and the fishing pole behind the door.) They reach a certain stage or age, some sooner, some later, when the old phrase which is supposed to epitomise the English country gentleman, 'It's a lovely morning; let's go out and kill something,' is no longer funny but obscene. Whether this has to do with the agony of the two great wars, or whether it arises from new ideas about humanity and suffering, I do not know. Nor do I know if this outlook is more common than it was, though I suspect it may be.

The comment by Thoreau which Peter quoted is from *Walden*, his great paean to the natural world, and the passage from which it is taken is worth quoting in full:

> We cannot but pity the boy who has never fired a gun; he is no more humane while his education has been sadly neglected. This was my

answer with respect to those youths who were bent on this pursuit, trusting that they would soon outgrow it. No humane being, past the thoughtless age of boyhood, will wantonly murder any creature, which holds its life by the same tenure he does ... Such is often the young man's introduction to the forest, and the most original part of himself. He goes thither first as hunter and fisher, until at last, if he has the seeds of a better life in him, he distinguishes his proper objects, as a poet or naturalist it may be, and leaves the gun and fish pole behind.

Peter certainly had the 'seeds of a better life in him', and he would most certainly have recognised his own life's trajectory in Thoreau's words. From the late 1940s onwards Peter shot only occasionally, while his distaste for the killing became increasingly clear. In 1949, on his expedition to the Perry River in Canada, it was necessary to obtain specimens of birds for scientific purposes. He wrote about shooting some king eiders in *Wild Geese and Eskimos*:

> We needed them for skins, so I shot four as they passed, two pairs. It was a strange feeling as I went to pick them up. One drake was only wounded, and I had to wring his neck. On the one hand it was horrible to shoot these tame and beautiful creatures, and to see them lying in the blood-stained snow. On the other hand, it was the first opportunity I had to see at close quarters their surpassing beauty of colour and pattern. And, then, since the skins were needed it was useful to have got two pairs neatly, so that we need never fire at king eiders again ... All the same, it was a crime which brought inevitable remorse.

In 1950, Peter was a guest of the royal family at Sandringham, where he had been invited to show the film he had made about the Perry River expedition. During the weekend, he was invited to join a pheasant shoot so felt compelled to borrow a gun and join the party. He continued to shoot periodically during 1951 and wrote to Mackenzie Thorpe in December about a trip he had just made to Ireland where he had shot eighteen Greenland white-fronted geese. A little while later, in early 1952, he wrote to Thorpe once more:

> After having a record season, you really ought to give the geese a rest. People won't think better of you if you slaughter geese

wholesale over decoys. Besides – like me – you've shot enough geese now. Why not let them off for a bit. You must have found, as I did, that when you get too good at it, it's too easy, and not much fun any more. (*Cambridge University Library MS Scott (Peter) A.142*)

Mackenzie Thorpe apparently thought Peter's letter a bit of a cheek.

In 1953, Peter was unhappy at the shooting at close quarters of sitting geese by Byron Goss for questionable scientific purposes during his trip to South America. Peter was no hypocrite though, and while he himself had more or less given up shooting by then, he saw no reason to urge everyone else to do the same. For him it was a matter of personal ethics, and he recognised that one's position changes over time. What did concern him was indiscriminate and careless shooting. If large bags of geese were taken there would inevitably be a long-term impact on the overall populations of wild geese. If people shot carelessly, aiming at birds that were almost totally out of range, there was a risk of wounding large numbers of birds without need.

In 1948, during his trip to North America, Peter had visited the Delta Waterfowl Research Station near Winnipeg in Canada, where for the first time he observed birds being X-rayed and could see for himself the damage that lead shot could do to the body of a goose or duck. He was also impressed by the way in which societies in North America promoted sustainable shooting. Gun clubs like the one at Cap Tourmente in Canada combined limited shooting with the protection of important habitat to ensure that wildfowl populations remained at sustainable levels. In the United States the shooting season was limited to six weeks, shooting was banned between 4 p.m. and 7 a.m., and bags were limited to five geese or ten ducks a day. Many less-common species were totally protected, and it was illegal to shoot them. In 1953, Dr Elder from the University of Missouri went out with the goose-netting teams in Scotland, armed with the equipment used by the Delta Research Station team. He discovered that of the geese captured, 41 per cent of the pink-footed geese and 37 per cent of the greylag geese had lead shot embedded in their bodies from previous strikes by wildfowlers.

Peter was not alone in attempting to curtail excessive shooting. In January 1953, he received a letter from a John Davey who, with a group of several hundred farmers and landowners, had signed a petition calling for the banning of shooting over decoys, in this case decoys being model geese laid out to attract flying geese down to land at a particular spot. They particularly wished to add the signature of Lord Yarborough, a significant landowner in their area, but Lord Yarborough had replied that he would only sign if he knew what Peter Scott thought about the matter. John Davey urged Peter to write to Lord Yarborough. Peter replied:

> I will certainly write to Lord Yarborough and encourage him to associate himself with the declaration against decoy shooting. And you may certainly quote me as being against any kind of excessive shooting, especially of shooting large bags of geese over decoys, which is not at all difficult, and by and large most unsporting. I should be in favour of legislation preventing shooting geese over decoys. Anyone who shoots more than 10 geese in a day probably feels slightly ashamed of himself – if he doesn't he ought to. If no one thought well of him for doing so, and he knew this, he might be less eager to make 'record' bags.

In the same month, the Trust also received a curt note from a member. Colonel Paynter enclosed a cheque for the renewal of his membership but said that he refused to sign a deed of covenant for his membership because the Trust still allowed the Berkeley family to shoot on the reserve. (A deed of covenant was the equivalent of a modern direct debit with Gift Aid to allow the Trust to recover the value of the associated tax.) Peter sent a long and detailed reply, explaining that under the terms of the lease through which the Trust occupied the land, the Berkeley family were allowed to shoot geese on eight days during the winter. He wrote:

> Somewhat optimistically I hoped that as the Trust developed our landlord would realise that the ultimate destiny of this very wonderful marsh was to be an inviolate sanctuary, and so we became the tenants. So far all efforts at persuasion have failed but it must be admitted that our landlord has used considerable restraint. Since we have been here (6 years) he has never shot on more than 5 days ... Nevertheless the shooting days here upset me so much that I have to arrange to be away on each of them ... Please forgive me for so long a letter, but I wanted you to know that my attitude to shooting has changed very much since my wildfowling books were written (whether as a result of the war or my advancing years I know not). I do not now care for shooting at all.

Colonel Paynter's subsequent reply contained an extraordinary admission. He owned to having been something of a wildfowler himself in former years and had lived and worked for many years in India. He went on to say he regretted that while living in India he had shot the last pair of pink-headed ducks he ever saw. If his claim is true, he personally contributed to the extinction of the species, as the last reliable sighting was in 1935. The Berkeleys continued to shoot wild geese at Slimbridge for many years, the final shoot taking place on 31 January 1983.

At the end of January 1953 came further news of Mackenzie Thorpe in a letter from a man called Michael Barling. It appeared that Peter's suggestion that Thorpe reduce the number of birds that he shot had been ignored. At a recent shoot, Thorpe and a friend had shot seventy-eight pink-footed geese, and he had had several other bags of twenty or more. Barling admitted that he and his own brother shot a few geese every season – it was what he called 'wholesale slaughter' that he objected to. Might it help if Peter approached Mackenzie Thorpe again? Peter replied:

I was very glad to get your letter about the over shooting of the Pinkfeet, as this is a problem which I feel very strongly about. I am trying to work on Mackenzie Thorpe. I heard from a friend who saw him a week ago that he was getting 'bored with shooting', but that may just have been a line to impress me. I certainly deplore the wholesale slaughter of the geese, but I am not against moderate wildfowling, although I doubt if I shall ever shoot another goose myself except for scientific purposes, or to eat when we are getting short on one of our expeditions.

I think the inevitability of wounding birds is what has chiefly spoiled shooting for me. Even a good shot is doing well to get one goose for every 3 cartridges expended and not all the other cartridges miss. Watching the geese here, we see dozens with broken legs, drooping wings and belly wounds. Time was when I could shut my mind off from this aspect of it, but I can't any more. So my enjoyment of shooting is spoiled and clearly it would be absurd to go on shooting when one doesn't enjoy it. I think also that when one has watched the creatures alive and kept them tame one is more than usually disgusted with their appearance when shot and dripping blood and mucus from their bills.

Some wildfowlers regard me as a traitor who has changed sides, but certainly the birds need some support, for they cannot compete with the spread of the human population unaided. Whether the destructive years of the war are responsible for my outlook, or whether I'm becoming a softie in my old age, I know not. But anyway I do not regard moderate wildfowlers as villains – only the immoderate ones ...

Peter was also talking to friends about his concerns over excessive shooting. In early 1953, one of his friends, Barry Hardcastle, had been to lunch with Peter at Slimbridge and wrote to thank him, asking if Peter had seen his recent letter to the *Shooting Times* extolling Peter's theories on moderate shooting. Hardcastle promised to discuss the matter further with his friends when he went shooting at Gleneagles later in the month. At the time, Peter was doubtless happy that his friends should spread the word about responsible hunting. He may not have realised quite what a reaction his ideas would provoke in certain quarters.

17

Open Warfare

The lecture about the 1951 Iceland expedition at the Royal Festival Hall in January 1953, Peter's subsequent magazine articles and radio talks on his work with pink-footed geese and the discussions he had with his friends, eventually brought his ringing activities to the attention of the wildfowling community and not everybody was happy. Peter was keen that any rings found on dead or injured birds should be returned to him, since in this way the evidence of their migration patterns could be built up. He had not reckoned however on the disgust of wildfowlers who shot birds only to find they were leg ringed. To some, this made the kill less exciting as the bird was not truly 'wild' having already passed through human hands. To these wildfowlers, the matter seemed all the more galling since Peter had been one of their own. Doubtless quite a few had been drawn to wildfowling in the first place through Peter's evocative descriptions of his adventures in the fens in the 1920s and 1930s as they appeared in his early books *Morning Flight* and *Wild Chorus*.

On 26 August 1953, an article written by Peter appeared in *The Times*. Headed 'Wild Geese in Iceland', the article described his most recent success in ringing over 9,000 geese that summer in Iceland. These birds formed a significant proportion of the birds wintering in England. On 20 October, while on a rocket-netting trip in Scotland, Peter received a letter from *The Times* accompanying a proof copy of a letter to the editor from a Mr Hammond; the letter from *The Times* informed Peter that Hammond had requested that the proof of his letter be sent to Peter. He had known Peter for some time and wanted him to have the opportunity to respond to his letter before it was published. The editor concluded that Mr Hammond's letter would appear in the columns of *The Times* within a few days.

Hammond's letter referred to Peter's recent article. He said that while he recognised the good work being done by the Severn Wildfowl Trust in collecting and breeding rare waterfowl, he and his 'grey-geese-loving friends' all cautioned against any further such goose ringing expeditions being undertaken. Hammond went on to say that the Severn Wildfowl Trust should reassure people about the inestimable harm he considered they were inflicting on the geese. He went on to list his concerns:

- By catching the geese in large numbers while flightless, the party showed to the Icelanders accompanying the trip an easy way of catching large numbers of birds. The locals knew where to find the flightless geese and the site was now accessible by lorry.
- The process would drive sitting birds off their eggs causing them to be abandoned.
- Goslings would be separated from their parents and would die of cold before they could be reunited.
- The rocket-netting used in Scotland was unethical as some birds were accidentally killed in the process.

It was Hammond's view that the damage done to the geese by shooting was slight compared to the harm done by the Trust's activities in Iceland. He stated that the catching of birds by netting should be made illegal, while under no circumstances should shooting them be banned as apparently suggested in a recent bulletin published by the Trust.

Peter must have been concerned to read the proof copy of the letter and knowing he had only a few days to reply he drafted a response straight away. He made a careful, considered refutation of Hammond's letter, point by point. Peter's letter concluded:

At present there is no indication that the Pinkfoot needs special protection from shooting or from anything else and no such suggestion has been made or intended by the Severn Wildfowl Trust, though most moderate wildfowlers deplore the very large bags which are sometimes made by individual sportsmen. Facts of the kind which have been and are being amassed by the Trust operate in favour of the geese, of the wildfowler, of the birdwatcher, indeed of all who are interested in these magnificent birds. No-one should feel that the methods used for obtaining these facts are in themselves disadvantageous to the geese. Were this to be the case the Trust would not be prepared to use them.

It must have been with a sense of relief that Peter sent off the letter in the post – he had made an excellent and complete rebuttal of the other's arguments.

If he thought that the matter was closed however, he was soon to be disappointed. Both letters were printed in *The Times* on 27 October and Peter shortly received a letter from the treasurer of the Severn Wildfowl Trust, Archie Jamieson, who clearly felt that Peter should have consulted other members of the Trust's council and in particular the president, Lord Alanbrooke, before replying. He wrote:

> I think your letter in today's Times is excellent. The only reason I suggested you might bring in the 'Master Gunner' (Lord Alanbrooke) is to show that you have the Council behind you. If the correspondence continues – and it attracts much attention – it might be as well that the next letter of yours – if there is one – should be signed both by Alan and yourself. The risk is that the Council will lose interest, or you will alienate them if they are not consulted, but if the President signs as well as you, the rest of them will follow. Just – every now and then – recall to yourself the loneliness of Dictators … It is one of the penalties of greatness that the 'curs' should yap at your heels: but the yapping can do a lot of harm.

Archie Jamieson's letter seems a little harsh and one is tempted to emulate the flapper and say 'Oh poor Peter'. Peter's feelings on receiving this letter are unknown but his reply is polite, tactful, considered and, as always, diplomatic; he wrote:

> I very much hope that it won't be necessary to involve the Master Gunner at all, partly because it might seem like hiding behind his name and reputation … I really didn't mean to by-pass the Council in the Times correspondence. I just felt that speed in replying was essential and that I was the only person who could answer at first-hand about Iceland and rockets. It was a pity that I happened to be in Scotland

otherwise I could have checked it with the President first. Anyway, I have written to him to explain the background of Hammond's letter. Meanwhile I am under fire as British Representative of the International Yacht Racing Union on an equally controversial issue concerning small boats, and am having a battle with the First Lord of the Admiralty about the fate of the old Discovery. What a life!

Peter need not have worried. On 8 November, Lord Alanbrooke wrote to Peter:

I have read the correspondence in the Times with the greatest of interest and I thought your letter was excellent. It was thoroughly well balanced and should satisfy the critics. I had gathered that the correspondence originated with those who feared that their sport might be curtailed as a result of your research work.

In December 1953, John Davey wrote once again to Peter, this time with a different concern. He had met Dr Elder from the University of Missouri who was working in the field with the Severn Wildfowl Trust's rocket-netting team, X-raying birds to determine the levels of lead shot in their bodies. Davey was aware that high levels of embedded lead shot had been discovered in birds in North America and was concerned at the public reaction if similar levels were found to occur in British birds. His main fear was that a public outcry would lead to a ban on all wild geese shooting. In light of this, perhaps Peter was preparing figures and facts that would show that injuries were so slight as to cause no difficulties to the geese? In any case, Davey added, any casual observer looking at a flock of pink-footed geese in flight would observe that they seemed perfectly healthy and that any injuries must therefore be insignificant. He finished by saying that any ban on shooting that might be invoked as a result of the findings would be 'an injury to our country'. Peter's reply was, as always, diplomatic but firm:

Of course I have given a great deal of thought to the point you raise about the proportion of geese carrying shot. I know there is a danger that our figures may be used by extremists, but nevertheless I do not think it would be right to suppress the results. (That way ends in 'burning the books'!)

I was very much distressed to find how high the proportion was. In adult geese it is 40%, and in those that are of breeding age it appears to be 50%. Biologically it does not seem to have affected the species very much, as in my view it is at least holding its own, (in spite of this, and an annual kill which is certainly in excess of 10,000 birds per year). But ethically I think that proportion which results from the universal habit of shooting at the geese when they are too high, is a serious blot on the sport of wildfowling. Whether publication of the figures would help to reduce the number of long shots taken I just don't know. I rather doubt it. It was this feature of wounding – pricking, call it what you will – which made me give up shooting geese, long before I knew what these X-ray figures were going to be.

Of course you are right that a bird showing shot may be perfectly fit – indeed most of them are. But if you could see the mess from which they have recovered you would realise that a large proportion must have suffered a good deal of pain. One bird had 23 pellets – of three different shot sizes. Another had 9BB shot in the head and neck, two of the pellets having flattened themselves on the vertebrae. One had a pellet in the brain, another a pellet in the heart – you could see it dilating with the heart beats. One had a .303 in the abdomen and two or three more had .22 bullets mushroomed out like flowers. Most of these birds were quite fit and their weights were up to average. But it isn't a nice thing to see, or to think about. And since it exists I believe that people ought to know about it.

Much depends, of course, on where and how it is published, and you may be sure that I do not want it to be used as a weapon against wildfowling, which is, as you say, a fine old sport. Also if we are to help the birds we must bring the wildfowlers along with us, and not make enemies of them all (though we are bound to make enemies of the extreme ones who know no moderation).

Trying to find a balance between the competing interests of wildfowlers, conservationists and the general public was almost impossible, but Peter was uniquely equipped to make the attempt and there is not the slightest doubt that his influence did much to resolve the conflict. He did have an occasional ally in the ranks of the shooting fraternity. In August 1953, he received a letter from a man who had recently paid a visit to Slimbridge. He wrote:

I have been a keen wildfowler all my life and felt ashamed of myself when all them [*sic*] wildfowl with you came to welcome me on my visit to you, I enjoyed myself more with a camera than I would ever with a shot gun.

Peter replied:

I am delighted you enjoyed your visit here so much. I also have come to realise – after many years as a keen wildfowler, that infinitely more enjoyment can be gained from watching and photographing the birds, than from shooting them.

Clearly Peter had made a convert. His problem was that there was still a whole army of wildfowlers at large who remained to be convinced.

In November 1953, Peter tried a new tactic. If he was experiencing difficulties with individuals on both sides of the debate perhaps a route forward could be found through better links with the wildfowling organisations. He already sat on the council of the British Field Sports Society so now decided to ask a friend, Edwin Parish, about the possibility of joining the other main wildfowling body, the Wildfowling Association of Great Britain and Ireland (WAGBI). Parish responded to say this was not the time to put his name forward as there was considerable hostility towards Peter in the organisation's ranks. Peter replied, 'I'm sorry to hear that I'm not allowed to be a member of W.A.G.B.I. It must be even more exclusive than I thought.' Nevertheless he decided to persevere. He wrote to Hugh Monahan of WAGBI to ask for a meeting to discuss ways in which WAGBI and the Severn Wildfowl Trust could develop better links and work together to their mutual benefit. One idea that was proposed was that there should be a liaison officer to improve communications between the two organisations though it is evident that the members of WAGBI were divided on this idea, many of them thinking they should have nothing to do with Peter and the Severn Wildfowl Trust.

Peter then turned his attention to the British Field Sports Society (BFSS) of whose council he was himself a member. He offered the BFSS a seat on the council of the Severn Wildfowl Trust but was somewhat dismayed when they declined on the basis that, in their view, the objectives of the two organisations might not always be aligned. Peter's response was to resign from the council of BFSS on the reasonable basis that if they saw no point in having a seat on the council of the Trust then he was wasting his time attending BFSS council meetings. In reply, the secretary of BFSS, Brigadier Pepys, wrote to express his concern at the possibility of Peter resigning from their council, adding that the link that Peter provided between the Trust and BFSS was of the greatest value to BFSS, as was his wide knowledge on the subject of wildfowl. Peter must have despaired at this point; BFSS were keen to gain insight into the thoughts of the conservation lobby but were unwilling to try and bridge the gap between the two sides; how could he possibly build any kind of consensus when one of the most influential organisations held such a position?

Despite their suspicion of Peter, the wider wildfowling community also felt that his knowledge and experience could be of value to them. In July 1954, he was invited to write an article for the *Shooting Times* on the provision for wildfowl in a new bill that was to be presented in Parliament, and his views continued to be sought by campaigners of different persuasions. Both sides of the argument were represented during the Parliamentary debates that followed later that year, and the Protection of Birds Act duly came into law.

In September 1954, Peter was asked to support a campaign to have wildfowling banned in Chichester Harbour and his response was, as always, even-handed:

> It is true that certain species of wildfowl are believed to be declining, and that wildfowl sanctuaries may be advisable in certain areas. On the other hand, the hunting instinct is deep in the human character, and I am personally opposed to too much restriction.

Peter also found himself embroiled in a dispute over the shooting of brent geese. Some of the most important wintering grounds for this attractive little goose are in south-east England. Numbers had been heavily depleted in the 1930s, when its major food source, eel grass, had been almost completely destroyed by a mystery illness, the population plummeting to between 10 per cent and 25 per cent of previous totals. Numbers subsequently rose, but the wintering population in England remained in the region of 10,000 to 15,000 birds, and thus the goose was under significant threat from wildfowlers. A WAGBI committee member wrote to Peter in October 1953, suggesting that the brent goose numbers could best be increased by protecting them from hunting on their Russian breeding grounds, presumably imagining that the Severn Wildfowl Trust might be willing and able to pursue such a campaign. Peter chose to ignore the hypocrisy implied in the proposal to persuade others to reduce hunting elsewhere in order to facilitate better sport in the UK. He replied:

> I very much agree with you that protection of geese and especially Brents in the breeding area would be the best possible means of increasing their numbers but, alas, under present international conditions there isn't much we can do about it. Therefore it is probably desirable to do what we can at this end.

The matter was resolved when the brent goose became a protected species under the 1954 Protection of Birds Act, though the Trust had to fight for the geese again in 1973 when the proposed siting of London's third airport at Foulness in Essex threatened one of the main wintering areas in England.

In the early 1950s, Peter also found himself under friendly fire from time to time. In the summer of 1954, the *Edinburgh Bird Bulletin*, an organ of the Scottish Ornithologists' Club, published, without permission, Severn Wildfowl Trust records of goose numbers and health records for wild geese caught in parts of Scotland. To make matters worse, much of the data were provisional, requiring further processing and analysis before publication. The bulletin also provided specific locations in Scotland where the geese had been recorded, making it easy for wildfowlers to determine where the best shooting might be found. It must have been intensely frustrating to Peter to have all his careful work on the distribution of pink-footed geese published in such a careless and reckless way.

Requests for Peter to arbitrate in shooting disputes continued to arrive in his postbag. In December 1954, Peter received a letter seeking his support in a dispute over shooting on the Solway Firth. This time Peter had had enough and he wrote back to say it might be better if he stayed out of it. Ever the diplomat, he used the triple negative to soften the blow: 'indeed I am not quite sure whether it would not have a greater effect if I did not enter the lists at this stage'. Peter's patience had been stretched far enough; he was clearly a little weary of the endless battles with a community that refused absolutely to engage in any kind of sensible debate about the future of wildfowl in Great Britain.

In subsequent years Peter had some success in persuading the conservation and shooting communities to work together for a common purpose. In 1956, WAGBI cooperated with a Wildfowl Trust survey of wildfowl concentrations and habitats on behalf of the Nature Conservancy with a view to establishing a series of reserves aimed at conserving wildfowl stocks. In 1960, when the Trust was carrying out scientific research into wildfowl feeding habits, wildfowlers cooperated by sending in to the Trust for examination over 400 viscera from birds that had been shot. In January 1963, during a particularly harsh winter, the Trust and WAGBI made a joint appeal on television to ask wildfowlers to refrain from the sport until the weather improved. The presence on the Trust's council of Dr Jeffery Harrison also improved links with the wildfowling community. Harrison was Honorary Scientific Adviser of WAGBI and chairman of the Wildfowl Conservation Committee of the Nature Conservancy. He did more than most to bring wildfowlers and naturalists together in the common cause of conservation, receiving the OBE for his work in 1971.

Whatever views Peter held on sustainable and responsible shooting, by 1954 his own shooting days were almost over as far as he was concerned. In November of that year, in correspondence with Scottish wildfowler Alex Barclay, he explained his ambivalence about the sport and added that though he still occasionally went wildfowling he had pretty much given up shooting geese since he was now convinced they were much nicer alive than dead. He added that the only advantage of wildfowlers shooting large bags of geese was that it was perhaps the only way of making them realise with distaste the folly of such excesses.

Peter gave up shooting altogether at some point before June 1960 when he finished writing *The Eye of the Wind*, because in it he wrote:

> I am quite sure that as soon as the doubts and the disquiet prevent
> you from enjoying shooting there can be no longer any good reason
> for going on doing it. So I have sold my guns and I no longer shoot.

There is a curious postscript to all this in Peter's book *Observations of Wildlife*, published in 1980. In it he wrote:

Wild Geese ... are very special birds because their society is based on a permanent pair bond and a family life which keeps the young with their parents until breeding time comes round again. It took me a little time after I had learned these things before I decided to give up all shooting. I have not fired a gun for 32 years.

This clearly cannot be true, as it implies he did not fire a gun after 1948. As we have seen however, he shot ducks or geese on several occasions between 1949 and 1954. It seems likely that it is either a miscalculation, a misprint ('22 years' would mean he had given up in 1958) or he simply got the years mixed up in his memory.

It was perhaps fortunate that Peter had begun catching geese in the early 1950s using rocket nets. As previously noted, the effort and guile required to outwit and catch the geese provided a kind of excitement not dissimilar from the thrills of shooting, with the added bonus that the birds were alive at the end of it. In addition, the process contributed to the advancement of science. Had this new kind of 'sport' not been available to him he might well have found it more difficult to give up shooting altogether. Whatever the case, it is certainly true that had he never been a wildfowler he would not have learned to love wild geese and by association, all types of wildfowl; nor would he have fallen under the spell of the magnificent wild places they inhabit. Without this impetus there would have been no Severn Wildfowl Trust, and Peter's invaluable contribution to conservation in Britain and around the world would have been diminished or absent altogether.

18

Good Science

It was clear to Peter in the early 1950s that he was not going to be able to win over the shooting lobby by reasoned argument and debate. What was needed was hard scientific evidence, facts and figures that nobody could refute. In addition, with the nene goose saved, at least for the time being, there were other species in urgent need of support and once again, good science would be the key to getting the support both moral and financial that the Trust desperately needed if its work was to be stepped up.

Another problem was that Peter was extraordinarily busy. In the early 1950s, his everyday management of the Trust, his travels, his painting, writing and broadcasting had become all-consuming and it was clear that he needed some additional support, and not just in administering the Trust. He was not alone in thinking this. Archie Jamieson, the Trust's treasurer, also had his views on the way in which Peter was single-handedly managing the Trust's affairs. In a letter to Peter in August 1953 he wrote:

I shall be seeing you on 2nd September, and in the meantime I believe Mike is having a talk with you about what form the future organisation of S.W.T. should take. You have really been so successful in arousing public interest that – in my opinion – the time has arrived to devise a more professional form of organisation and one which is not so entirely dependent upon yourself. I think you will find we all agree about this, and we can have a talk about it when we meet on the 2nd September, and perhaps put it into force at the beginning of next year.

It is not clear whether this had been a point of discussion between other members of the council or if it was simply Archie Jamieson's point of view. In the early days of the Trust it had just been Peter and some friends who, through sheer hard work and determination, had made things happen, building up the Severn Wildfowl Trust from nothing. Now, seven years on, with the Trust established and its work expanding at an exponential rate, something had to change.

The solution, when it came, would satisfy Peter's desire to maintain his hands-on approach while dramatically widening the scientific expertise available to the Trust. Scientific research had been one of the founding aims of the Severn Wildfowl Trust so it was entirely fitting that in the summer of 1954, the Trust announced the formation of a Scientific Advisory Committee. This committee would bring together experts from different but related fields to advise and provide guidance on the research work carried out by the Trust. This solution had the advantage of dramatically widening the expertise available to the Trust without adding a significant financial burden. At the same time it would enhance the provenance of scientific data used in support of the Trust's work and make it easier to obtain grants for future projects.

Through his extensive network of connections, Peter was able to assemble a formidable group of people. Among the twenty-eight-strong committee were Prof. Konrad Lorenz, the man who invented the science of ethology, the study of animal behaviour, Prof. Julian Huxley FRS, Jean Delacour, author of the prestigious four volume work *Wildfowl of the World* that Peter was in the process of illustrating, Dr David Lack FRS, head of The Edward Grey Institute of Field Ornithology at Oxford University (and who had discomfited Philippa some years before in Sweden), Dr F. Fraser Darling FRSE, Sir Ronald Fisher FRS, Bruce Campbell, secretary of The British Trust for Ornithology, Dr L. Harrison Matthews FRS, director of The Zoological Society of London, Niko Tinbergen, the Dutch biologist who would share a Nobel prize in 1973 and Prof. Vero Wynne-Edwards FRSE, an ornithologist who would later engage in a bitter dispute with David Lack over the science of bird behaviour. One other member was George Yeates, who like Peter had been a keen wildfowler. A member of the Trust since 1948, Yeates developed a passion for photography and for him, eventually, the camera replaced the gun. Peter welcomed having someone on the committee who, like him, understood the other side of the wildfowling debate. The committee included eight Fellows of the Royal Society and was, by any standards, an extraordinary group of scientists, probably the most influential body of biologists and ornithologists ever gathered under one roof.

At the first meeting of the committee, Sir Landsborough Thompson was elected as chairman. He was the perfect choice: an ornithologist of international distinction, he had established organised bird ringing in the UK, and in 1954, the same year he took up the chair of the scientific committee, he was appointed President of the Eleventh International Ornithological Congress in Basel, Switzerland. One of the committee's first actions was to appoint a scientific director for the Trust. The selected candidate, ornithologist Geoffrey Matthews, was a Cambridge academic engaged in post-doctoral research into bird navigation. He arrived in May 1955 and began building a team of researchers as the Trust's scientific work expanded. He was to continue to work for the Trust for the next thirty-three years, becoming deputy director in 1973.

Peter was able to secure funding from the Nature Conservancy to pay the salary of Geoffrey Matthews and of a number of other scientists, so the new committee was able to get off to a flying start. A new laboratory had been established in the old stable buildings and was put to use in the summer of 1954, when research began into parasitic nematode worms and aspergillosis, both of which had caused significant problems among birds in the collection. The laboratory also contained a darkroom equipped free of charge by Kodak Ltd. It was at this time that the word 'Severn' was dropped from the name of the Trust as its work and influence became more international in nature.

In May 1954, Peter attended the Eleventh International Ornithological Congress, held at Basel in Switzerland. The list of delegates included Bruce Campbell, Julian Huxley, Richard Fitter, Roger Peterson, David Lack, James Fisher and Eric Simms. Peter presented a paper on his work on the distribution of pink-footed geese and showed a film of his recent work in Iceland. The following day, certain delegates were invited to show films on various topics at a delegates' film evening. Peter was selected to show his film about pink-footed geese again but instead chose to replace it with *Ring of Fire* about his expedition to Tierra del Fuego the previous year. Another film selected for inclusion was a short one about woodpeckers called *Carpenters of The Forest* by a German film-maker, Heinz Sielmann. Peter was deeply impressed by the film but could not have guessed the impact that it would have on his future career.

During the Congress at Basel, Peter was elected to the International Ornithological Committee, an appointment that reflected the growing importance of his work in the international community and one which gave Peter some justified pride. Unfortunately he was not present when the announcement was made as he had had to return early to England to be present at the birth of his son, Falcon. Back home, Peter was invited to take up a further post as a member of the Home Office Advisory Committee on the Protection of Birds for England and Wales.

The main purpose of Peter's rocket-netting activities in the early 1950s had been to build up accurate numbers of geese wintering in Britain, with a particular focus on the pink-footed goose. As mentioned in Chapter 11, the National Wildfowl Count was established in 1947 to gather data on numbers of all kinds of waterfowl wintering in Britain. In 1954, responsibility for the count passed to the Wildfowl Trust. At the time, the scheme was supported by 700 amateur ornithologists who counted wildfowl species at over 500 wetlands and bodies of water throughout the country. The information received through the scheme helped Peter and the Trust gain an accurate picture of the numbers of all wildfowl species in winter. By 1986, the scheme included 1,500 sites surveyed by 1,100 recorders.

Between 1957 and 1960, the Trust carried out an investigation on behalf of the Nature Conservancy to consider the value of aerial surveys in establishing accurate wildfowl counts. The Trust determined that aerial survey was particularly effective with certain species such as barnacle geese, brent geese, shelduck and swans, presumably because the plumage of these species made them easier to identify and count on aerial photographs. One of the areas chosen for survey was the Bristol Channel where the work cast new light on the concentrations of moulting shelduck in Bridgwater Bay; the information gained could not have been achieved by any means other than aerial survey.

As research activity increased, it became apparent that the laboratory in the stable yard was too small. In August 1962, it was announced that a donation of £10,000 had been received from the Trustees of the Wolfson Foundation for the development of a new research building. Work commenced on the research centre in April 1964; the design allowed for research rooms, a post-mortem room, a darkroom and a library on the first floor, with an exhibition room and a lecture hall on the ground floor. The entry to the grounds would be through one of the exhibition spaces which would have large windows looking onto the bird enclosures. Further funding came from the Nature Conservancy and City of London institutions, and the Wolfson Foundation increased their donation to £25,000. The lecture rooms were occupied in February 1965. Peter painted a large canvas for the entrance hall depicting nene geese in flight in front of the peak of Mauna Loa in Hawaii; the painting still hangs in the foyer at the current centre in Slimbridge. The new research centre, called Wolfson Hall, was opened by Her Majesty the Queen on 23 April 1966. The Wildfowl Trust Guide for 1969 gives an outline of the research work carried out, accompanied by several photographs of scientists 'at work' including a post-mortem being carried out on a dead swan. Peter was deeply interested in such matters; he was convinced that visitors to Slimbridge who purchased the guide would be too.

One of the first exhibitions mounted in Wolfson Hall presented to the public the four main objectives of the Wildfowl Trust: research, conservation, education and recreation. These four stated aims were seen by Peter as the fundamental pillars or building blocks of the Trust; they are still at the heart of everything it does today. The idea for the first exhibit was Peter's: a full-length mirror with the caption 'You are now looking at the most dangerous animal on the planet'. It proved to be an extremely effective way of getting the conservation message across to every person who stepped through the door.

In July 1966, the International Ornithological Congress was held at Oxford. The main mid-week excursion for participants was to the Wildfowl Trust and 400 delegates descended on Slimbridge. The Trust bulletin for August 1966 noted:

> There has been a constant flow of international ornithologists before and after the Congress and the Research Centre's Visitor's Book, graciously opened by H.M. The Queen when she inaugurated the Centre on 23rd April, is filling up rapidly!

The presence and interest of over 400 of the world's leading ornithologists can only have helped promote the Trust's credentials on the international stage and improve the kind of links without which no scientific foundation can prosper.

In the same month, July 1966, the Wildfowl Trust hosted a meeting of the executive board of the International Wildfowl and Wetlands Research Bureau (IWRB), an event which would have far reaching consequences for science and research at Slimbridge. Initially founded in 1937 as the International Wildfowl Inquiry, part of the British section of the International Committee for Bird Preservation, IWRB was reformulated and renamed in 1954 when its scope was extended to include protection for wetland areas. Its stated aims were to stimulate and co-ordinate research and conservation work on waterfowl and their wetland habitats at an international level. It was clear that IWRB and the Wildfowl Trust had many common interests and that working together would be mutually beneficial. The meeting in July 1966 saw scientists gather from Belgium, Denmark, France, West Germany, Ireland, Israel, the Netherlands, Sweden, Switzerland and the United Kingdom. Good connections were clearly made because that winter IWRB launched the first ever International Waterfowl Count based on the principles of the British operation run from Slimbridge. The new international count was also run from Slimbridge and included 3,500 locations in thirty countries in Europe, western Asia and North Africa, each of which was surveyed twice during the winter. This would inevitably include counts for all species wintering in Western Europe and provide a valuable resource to both organisations. By September 1967, records had been gathered for 2,685,000 swans, geese and ducks. A further 3,000,000 records were awaited from the Soviet Union. With support from the Nature Conservancy and the Forestry Commission, data were transferred to punch tape prior to subsequent computer analysis.

At this time, the headquarters of IWRB were in the Camargue in France, but in January 1969, Geoffrey Matthews, Director of Research at the Wildfowl Trust, became director of IWRB, and its headquarters were moved to Slimbridge where office space and facilities were made available. One of IWRB's most important achievements came in 1971 when it was instrumental in establishing the Ramsar Convention on Wetlands of International Importance. This protocol, signed in 1971 at the International Conference on the Conservation of Wetlands and Waterfowl at Ramsar in Iran, required signatories to list wetland reserves as sites of scientific importance and commit to their protection, becoming the first major agreement between governments to protect wetlands and their biodiversity. Participation signified a binding agreement to safeguard the selected areas against any kind of threat or development. By 1985, thirty-eight countries had become signatories to the Convention, incorporating 300 protected wetlands around the world and covering a combined twenty million hectares. The Trust's reserve at Slimbridge is a Ramsar listed site.

In 1985, IWRB was commissioned by the World Wildlife Fund to carry out inventories of wetlands in Central and South America and in Asia. Scientists from the Netherlands and Spain came to Slimbridge to work on the project, further increasing the international diversity of the team on-site. As a result of this project, two sister organisations were formed, Wetlands for the Americas and the Asia Wetland Bureau. In 1996 the two organisations merged with IWRB to form Wetlands International which is managed today from its headquarters in the Netherlands.

On 18 March 1967, the oil tanker *Torrey Canyon* went aground on the Seven Stones Reef off Land's End, spilling most of its cargo of 119,000 tonnes of crude oil into the sea. Over 10,000 tonnes of highly toxic dispersant were poured into the surrounding waters over the next few days, and the impact of both oil and dispersant on the seabirds in the area was devastating. Oiled birds poured into RSPCA centres in Cornwall and the organisation was soon swamped. The Wildfowl Trust offered its services as part of the huge operation to rescue the oiled seabirds. Ninety-seven birds including guillemots, razorbills and shags were sent to Slimbridge, though only eighty-six survived the journey from Cornwall. Despite treatment, most of the remaining birds died. One of the main problems in bringing the birds back to health was that the chemicals used to disperse the oil on the feathers also removed the waxes spread by the birds from their preen glands. This was a common problem at all the cleaning centres, but Peter and the Trust used their scientific resources to solve the problem. A scientist studying the composition of preen gland secretions was invited to Slimbridge from Sweden, and a chemical company was commissioned to make up aerosol sprays containing common chemical compounds which simulated the natural ones secreted for preening. The sprays were distributed to other centres, and overall the waterproofing of the birds' feathers was improved. Of the 8,000 birds recovered alive on the beaches of Cornwall, 97 per cent subsequently died. Nevertheless, the work carried out by the Trust meant that, in future disasters, the impacted birds would stand a better chance of survival, and it was agreed that further research work would be carried out to improve the efficacy of the chemical sprays.

An expansion to the Slimbridge research centre was announced in 1972, when a donation of £30,000 was given by council member Jack Hayward. This second phase of building included specialist laboratories, a museum, space for visiting scientists and facilities for the new education department. Both phases of the research centre still stand, though the first phase was significantly modified to incorporate the current reception building and observation tower. The second phase of building has remained relatively unchanged with the original rooms overlooking the Big Pen now used as administrative offices.

An important part of the work of the Trust was the breeding and rearing of waterfowl, especially of endangered species. For many years, this work was carried out in a ramshackle shed called the Top Hut in the north-west corner of the Rushy Pen. The facilities were hardly adequate, so when an inspection tour was made by experts from the Federation of Zoological Gardens of Great Britain and Ireland prior to the acceptance of the Trust into the Federation, the upgrading of the breeding facilities was strongly recommended. In August 1969 came the announcement that funding had been obtained for the construction of a new propagation facility to include a food preparation room, an egg room, an incubator room, a room for breeding food insects and a large internal duckery for rearing ducklings.

The Trust Bulletin published in August 1969 added, 'We shall not of course be able to call this fine new building the "Top Hut". It will be known as the "Propagation and Service Building".' The building was put into operation in 1970 and continues to provide the same facilities fifty years on. The building is known today, of course, as the Top Hut.

Some scientific problems seem to be ever-present. Take for example the use of lead shot by wildfowlers and fishermen. The dispersal of lead shot on the ground by hunters and the loss of lead fishing weights in rivers and lakes causes wildfowl to suffer severe lead poisoning through ingestion of lead pellets. Many species of wildfowl swallow small quantities of grit to aid digestion of cellulose in the gizzard. Unable to differentiate between gravel and lead shot, the birds swallow the lead, which often leads to their death. In 1986, the Trust's *Wildfowl World* magazine commented, 'The Trust has been actively involved in the efforts to find a solution to this problem, which seems to be in sight.' Use of lead shot in fishing was indeed banned but the problem didn't end there. Fast-forward thirty-four years to 2020 and an article in the Trust's magazine, now called *Waterlife*:

> The end of lead poisoning looks another step closer as leading members of the UK shooting community call for a voluntary ban on lead shot. This major success follows decades of campaigning by WWT and other conservation organisations.

Nothing could better illustrate the need for ongoing 'Good Science'.

19

Expanding the Trust

In addition to his involvement in developing facilities for science and research, Peter was also directly and personally involved with the development of the wildfowl collection and the associated facilities for visitors at the Trust, relying initially on a small team of people to help him manage day-to-day affairs and expanding the team in later years. Walking around the enclosures today it is difficult to imagine just how primitive things were in the first years of the Trust. Bulletin number five of the Severn Wildfowl Trust issued in September 1951 contained the following announcement:

> A road with hard core, gravel and a bitumen surface has been laid from the main gate down to the end of the Big Pen (nearly half a mile). Those members who struggled through the deep mud in order to see the birds in these furthest pens last winter will appreciate the necessity for this rather costly venture.

Gradually, a visit to the Trust became less of an ordeal as more and more facilities were developed. In 1954, a new water supply system was installed allowing better and cleaner flow of water through the pools in the enclosures. The water was pumped from local drainage ditches at the north end of the site but flow still couldn't be guaranteed until 1982, when two pipes were installed to bring water from the canal under gravity feed. More bird hides were added and in 1956 it became possible for Trust members to make visits to the sea wall without the supervision of a warden. The winter flocks of geese on the Dumbles continued to be a huge draw for birdwatchers and enthusiasts, and the numbers rarely disappointed during the early years of the Trust. Numbers of geese were regularly above 3,000, peaking in 1970 with a staggering count of 7,600 white-fronted geese.

By 1957, the collection had grown to fill the space available in the seventeen acres that had originally been enclosed by the fox-proof fence. At the end of that year there were just over 1,300 birds in the collection representing 116 different species. A neighbour who farmed the adjacent land offered to transfer a further seven acres to the Trust, an offer which Peter gratefully accepted. The new area was next to the Big Pen on the south-east side, and its acquisition led to a reorganisation of the collection. In the new area were added a large covered aviary donated by Arthur Guinness Ltd which would contain breeding pens and five large enclosures in which for the first time, at the request of a number of Trust members, birds were organised by continent of origin. The new section was opened to the public at Easter, 1959.

More developments followed, starting with a restaurant in December 1962. The year 1967 saw the construction of the Tropical House, the funds for which came from an anonymous donor, with plants donated by Kew Gardens. The building opened its doors on 11 November 1967 to celebrate the twenty-first anniversary of the Trust. Now Peter was able to keep tropical species such as hummingbirds and tanagers, and the lush vegetation and warm, humid atmosphere provided a welcome respite for visitors on cold winter days. In the same year, the Holden Tower was erected adjacent to the sea wall, giving unrivalled views across the Dumbles where the wild geese gathered in winter. In 1968, the car park was enlarged and surfaced and the Swan Observatory was opened. This overlooked the Rushy Pen and was reserved for the use of members only.

In 1973, came a major expansion. A further sixty-two acres were enclosed on both the west and the east sides of the Big Pen, bringing the total enclosed area to 100 acres, of which sixty were open to the public. Existing pens were extended, new flamingo pools were added and the whole collection was reorganised. Beyond the centre, things were changing too; in the same year a further 300 acres were added at the north end of the reserve. In 1982 the South Finger was opened up to visitors with three new hides looking north to the river, offering uninterrupted views of the winter geese flocks.

Above left: Peter with pet lizard, Zonure, *c.* 1920. (Dafila Scott)

Above right: Back from the hunt, *c.* 1930. (Dafila Scott)

Below: Peter with roe deer fawn at Oberau, 1933. (Dafila Scott)

Above left: Billy Williams, ringing a teal at Borough Fen duck decoy. (Dafila Scott)

Above right: East Lighthouse at Sutton Bridge, *c.* 1935. (Dafila Scott)

Below: The first trip to Slimbridge with Harry Savory (centre) and Howard Davis (right), 1937. (Martin Davis)

Above: The window at the Cap Tourmente Gun Club, 1938. (Dafila Scott)

Below: Playing cards in the wardroom. (Dafila Scott)

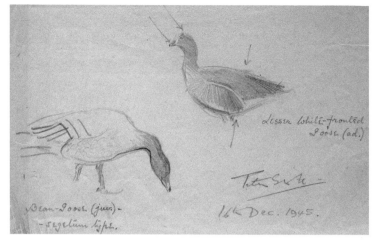

Peter's drawing of a lesser white-fronted goose which helped identify the two birds seen at Slimbridge in December 1945. (Martin Davis)

The cottage at the New Grounds in 1946. (Wildfowl and Wetlands Trust)

Philippa feeding greylag geese, 1949. (Dafila Scott)

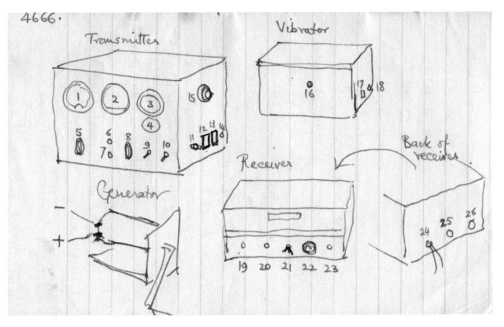

Above: Peter's diagram of the radio transmitter in one of his notebooks from the 1951 Iceland expedition. (Wildfowl and Wetlands Trust)

Below: Peter ringing a pink-footed goose in Iceland, 1951. (Dafila Scott)

Peter and Philippa's wedding in Reykjavik, 1951. Finnur Gudmundsson towers above Philippa in the front row while Jack Greenway stands at the back top right. (Dafila Scott)

Peter with the first nine nene goslings hatched at Slimbridge, 1952. (Dafila Scott)

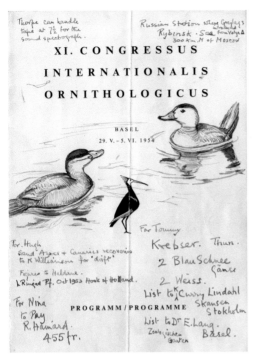

Above left: Peter's copy of the programme for the International Ornithological Congress in Basel, 1954, enhanced by his doodles. (Wildfowl and Wetlands Trust)

Above right: Kathleen Scott's statue of her husband in Christchurch, New Zealand, 1956. (Dafila Scott)

Below: Encounter with a koala bear in Australia, 1956. (Dafila Scott)

The family home at Slimbridge, 1960. The studio window was much narrower at that time. (Dafila Scott)

Peter and Dafila feeding snow geese in the Big Pen at Slimbridge, 1961. (Dafila Scott)

Above left: Peter at the helm of *Sovereign*, during preparations for the America's Cup, 1964. (Dafila Scott)

Above right: Peter in the studio window with his beloved Bewick's swans behind him, 1970. (Dafila Scott)

Below: Preparing a canvas on the studio floor. (Dafila Scott)

One of Peter's many copies of underwater writing boards, listing the fish he had seen, in this case at Kai Besar in Indonesia. (Wildfowl and Wetlands Trust)

Peter with Max Williams and a Volkswagen Beetle converted into an emergency bird hide in Romania, 1971. (Dafila Scott)

Time off from meetings – gliding in New Zealand, 1971. (Dafila Scott)

Right: Peter with Tommy Johnstone, Curator of Birds at Slimbridge for twenty-four years. (Dafila Scott)

Below: Close encounter with a royal albatross on Campbell Island, New Zealand, 1971. (Dafila Scott)

Peter among Adélie penguins in Antarctica. (Dafila Scott)

Painting Egyptian geese on a large canvas in the studio. (Dafila Scott)

Peter diving off Greenland, 1972. (Dafila Scott)

The *Lindblad Explorer* at Larantuka, Flores, 1977. (Dafila Scott)

Philippa and Tenzing on Mount Flora, Antarctica, 1978. (Dafila Scott)

Peter and
Philippa
outside
the hut at
Cape Evans,
Antarctica,
1979. (Dafila
Scott)

Peter painting
in his travel
diary, Virgin
Islands.
(Dafila Scott)

Peter with a
giant panda in
China, 1980.
(Dafila Scott)

Right: Philippa helping to ring Bewick's swans, 1980. (Dafila Scott)

Below: Peter and Philippa in the studio window, 1982. (Dafila Scott)

Peter meeting Konrad Lorentz at Grunau, 1985. (Dafila Scott)

A corner of the studio, Scott House Museum, 2019. Peter's last painting still stands on its easel. (Wildfowl and Wetlands Trust)

As the facilities at the Trust improved, the number of visitors increased. In April 1948 Peter estimated that there had been around 2,500 visitors to Slimbridge during the previous year. In November 1955, Slimbridge had received 80,000 visitors by mid-November, and in December 1956 the one-hundred-thousandth visitor that year was met by Peter and presented with a signed print. One impediment to visitor numbers at that time was the swing bridge over the canal which, being made of wood, was unable to carry buses and coaches. The bridge was hand-operated and built in two halves which had to be opened and closed in tandem from both banks of the canal. Anyone arriving on a coach disembarked on the other side of the canal and walked half a mile down the road to the Trust. This was clearly undesirable for infirm or older visitors, so the Trust was delighted when it was announced that the old bridge was to be replaced with a new metal one. During construction at the end of 1957 there was no road access to the Trust, visitors crossing the canal by ferry boat. The new bridge opened to traffic in January 1958 and has been in service ever since. In 1979 the Trust welcomed its six millionth visitor and by 1980, numbers visiting Slimbridge had increased to 222,000 visitors each year. To be fair, not everybody was entirely happy with their visit to Slimbridge. Peter wrote in a letter in April 1955:

> The other day I gave a lift up the lane to two girl students who did not recognise me. 'Well, what did you think of the ducks?' said one of them. 'I thought they were rather exciting,' I said. 'What did you think?' 'Well frankly we were disappointed,' she said. 'We didn't think it was worth half-a-crown.' I asked why not and received this astonishing answer '… we thought we should see more different kinds.'

Accommodation was always a problem for people who wanted to stay for a few days, or for short-term staff who could not afford to find lodgings in the surrounding area. When the narrowboat *Beatrice* was sold in 1952, there was no accommodation for visitors or staff until a hostel was established in the stable yard in 1954. When the hostel was full, the overflow could be accommodated at the Patch Bridge guest house by the canal bridge. By 1967, as numbers had continued to grow, the problem of accommodation had become acute. The Trust was now offering field study opportunities for students, who naturally needed somewhere to stay. A new joint venture with the Youth Hostel

Association saw the building in 1968 of a fifty-bed youth hostel with facilities for field studies at Shepherd's Patch across the canal.

When the Trust was first formed, it was never imagined that it would manage any wildfowl collections other than the one at Slimbridge. However, as Peter's popularity soared due to his radio and television appearances and the numbers of visitors to Slimbridge increased, it became apparent that revenues from door takings and memberships were becoming a valuable addition to the Trust's funding. For a large proportion of the British population Slimbridge was not the easiest place to reach, so Peter began to think about the possibility of opening another centre elsewhere. In 1953, a proposal was made to the Trust's council to open a second centre in Scotland at the home of the Earl of Wemyss, Gosford House, fourteen miles east of Edinburgh. The house had extensive grounds with three lakes fed by a burn and much attractive woodland. The proposal called for the enclosure of twenty-three acres which it was thought would support a collection of around 1,000 birds. The wildfowl collection would be open to the public, and given the proximity of Edinburgh, it was thought that the centre would do well. The nearby nature reserve at Aberlady Bay supported a flock of several hundred pink-footed geese in winter, raising hopes that the Trust could make scientific and educational use of the reserve. In the end the proposals fell through and the centre was never established.

Peter was undeterred and remained determined to develop at least one additional site somewhere in the UK. In Bulletin number seventeen, dated 4 February 1955, appeared the following item:

> The Council wishes to know whether, now that the Trust had become a national organisation, the formation of Branches would be welcomed by Members who live too far away from the Severn Estuary to enjoy the privileges available at Slimbridge. Branches might provide a nucleus for holding lectures and other social entertainments, or for field excursions, they might establish and administer special facilities for studying wild waterfowl, such as observation huts etc., or they might even consider the creation of branch collections of live waterfowl. Members' views on this subject will be welcomed by the Council.

The view of the Members was clearly supportive. The first additional site opened in 1957 at Peakirk, near Peterborough, with the aim of supporting the decoy at nearby Borough Fen. The first warden at Peakirk was Billy Williams who had been the decoyman at Borough Fen since Peter first met him there in 1932. In 1956, the Trust had become tenants at Borough Fen after which it was used purely to catch ducks for ringing purposes. Called 'The Waterfowl Gardens', the centre at Peakirk was much smaller than Slimbridge, covering just fifteen acres. It also differed from Slimbridge, and from all the other centres that followed, in that there were no bird hides looking out into the surrounding area as it was surrounded on all sides by agricultural land. However, on certain days, Trust members were allowed access to the decoy at Borough Fen. Billy Williams continued to combine management of the Peakirk centre and the decoy at Borough Fen until his death in 1958. Billy's wife, Annie, continued to be associated with the Peakirk operation and was still actively involved at the age of ninety-two, twenty-five years after it opened.

For thirteen years there was just Slimbridge and Peakirk until, in 1970, a centre was opened at Welney in Norfolk. Welney is on the Ouse Washes just a few miles from where Peter used to go punt-gunning in the 1930s. In winter it is home to thousands of ducks as well as hundreds of whooper and Bewick's swans and therefore was a natural choice for a new wetland centre. Unlike Slimbridge and Peakirk, there was to be no collection of non-native species at Welney; the focus was, and remains, entirely on the spectacle of the summer wildlife and the thousands of waterfowl that visit in winter. As always, money was the main problem. In April 1969 a campaign was launched to raise £320,000 to support the three existing sites at Slimbridge, Peakirk and Welney. The construction work at Welney was complex and costly, requiring as it did a bridge over the road from the new centre to the observation hides. The construction of this was resolved when the Royal Engineers offered to build the bridge free of charge as a training exercise.

Other centres followed. In 1971 Caerlaverock opened on the north shore of the Solway Firth where, in winter, huge flocks of barnacle geese gather to feed. In 1975 came Martin Mere in Lancashire, home in winter to large numbers of pink-footed geese. Peter was familiar with both these locations from his rocket-netting adventures in the 1950s. The year 1975 also saw the opening of the Washington centre in Tyne and Wear, followed by Arundel in 1976. Wildfowl Trust Bulletin number 70 published in October 1974 clearly stated the case for the expansion:

Great progress has been made towards the completion of our three new refuges at Martin Mere, Washington and Arundel. These will bring the facilities of the Trust to within reasonable reach of most of the major centres of population in the country. It is only through education that the support of the mass of the people for conservation can be obtained. The Trust's well-tried formula of the wildfowl collection, where the birds can be seen at close quarters in nearly ideal conditions and alongside a wild refuge in which other birds can be seen in their natural habitat, will shortly reach many more people than the quarter million who come yearly to Slimbridge and Peakirk.

The opening of the new centres led to a significant increase in visitor numbers. By 1980, there were 662,000 visitors across all the centres; by 1989 over 10.5 million visitors were thought to have visited the Trust since 1946. Trust membership too increased from 1,102 at the end of the first year to 14,000 thirty years later. Today, membership of the Trust stands at 85,000.

The numbers of birds in the collection across all centres also increased over the years. The first Annual Report, published in 1947, indicated that the Trust had 400 birds representing sixty-seven species in the collection. In January 1975, the Slimbridge collection was recorded as 2,300 birds representing 171 species, while in the following year the Trust overall held 5,000 birds representing 189 species. The year 1975 was good for breeding, with 2,660 young raised from 128 species.

During the first thirty years of the Trust, some of the collection birds were free-flying, including some rather rare species. This led to some problems, as for example in 1952 when a small flock of greater snow geese at Slimbridge became disoriented in fog and flew off. A search was made by aeroplane to no avail, so a number of messages were broadcast on the radio and the Trust received over 200 sightings, nearly all of them false alarms. It was later discovered that the birds had landed at Cheltenham; two eventually returned and two were shot. This didn't deter Peter and he continued to keep free-flying specimens. By 1959 more than 250 birds from forty-nine species could fly and that year another forty birds were lost in fog. By 1973 the free-flying flocks included twenty-six nene geese which must have been a remarkable sight in the skies over Slimbridge. Such flights were not always by design. In 1960, a Falkland Islands flightless steamer duck surprised everyone (and possibly itself) by taking to the air in a high wind, clearing the fox-proof fence and landing three fields away.

One species that escaped from the collection at Slimbridge was ultimately to cause considerable problems. A number of ruddy duck were imported from North America, but it was discovered that they did not thrive if the eggs were taken in for incubation like other species. The ruddy ducks were therefore left to breed in the grounds, with the result that a number of birds escaped before they could be pinioned as they were supposed to be. Gradually, over time, flocks of the species became established in various parts of the West Country and the Midlands. Due consideration has to be given to any escaped species; one only has to consider the impact of the American grey squirrel on the native British red squirrel to understand the potential gravity of any escape. On balance, Peter thought there wouldn't be a problem and wrote in 1980:

> ... it seems doubtful to me that the Ruddies will ever become a pest or drive out any other species. Like the Mandarin Duck, they will, I believe, prove a harmless and attractive addition to the British avifauna.

What Peter could not have foreseen was that the ruddy ducks would eventually spread across the English Channel and onwards through Europe. In 1986, the first birds reached Spain where they began to mate with female white-headed ducks, a species they would not have encountered elsewhere. The rarest of native duck species in Spain, the white-headed duck had been reduced to twenty-two individuals in 1977, but by means of an extremely expensive rescue programme, numbers had been increased to 400 birds by 1988. Now it looked as if all that good work might be wasted if the purity of the species was lost through interbreeding. A major cull of the ruddy duck was put in place, and the white-headed duck was eventually saved; numbers have now increased to around 2,500 individuals in 2020. To be fair to Peter, the Trust was not the only culprit, as a number of bird collections held pairs of ruddy duck and it is clear that escapes came from other places too.

One of the Trust's greatest successes in captive breeding over the years has been with flamingos. The six species of flamingo were all notoriously difficult to breed when the Trust received its first specimens in 1960. In this first group of thirty birds were greater, lesser and Chilean flamingos. In 1963 Caribbean flamingos were added and by 1966 all six species were represented. There followed a number of flamingo breeding 'firsts'. In 1968 the Caribbean flamingos produced the first ever flamingo chick to be hatched in the UK. The following year saw the first Andean flamingo chick hatched in captivity anywhere in the world and the first Chilean flamingo chick in the UK. In 1972 four different species bred at Slimbridge for the first time. Over the years, the Trust's expertise in breeding flamingos has increased; practices developed have been shared with other collections in the UK with which birds are regularly exchanged.

One of the primary aims of the Trust from early on had been education. It seemed obvious to Peter that the activities of the Trust and the collections of waterfowl naturally educated the general public in the widest possible sense. Writing in 1986 on the fortieth anniversary of the Trust he noted:

> The ideals of effective education and educative recreation have been pursued simultaneously, and these are two of the four aims of the Trust. Indeed, for education to be effective it must be enjoyable – even at times subliminal … What is important is to make the process of 'education' undetectable.

Peter was keen however to also provide more focused and formalised education on natural history and conservation for young people visiting the Trust's centres around the country. In 1966, 444 school parties and fifty-three natural history societies visited Slimbridge, and in September that year the Trust's first Education Officer was appointed, tasked with developing specific learning programmes for school children at Slimbridge and Peakirk. By 1977, over 70,000 children from almost 1,000 schools around the country were visiting the centres on organised trips each year. Activities became more carefully targeted to dovetail more closely with the national curriculum, and attention was given to the needs of pupils of different age groups. When the second phase of the education and research facility was completed at Slimbridge in 1975, classrooms and a lecture theatre were added to the facilities available for visiting schools. Anyone who visits Slimbridge on a weekday today is very likely to see a large cohort of excited children heading down the ramp for a day of pond dipping or a visit to the Arctic Adventure hut. Higher education too was considered important, and the Trust established links with a number of universities including Bristol, Cardiff, Liverpool and Bath. Educational staff were appointed at Washington, Peakirk and at Martin Mere, where an educational wing was added with teaching staff seconded to the centre by Lancashire Education Authority. Martin Mere very soon became a magnet for school visits.

As the years passed, the number of staff grew, and Peter became less directly involved in the day-to-day running of the collection and the reserve at Slimbridge; by 1955 the Trust employed twenty-five full-time staff. A new arrival that year was Mike Garside who was appointed as a temporary replacement for Douglas Eccleston in the role of Peter's personal assistant. He ended up staying twenty-five years, becoming one of his most loyal and hard-working staff members. Mike assisted Peter in a variety of ways, fielding telephone calls, helping Philippa to organise Peter's diary, driving the children to school when the Scotts were away, helping to feed the animals and insects in the conservatory and driving for miles to retrieve Peter at the end of long glider flights. When Peter set off on his frequent overseas trips, Mike would accompany him to the airport. The driving was shared; Peter drove for part of the time so he could dictate letters to Mike, then they would switch over and Peter would sign correspondence and make notes. Peter was always anxious not to waste a moment's time. He would often take someone to appointments, for example at the opticians, so that he could work while he sat in the waiting room. His focus on his work was absolute and he expected those around him to have the same approach. Mike Garside was paid a modest wage and lived on-site with a bedroom in the hostel, where there was a shared kitchen and dining room. After nine months in the job he asked Peter for a weekend off. Peter was taken aback and asked why Mike wanted to go away; wasn't he happy at Slimbridge? Mike said he had some family business to attend to and so Peter agreed he could go. Everyone who knew him remembered Peter as one of the kindest and most generous of men; he simply couldn't imagine why Mike would want to be anywhere else other than Slimbridge.

Other people came into Peter's orbit by accident rather than design. One such was Paul Walkden who long admired Peter and his work and who moved to Gloucestershire in 1972. He had been collecting Peter's books and articles for some years and began to compile a list of his published works. Noticing an anomaly in the recording of a particular publication he contacted the Trust for clarification on the point and was invited to meet Peter. During their discussion, Peter reflected that perhaps what he needed was a bibliographer and asked Paul 'Why don't you do it?' So, Paul became his bibliographer, compiling a comprehensive list of everything Peter had written. Paul recalled that when Peter was due to make a foreign trip, he would ask Paul to find him the relevant field guides and reference books, which were then added to his library. The complete bibliography was published in *Peter Scott at 80,* the catalogue which accompanied Peter's retrospective exhibition in 1989, and Paul went on to write his own book *The Wild Geese of the Newgrounds* in 2009 and to compile *Peter Scott, Collected Writings,* published in 2016.

Though Peter gradually relinquished his day-to-day duties to staff members, he still kept a very close eye on proceedings. In winter he would observe the daily feed of the wild birds in the Rushy Pen and would be quick to send a note to the warden if he thought something should be changed or could be improved. He still had, suspended over his bed, two sheets of glass between which he would slide plans of drawings for whatever project he was thinking about so that when he woke in the morning he could lie in bed and mull things over. Always thinking, always planning, Peter had a restless mind and a determination to put it to good use.

The house by the lake continued to be both the centre of operations and the heart of the family. The children grew up, as their father had, in a family home that was also a workplace. Dafila shared her father's love of wild birds and also his gift for painting, becoming, in time, an artist in her own right and achieving a PhD in the behaviour of Bewick's swans. Nicola spent her summers at Slimbridge and was given a pony, which was her pride and joy. Falcon's interests lay elsewhere; as he grew he became interested in building things, but whereas most boys would settle for building a den in the woods, Falcon's ambitions were much larger. Around the age of fifteen he set himself the task of building an observation tower at Slimbridge which would be a little over fifty feet in height. Many parents might discourage what, on the face of it, seemed like a slightly risky venture, but Peter bought the materials Falcon needed and let matters take their course. After much trial and error the tower was built, and though at forty-five feet it fell slightly short of the original target it was completely viable as an observation tower. By 1976 Falcon had qualified as an engineer and

decided that the tower needed his attention once again. An article in
Wildfowl News, the Trust magazine, told the story:

> As a professional engineer he recently decided that the tower no
> longer did him justice. He therefore re-designed the top half and has
> been re-building it, again single-handed, at week-ends and largely at
> his own expense ... Visitors may have seen him perched perilously on
> his scaffolding with large pieces of timber, glass or other equipment
> dangling from a rope. The Wildfowl Trust staff will be able to use the
> tower for observing the numbers and movements of the wild geese
> and swans in the winter and checking the causes of any disturbance.
> The Trust is most grateful to Falcon Scott for his efforts.

Falcon may have chosen a career path divergent from his father's but
one cannot help but see an affinity in the single-minded pursuit of a
project that might to others seem difficult or impossible to achieve.

The family home was also the nerve centre of the Trust and the
children were used to the constant stream of visitors who came to
see their parents. The visitors book in the studio reads like a Who's
Who of twentieth-century Britain including as it does, Her Majesty
the Queen, Prince Philip and Prince Charles, the Duke and Duchess
of Kent, Prince Bernhard of the Netherlands, David Attenborough,
Douglas Bader, James Robertson Justice, Miriam Rothschild, Konrad
Lorenz and many others. Both Prince Philip and Prince Charles stayed
at the house, and Charles later wrote of his delight at waking up to the
spectacle of the birds on the lake outside the window.

As a result of his television appearances, his lectures and his books,
Peter's postbag was enormous, full of letters from all sorts of people
asking his advice on a range of matters, the most common request
being 'How do you get a job working with wildfowl like Peter
Scott?' In the early years of the Trust, Peter received many letters
from ex-servicemen who were seeking work after demobilisation.
One interesting letter came from Air Vice-Marshal Traill who had
served in the Air Force with distinction in both World Wars. Traill
wrote seeking employment, and while acknowledging that he knew
little about wildfowl, he reminded Peter that in 1945 he had taken
to chasing flights of duck in his aircraft and measuring their speed.
The information so gained he had passed to Peter as he thought it
might be of interest. Other correspondence asked for information on

how to keep waterfowl or contained information about a particular bird that had been sighted and which the correspondent thought Peter might like to know about. Non-native waterfowl discovered anywhere in the country were assumed to have escaped from Slimbridge and Peter would be asked when someone would be coming to collect them. There were also sightings of rare native species from every quarter; occasionally these were genuine, more often they were flights of fancy inspired by Peter's television programmes.

Another raft of correspondence was from individuals who were due to visit Slimbridge and hoped that Peter would be able to find the time to show them round. In fact, Peter very often would show people round whether they were professional ornithologists, old school and university friends, people he had met on his travels around the world, members of government bodies or working in other branches of conservation at home or abroad, or potential sponsors, supporters or donors. If he thought they would have something interesting to say or might be able to help the Trust, Peter was more than happy to make himself available, assuming he was at home at the time of the visit. As for the rest of his postbag, Peter, Philippa or one of the secretaries punctiliously responded to every letter and query, and looking through the vast array of letters it is striking that every single answer was thoughtful and considered, no matter how unimportant the matter in hand might seem to be. Dealing with this explosion of correspondence must have taken up quite a bit of Peter and Philippa's time and that of their team.

There were frequent requests from natural history societies up and down the country to borrow Peter's nature films, many of which had been used by Peter at his illustrated talks or as part of his early television programmes. Peter always had to reluctantly refuse. Apart from the cost of duplicating the films, they were all made without a soundtrack so Peter would have to be present when they were screened to provide the commentary, and his time was severely limited.

One other kind of request, received fairly regularly from a wide range of bodies and organisations, was for Peter to accept some form of honorary position on their board. It might be thought that with the work involved in being honorary director of the Wildfowl Trust, a member of council of the Zoological Society of London (London Zoo), vice-president of the Inland Waterways Association, vice-president of IUCN, and head of its Survival Service Commission, vice-president of the World Wildlife Fund, chairman and then president of the Fauna and Flora Preservation Society, president of the British Butterfly Conservation Society, vice-president of the Camping Club of Great Britain, president of the International Yacht Racing Union and president and then vice-president of the British Gliding Association, as well as with his constant travelling, broadcasting, writing and painting activities, Peter would have enough on his plate, but nevertheless he did from time to time accept additional responsibilities, some of which made more demands on his time than others. In 1960 he became Rector of Aberdeen University, in 1962, Admiral of the Manx Shipping Fleet, and in 1974, Chancellor of Birmingham University. The two university posts in particular added to Peter's workload but he always found the time, somehow, to fulfil the requirements that all of these posts imposed upon him. Why did he agree to these additional obligations? Certainly he had doubts about what he might bring to such positions. In *The Eye of the Wind* he wrote, 'I have never thought much of my capacities as an organiser or administrator.' Perhaps though, his acceptance stemmed from two things. Firstly, the ingrained sense of duty derived from his father's example and his wartime experience, that if called upon you should serve if you can. Secondly, Peter was aware just how closely his own personality and the Wildfowl Trust were entwined in people's minds, knowing that whatever good he could do for others would bring benefit in equal measure to the organisation and the causes that were closest to his heart.

Peter and Philippa did occasionally find time to take holidays with the children. In 1962, they rented a cottage in the South of France with John Winter and his wife and family, while on a couple of occasions in following years they borrowed the house of an acquaintance in the Bahamas; these holidays were rare opportunities for the couple to escape the pressures of work and the constant demands made on them and to enjoy life as a family without the interference that came from combining home and workplace. Peter was always happy to get back to Slimbridge however. Despite his occasional frustration at how desperately busy he always was, he cared so deeply about the causes that he engaged with that it didn't seem to him like work in the normal sense of the word. Being enthusiastic was all to Peter. He wrote, 'My great key to the enjoyment of living is enthusiasm,' and on another occasion, 'Over-enthusiasm is one of my most tedious social shortcomings' (*Cambridge University Library MS Scott (Peter) M.2742*). Fortunately for everyone around him, he usually knew just how far his enthusiasm should be taken. He was also fortunate in being able to recognise that he was happy for most of the time, a state in society not as common as might be wished. In a letter to a correspondent in Iceland Peter commented, 'What a lot of wonderful things there are to do in this wonderful World.' And in the final paragraph at the end of *The Eye of the Wind* he wrote:

> As I contemplate all these things I am more than ever convinced that I am the luckiest man I know. I say this not with smugness or self-satisfaction but because I can think of nothing sadder than to live a happy life without recognising it. Maybe I am an ostrich with my head in the sand. Maybe Fate or my own or other men's folly has all kind of disasters in store for me, but they cannot take away these exciting and happy years. Not to acknowledge such good fortune would be inexcusable.

20

Spreading the Word

Today, we tend to think of Peter as a conservationist first and painter second. He however, when asked, described himself as an artist with a passion for conservation. On an application for a travel visa to visit Indonesia he took a different view. Under the heading 'Occupation' Peter wrote 'Writer, Artist, Conservationist'. He might well have added 'Broadcaster' or 'Scientist', but perhaps there wasn't room on the form. These different spheres of endeavour were to a considerable extent interdependent; without his writing and broadcasting for example, his conservation work would not have had the impact that it did.

Peter started writing and broadcasting long before the founding of the Severn Wildfowl Trust in 1946. In 1932, as we have seen, while working at Borough Fen, he had borrowed a cine camera and made a film of the birds on the decoy. He had a strong urge to share his passion for wild geese with others; if he found the birds fascinating and their life stories compelling, surely others would too? With this thought in mind he gave a talk to the Spalding Gentlemen's Society about the birds at Borough Fen and the operation of the decoy. From an early age Peter had kept a diary full of information about his wildfowling activities. Details of shooting expeditions, the locations, his companions and the numbers of birds shot were entered with meticulous detail. The urge to communicate his passion to others led him to write his first article on shooting which appeared in *Country Life* in 1929 when Peter was just nineteen. His first book, *Morning Flight,* was published in 1935 and with its companion volume,

Wild Chorus, published in 1938, contained vivid descriptions of wildfowling on the fens. The diaries that he kept during these years and the detailed records they contained, provided the source material for his subsequent writings about his wildfowling exploits.

Peter continued to write during the war, though he had very little time in which to do it. In 1940 for example, while HMS *Broke* was in Plymouth Dockyard for a refit, he wrote an article for *Country Life* on the greater snow geese that he had seen at Cap Tourmente in Canada in 1938. Before and during the war, the impulse had been an instinctive desire to share his love of the natural world with others. With the setting up of the Severn Wildfowl Trust, Peter's urge to write and lecture on natural history had an additional purpose; to draw people's attention to the work of the Trust and hopefully encourage their support both as donors and as paying visitors to the New Grounds at Slimbridge.

His output was prodigious; in the late forties and early fifties you would be forgiven for supposing that he was a full-time professional writer, speaker and broadcaster. During this period, articles by Peter featured in, among other magazines and newspapers, *Country Life, Country Sportsman Magazine, Boy's Own Paper, RSPB Magazine, Ladies' Journal, The Mystery Magazine, The Times, The Sunday Times, Lilliput Magazine, Meccano Magazine, Animals Magazine, The Cornhill Magazine, The New Naturalist* journal and *The BBC Naturalist* with topics covering a wide range of subjects. In 1951 he wrote the book *Wild Geese and Eskimos* about his trip to the Perry River region of Canada in 1949, and in 1953 he co-wrote with James Fisher the book *A Thousand Geese* about the 1951 Iceland expedition. Extracts from these books and from his two wildfowling books from the 1930s were also published in magazines and newspapers.

As demands on his time increased, he was sometimes forced to turn down requests for articles in various publications. In 1954, Peter was approached by sound recordist Ludwig Koch to contribute an article to a forthcoming publication *The Encyclopaedia of British Birds.* The fee was to be £25. Peter initially declined the request but Koch badgered him to agree and said he would be sorry if he wasn't included. So Peter changed his mind and agreed but was unable to find time to write the piece as the publishing deadline approached. Under increasing pressure, Peter circulated to his staff the latest strongly worded reminder from Koch's secretary, adding at the bottom,

'Anyone like to earn £15 by ghosting it for me? I keep the other £10!!'
William Collins, publishers of the popular *New Naturalist* series
apparently had a shortlist of authors from whom they would have
accepted a book on almost any topic. The names on the list included
Vero Wynne-Edwards, Julian Huxley and Peter Scott. Intriguingly,
there was no volume on British wildfowl in the series until twenty
years after Peter's death when, in 2009, *Wildfowl* by David Cabot was
published. Had it been suggested thirty years earlier, Peter would have
been the obvious choice as author.

Over time, Peter's lecture appearances became more and more
frequent, and he was continuously in demand as a public speaker.
During 1948 and 1949 Peter gave talks to over 20,000 people.
The narrowboat *Beatrice* was used in 1950 for a lecture tour by canal
though this venture proved problematic. Progress on the canal system
proved slower than expected and Peter was forced to take a taxi
each evening to his speaking venue, the trips to and fro taking longer
and longer as *Beatrice* fell further behind schedule. During this trip
Beatrice made the first crossing of the River Mersey by a converted
narrowboat, a journey of fifteen miles from Liverpool to Weston
Mersey; Peter was taking a bit of a risk as the boat was insured for
cruising on non-tidal waterways only. During 1950, he gave thirty-one
lectures, mostly about his trip to the Perry River in northern Canada
the previous year. As well as promoting the Trust and its activities, the
lectures provided a steady source of income. In 1953 over 100 requests
for lectures were unfulfilled, either because Peter couldn't fit them in to
his schedule or because the organisation concerned was unwilling to
pay his fee of fifty guineas. By 1955, Peter was charging 100 guineas
a time for his appearances, and by 1956 there was a twelve month
waiting list for those anxious to secure him to speak. An indication of
Peter's hectic working life in December 1953 is found in a letter to a
friend in Northumberland with whom he had stayed prior to giving a
lecture in Middlesbrough:

After Middlesbrough I motored till 1.00am when I got to Newark –
was roused at 4.45 and went on to London for this boring meeting
about the future relation between the Trust, the Wildfowl Enquiry
Committee and the Nature Conservancy. It reached no conclusion
and wasted a lot of people's time. Then for two days I was plunged
into the whirl of television in which pretty well the only nice thing

was your telegram. Since then more lectures interspersed with wild activity on the committee stage of the Protection of Birds Bill, plans for the next television, a little man who descended on us for being dilatory about the preparation of a film strip for schools and a conference of animal behaviour experts from Oxford – 57 of them here in 2 buses! So life has been hectic to the point of not being any fun at all. And still it goes on – a broadcast on the Nature Conservancy all day tomorrow and a meeting at the Bristol Zoo as well! Oh dear oh dear!

There can be no clearer indication of the pressure Peter was working under at the time. This was not the only occasion when Peter admitted to letting himself get over-stretched. In a BBC broadcast for American radio listeners in the same year he commented:

For as long as I can remember I've been obsessed with the urge to use such talents as I possess … it's a sort of creative itch. I'm not really happy unless I'm making something, whether it's a picture, a book, a scientific paper, a wild life movie, or a research station. And my perpetual concern is that life's too short for all the thing I want to do. Perhaps I should do some of them better if I didn't try to do so many.

In that famous letter to his wife, Peter's father had added a further comment about Peter:

Above all he must guard, and you must guard him, against indolence. Make him a strenuous man; I had to force myself into being strenuous as you know, had always an inclination to be idle.

Robert Falcon Scott need not have worried.

Given the number of lectures he was presenting, it is surprising to note that public speaking made Peter nervous. One solution was to use humour to get the audience going. Once he had made them laugh with an anecdote or a comical drawing on a blackboard, he could relax and continue with his talk. The quick cartoon of a bird or person was clearly a particular trick of his and may have stemmed from that first lecture at the Spalding Gentlemen's Society in 1932 when the projector failed and he was forced to draw ducks and geese on the blackboard to keep his audience amused while the equipment was repaired.

As a popular naturalist and broadcaster, Peter's lectures were always well attended. His lecture on the 1951 Iceland expedition, given in 1953 to a full house at the Royal Festival Hall has already been noted. He returned to the Royal Festival Hall twice in January 1954, first to show his film *The Land of Fire* and then, a week later, to show a second film *The High Andes*, both filmed during his South American trip. In January 1955, a further talk at the Royal Festival Hall was held in the afternoon. Entitled *Ducks and Drakes*, it was aimed at children as much as adults.

Peter was in demand to address scientific bodies as well. In 1954, he presented a paper entitled *Population Study of the Pink-footed Goose* at the Linnean Society and at the Royal Association for the Advancement of Science (now known as the British Science Association). On another occasion, invited to speak at the Royal Institution, Peter was presented with a slight dilemma. Tradition demanded that speakers walk straight to the podium and begin their address without introduction. How to begin? In the end he took an idea from his public lectures and on entering the room stepped silently up to the drawing board and drew a dodo adding a twinkle in its eye with a final flourish, managing to get a roar of laughter. The dodo evidently made it onto the small screen. In November 1953, a member of the public wrote to Peter after he had presented a television programme about catching pink-footed geese by rocket-netting. The purpose of the letter was to enquire whether the nets ever injured the geese, but as a postscript the correspondent added that he had particularly liked the twinkle in the eye of the dodo.

In 1972, the formation of the Wildfowl Trust film unit was announced. Two film-makers, Eric Soothill and Peter Whitehead toured the country showing two films. One, an Anglia Television *Survival* production, was called *A Wealth of Wildfowl* and featured the Trust's centre at Welney with a commentary by Peter, while the second was a film they had made about birdwatching in Spain. Between October 1972 and March 1973 they showed the films at sixty-five venues from Plymouth to Ayr, all of this activity providing valuable publicity for the work of the Trust.

Despite his other commitments in later years, Peter still found time to give lectures in support of the Trust and those other endeavours closest to his heart. In the early 1980s he and Philippa gave a series of talks at Slimbridge under the title *Have Camera – Will Travel* in aid of the Trust's Special Appeal, a major fundraising campaign. In 1986, Peter and Philippa went on the road with a talk entitled *Forty Years,* visiting all the Wildfowl Trust centres to celebrate the fortieth anniversary of the Trust. Writing in the Trust's magazine, *Wildfowl World,* that year he noted, 'The missionary fervour has lost little in 40 years.' As so often with Peter's talks on home ground, the notice announcing the talk at Slimbridge added, 'Includes late-night shopping'.

It was perhaps through broadcasting that Peter made the biggest impact on the British public. As already noted, in August 1936 he had been invited to give two short talks on the radio, one about dinghy racing and one about his life at the lighthouse and his travels in Hungary. He clearly proved a hit because further invitations from the BBC quickly followed. Peter was skilled at reusing material and that early broadcast about his life at the lighthouse became a chapter in *Wild Chorus* two years later, the script repeated verbatim. In August 1939, Peter made a radio programme about badgers, followed a month later by a programme entitled *September in the Country,* written and transmitted while he was waiting to be called up for service. The war had begun, and Peter talked about the effects of war and of the recently imposed blackouts on migrating birds. It is clear that Peter's love for the wild places had been sharpened by the thought of the coming conflict:

> My first thought on a bright September morning is: 'It's perfectly impossible that there can be such a thing as a war when the world is so beautiful,' and my next is: 'that for some reason the world, the fields, and the trees and rivers are so much more beautiful because there is a war ...'

Listeners' responses to Peter's broadcasts were universally complimentary; he combined a clear, well-modulated voice with the assurance of someone who knows what they are talking about and his confident presentation belied any nervousness that he might have felt. It was not surprising therefore that he was approached by the BBC after the war to resume his broadcasting career. An early performance was as a commentator on the Forces' victory parade in London in June 1946 where he found himself in the unique position of reporting on an event in which he was simultaneously taking part. A clip of this broadcast is still extant and Peter's commentary is vivid and convincing. Given that it was recorded over seventy years ago, it sounds remarkably modern, lacking that starched and artificial intonation that characterises so many recordings from that time. Peter's mother was with her husband at the saluting base in The Mall for the parade and wrote of the occasion in her diary:

> I had the felicity of seeing my son as he passed by standing in uniform in a duck (an amphibious vehicle), gallantly struggling with a commentary for the broadcast and saluting the King all in one breath.

Two years later, he was part of the BBC team that provided the radio commentary on the wedding of Princess Elizabeth and Prince Philip, while in June 1953 he found himself again commentating on a major national event, providing live commentary of the Royal Naval Review at Spithead off Portsmouth.

Despite these forays into mainstream broadcasting, Peter's interest lay in nature programmes; he did not want to go down the route of the conventional commentator who was called upon to talk about any subject on demand. In 1946, he was invited to take part in a new *Children's Hour* programme on the radio about natural history which was to be called *Nature Parliament*. Children were to be invited to send in their nature questions which would be answered by a panel of experts. These would be Peter, Hugh Newman and Brian Vesey-Fitzgerald. Peter was unsure about the title but he need not have worried. The programme, which was broadcast monthly, was a huge success and ran for many years. Peter's colleague from the 1951 Iceland expedition, James Fisher, would become the fourth member of the panel.

In early 1946, a young radio producer called Desmond Hawkins, based at the West Region of the BBC, arranged with the German sound recordist Ludwig Koch to make a series of recordings of the flocks of white-fronted geese on the New Grounds at Slimbridge. When they visited the New Grounds, the cottage at the end of the lane was empty but Koch confided in Hawkins that Peter Scott was planning to move in to study the geese on the estuary. Hawkins returned to Slimbridge a few weeks later and found the lane to the cottage blocked by a car with a 'compact and resolute figure in an authentically naval dufflecoat' sprawled across the bonnet watching the geese through a telescope. Guessing the figure was Peter Scott, Hawkins walked down the lane to introduce himself and immediately had the telescope thrust into his hands with the invitation to take a look at the fourth lesser white-fronted goose ever to be recorded in Britain. From this chance encounter developed a collaboration that would change the face of wildlife broadcasting in the 1950s.

Hawkins was keen to develop natural history radio programmes from his base in Bristol, and under his management two new radio series were created. These were *The Naturalist* chaired by Brian Vesey-Fitzgerald, and *Birds in Britain* introduced by James Fisher. With Peter based nearby at Slimbridge, his experience of radio broadcasting and his friendship with James Fisher, it was inevitable that he would become involved, and he soon began to make regular contributions to both programmes. Peter and Desmond Hawkins became good friends and in January 1953, Hawkins told Peter that he was going on a course for television producers. Peter was intrigued and raised with Hawkins the possibility of a television show based on the style of his lectures. These started with an introduction, during which he would often use a quick drawing to break the ice; then he would show a film and afterwards talk about what his audience had seen. Occasionally there would be two reels of film, in which case it was necessary to fill the gap while the reels were changed. Peter was in the habit of using his drawing skills to keep the audience amused during the changeover.

In *The Eye of the Wind,* Peter recalled Desmond Hawkins asking him if he would give a talk along these lines at his son's school so that he could see Peter in action. Peter agreed and Hawkins was suitably impressed. Another young radio producer based at Bristol was Tony Soper who remembered going with his boss to a lecture given by Peter at the Colston Hall in Bristol. Soper recalled that afterwards there was immediate agreement between them; Peter would be perfect on television. At this time there were no television studios at the BBC in Bristol, but Desmond Hawkins solved the problem quite simply by bringing a television outside broadcast unit to Bristol and connecting it up to the radio studios. Before long the West of England Light Orchestra were turned out of their theatre, which was converted into a television studio. So was born the BBC Natural History Unit which continues to operate out of studios in Bristol to this day.

Peter started out with something of an advantage. Not only did he have an established reputation as an accomplished radio presenter, but in addition he had a stock of films taken by him both at Slimbridge and on the various expeditions he had undertaken in South America, Canada and Iceland. In 1953, as his television broadcasting career developed, he appeared in two kinds of programmes. First, there were broadcasts on different natural history topics based around his existing collection of films. As with his lectures, the films were interspersed with Peter talking to camera and occasionally doing a quick drawing or two. It is interesting to think that this format continues on the BBC nearly seventy years on with the flagship natural history series *Springwatch* and *Autumnwatch* following exactly the same format with the only difference that the drawings have been replaced with an impressive range of charts and diagrams. The other sort of programme saw Peter starting with a blank canvas at the beginning and creating a dramatic painting of waterfowl in the space of half an hour while talking about the birds he was depicting. The first of these was called *Painting Aloud* and caused something of a sensation, with viewers flooding the BBC's telephone lines wanting to buy the painting they had seen completed on the television. Two or three more such programmes followed.

During 1953, among other topics, Peter presented television programmes on the story of the pink-footed geese and his development of rocket-netting, making use of his own film material. Two live outside broadcasts from Slimbridge proved popular among both children and adults. Transmitted on consecutive days, the first live broadcast formed part of *Children's Hour* while the second broadcast, again live, was transmitted at 7.30 in the evening. Afterwards an enthusiastic viewer in Edinburgh wrote:

> Hearty congratulations on an excellent performance this evening. We found this half-hour with you at Slimbridge most interesting and instructional. My family were enthralled and now, of course, a visit to the New Grounds is a 'must'.

He wasn't the only person to head for Slimbridge as the following item from Severn Wildfowl Trust Bulletin number twelve, dated June 1953, testifies:

> Television broadcasts from the Trust on 30 April and 1 May followed on Whit Sunday by a sound programme have produced very large crowds at subsequent weekends. These help to broaden

the Trust's educational field, and increase the income from the gate, but Members are advised, during the summer, if possible to avoid Saturday and Sunday afternoons at the New Grounds, when the enclosures sometimes contain more visitors than birds'

During this time, Peter never saw his own programmes transmitted as there was no electricity in the cottage at Slimbridge where he was living at the time. He received a regular postbag of letters as a result of his television work and gave an insight into his thoughts on the medium in a reply to a viewer who had written to say that his children had especially enjoyed a recent broadcast. In reply, Peter wrote:

I am so glad your children liked the Television show. It seems to have gone pretty well. We are debating whether or not to have it when we get electricity down here in our new home which is due to be completed by September. Neither of us like the beastly invention, but I feel that I ought to know something about it since I have to do it fairly often.

There can never have been a better excuse for buying a television.

In early 1954, Peter got into hot water as a result of a live broadcast he made from Lime Grove Studios in London. The programme was about ringing ducks, and Peter brought three mallards into the studio as demonstration models. At the end of the ringing process Peter, wanting to create a completely authentic experience, released the birds from the studio window, live on air. All might have gone well were it not for the fact that it was night at the time, and one of the birds, becoming disoriented, was picked up in the road nearby shortly after the transmission and taken to the nearest RSPCA centre. Since the 'crime' had been witnessed by several hundred thousand people and a number of them had written to complain about the incident, Peter had no choice but to make an apology when he received a stern rebuke from the RSPCA.

It didn't take long for Peter to run through his own stock of nature films. The BBC were reluctant to give up on a format that looked promising so it was decided in 1954 that Peter would chair a number of programmes and show films made by other wildlife cameramen. At this stage the programmes appeared at irregular intervals in the schedules and were not considered to be a wildlife series as we would recognise it today. The BBC were not sure if the idea had longevity and were reluctant to create a new series while there was a risk it might run out of steam at an early stage. Nevertheless, Peter was clearly devoting a lot of his time to his television appearances during 1954. In a letter to zoologist Harold Munro Fox, Peter apologised for the delay in replying to him, adding, 'This TV lark is all very well in small doses, but I'm suffering from a surfeit.'

Towards the end of 1954 began a revolution in wildlife broadcasting that continues to influence the kind of programmes we watch today. In December 1954, the first *Zoo Quest* series was aired on the BBC and the world changed for ever. Presented by a young, charismatic and virtually unknown naturalist, David Attenborough's *Zoo Quest* brought to British television screens amazing wildlife films captured by a young Czech cameraman called Charles Lagus during an expedition that he and David had made to Sierra Leone on behalf of London Zoo and the BBC. The series ran from December 1954 to mid-January 1955 and convinced BBC producers, if they didn't know it already, that there was an insatiable thirst for natural history amongst the British viewing public. From November 1954, Peter's own television appearances became a more regular occurrence with a programme on Saturday evenings once a month.

At the International Ornithological Congress in Basel in 1954, Peter had been immensely impressed by the film *Carpenters of The Forest,* which had shared the bill with his own film *Ring of Fire* during the conference. The film, by German naturalist Heinz Sielmann, created quite a stir, since for the first time black woodpeckers were filmed on the nest. Sielmann achieved this by cutting a section out of the back of the tree and inserting a camera and lighting, to which the birds quickly became accustomed. Peter realised that the film was hugely significant; nothing like it had been done before and on his return to England he persuaded the BBC to buy the rights to show the film in the UK. Negotiations with the Bavarian Department for Education took some time, but eventually a contract was agreed and Heinz Sielmann came to England for the broadcast in January 1955, when Peter introduced him and the film to the viewers. The programme was an absolute sensation when it was aired and the BBC switchboard was jammed after transmission with people wanting to congratulate all concerned on the broadcast. The event was a triumph for Peter and afterwards, of course, most people would remember the name of the man who introduced the film, Peter Scott, rather than the man who made it, Heinz Sielmann.

More natural history programmes hosted by Peter followed on a monthly basis during the spring of 1955. On 6 June, there was a further live broadcast from Slimbridge transmitted at the peak evening viewing hour of 7.15 p.m. Peter sat facing the camera with the studio window behind him and as the cameras rolled he welcomed his viewers to his home and talked about the birds they could see behind him through the window.

By early 1955, Desmond Hawkins had realised that the popularity of Peter's programmes meant that they should become a regular series with a name and a recognised format. The name chosen was *Look* and one of the most successful natural history series ever broadcast by the BBC was born. The programmes would be broadcast live from Slimbridge from where Peter would conduct interviews and introduce wildlife films. The first *Look* programme was broadcast from Peter's studio on 14 June 1955; that evening Peter introduced a film by Heinz Sielmann about foxes, and the programme was watched by nearly six million viewers. As with his previous live transmissions from the Trust in 1953, a direct consequence of the two live broadcasts in June 1955 was a desire among the public at large to get down to Slimbridge and see his collection of ducks and geese for themselves. The Wildfowl Trust was on the map.

Initially, the programmes were transmitted monthly, but they rapidly became so popular that it was decided that *Look* should become a fortnightly affair, broadcast on two consecutive nights, twice a month. This presented some difficulty however as the effort of taking an outside broadcast unit to Slimbridge twice a month was deemed to be too costly. The disturbance to the family's daily life was also great. The large cameras had to be brought in on a lorry and set up in Peter's studio. Cables snaked through the doorways and into the yard, the dogs were banned from the house and Philippa recorded that she felt like a stranger in her own home. In the end, the solution was obvious. The BBC constructed a replica of Peter's studio at their Bristol studios, complete with the giant window and a photograph of the lake behind. Thereafter, Peter simply motored down to Bristol twice a month and made his broadcasts in his new home from home.

There was some debate in the BBC at the time about how responsibility for natural history programmes should be co-ordinated in future. They now had two highly successful series being produced at different locations under different management and with two highly charismatic presenters. *Zoo Quest* had been made as part of the Talks Department in London while *Look* had been devised and produced by Desmond Hawkins in Bristol. David Attenborough was offered the opportunity to head up what was to be called the BBC Natural History Unit in Bristol, which would manage all wildlife programming, but he was reluctant to leave London both for family reasons and because he felt there were more exciting possibilities where he was, at the heart of the BBC. In the end, a compromise was reached. It was agreed that the Natural History Unit in Bristol would concentrate on British wildlife while a new group would be set up in London called the Travel and Exploration Unit which would include series like *Zoo Quest*. Both *Look* and *Zoo Quest*, and their respective presenters were hugely successful during the years that followed. The hundredth episode of *Look* was broadcast during National Nature Week in May 1963 when Peter was joined as presenter by Prince Philip.

A perennial problem for Peter was finding enough film material for his programmes, so in 1956 it was decided that he would make a travel documentary about wildlife. He was planning a trip to Australia as part of his responsibilities for the Olympic sailing competition which was to take place that year in Melbourne. This provided a perfect opportunity to make a series of programmes about Australian wildlife. Peter had considerable experience in taking wildlife films, but given the other demands on his time during the trip it was decided that he would take a professional cameraman with him, so Charles Lagus, who had worked so successfully on the first *Zoo Quest* programme, joined Peter and Philippa.

The most comprehensive description of the trip was published seventeen years later in *Travel Diaries of a Naturalist: Volume I.* The party filmed in the Northern Territories and Western Australia before Peter and Philippa flew to Melbourne for the Olympic sailing events. Further filming took place in New South Wales and Victoria as well as Tasmania. The trip continued to Papua New Guinea, Queensland and then on to New Zealand. The resulting television series was called *Faraway Look* and was, once again, a great success. At BBC HQ they no doubt took a pragmatic view of the fact that the Natural History Unit in Bristol had exceeded their brief by making a foreign travel documentary, but given the success of both Peter and David Attenborough's programmes nobody was likely to complain.

More media successes were to follow. In 1966, British Transport Films made a short film called *Wild Wings* which featured the conservation work carried out by the Trust. Much of the film was shot at Slimbridge and Peter provided the narration. The film won a top prize at the Vancouver Film Festival that year, following up that success with an Oscar in the Best Short Subject category at the thirty-ninth Academy Awards in Los Angeles in 1967. The Oscar-winning film was shown at Slimbridge on 11 November that year, during the twenty-first anniversary celebrations for the Wildfowl Trust.

A further example of the power of television as a means of promotion came on 8 February 1980, when the BBC devoted a good deal of the day's programming to activities at the Wildfowl Trust at Slimbridge. In a series of four live outside broadcasts throughout the day, viewers were shown many of the wildfowl in the collection and the wild birds on the reserve. Commentators, including Peter and Tony Soper, talked about the daily routines of the birds and the work of the staff. The following weekend, all the centres and Slimbridge in particular, experienced a huge influx of visitors, all anxious to experience for themselves what they had been shown in their homes the week before.

In 1961, Peter became involved in an entirely new television venture when his friend Aubrey Buxton created a new natural history series for Anglia Television; Buxton was also a founder member of the Council for Nature and the World Wildlife Fund. The original title for this series had been *Tooth and Claw* but it was felt that the title might limit the scope of the films they wanted to make and might not appeal to some viewers, so almost by accident the series was given the title *Survival*. Quite how the series might have fared with its original title is impossible to know. What is known is that the series became a massive hit, with Peter and fellow naturalist David Bellamy among the earliest of narrators for the programmes. Peter was also appointed scientific adviser to the series. Hugely successful, the first iteration of *Survival* ran for forty years and notched up nearly 1,000 episodes. There was no presenter to interrupt the action with the advantage that the programmes could be prepared for export sales by simply translating and re-recording the narration. By this simple means, the programme would eventually be sold to 112 countries around the world. Narration was later taken up by a host of cinema and television stars and celebrities, adding yet more lustre to the series. Prince Philip would narrate three of the programmes over the years including, in 1967, a programme about the Galapagos Islands entitled *The Enchanted Isles*.

Peter was always slightly ambivalent about the fame that came with his television success. He admitted that doors were now opened to him that might not have been otherwise, but he was no longer able to go off on the kind of expeditions he had enjoyed in Iceland and on the Perry River; television imposed new demands and responsibilities on top of his already hectic schedules. The most important impact however was that there were now legions of viewers who were interested to hear what Mr Scott would say and do next. On his lecture tours, Peter had been used to connecting with thousands of people. The thousands had now become millions.

21

Riding the Wind

After the war, Peter had wanted to return to his pre-war life in as many ways as possible. This inevitably included sailing, though now, with his growing workload at the Severn Wildfowl Trust, he had less time to pursue the sport. During the 1930s, his summers had been dedicated to racing and his campaign to win the Prince of Wales Cup; now there were many other demands on his time. Having had no practise during the war years, Peter doubted whether he could still sail at the levels he had previously attained. Nevertheless, in 1946, he and John Winter got their dinghy *Thunder and Lighting* out of mothballs and entered her for the Prince of Wales Cup at Brixham. To their surprise, the boat was still the fastest around, and they had not lost their skills. *Thunder and Lightning* won the cup with three minutes to spare.

As a winner of the Prince of Wales Cup in 1937, Peter had become a member of the dinghy committee of the Yacht Racing Association (YRA). Now, in 1946, Peter was invited to join the council of the YRA and was present at one of their meetings when a volunteer was sought to go to Lausanne in Switzerland to represent British interests in the planning for the sailing competitions at the 1948 Olympic Games. London was the host city, and the sailing events were to be held in Torquay. Peter thought it might be interesting to go so volunteered. He assumed that he would be working with yachtsmen from other nations, but on arrival he found that he was solely responsible for planning the sailing competition as preparations for each sport had been put in the hands of a single individual. Back in the UK, given his experience at Lausanne, Peter was appointed as chairman of the YRA's

Olympic committee and told to organise the sailing events in Tor Bay, a task which he undertook with his usual flair and attention to detail.

Peter wasn't yet ready to give up sailing altogether however, and he continued to sail competitively for a number of years in the 1950s. There was another international event in Montreal which recaptured some of those exciting days in Canada before the war. Peter and John Winter had one last attempt at the Prince of Wales Cup in *Thunder and Lightning* in 1956 when they came halfway down the field. There were plenty of other opportunities, for example at the Fowey regatta, where he stayed once more at Menabilly, the house his family had rented before the war, this time as the guest of author Daphne du Maurier.

In 1955, during Cowes Week, a challenge was issued to determine the fastest sailing boat over a measured half mile in the Solent. This was the first time such a competition was held, and Peter was determined to enter. In the event, at the age of forty-six, he won against all comers – the urge to be the best had not been dimmed. In the 1950s, Peter sailed regularly during Cowes Week, switching in 1957 to catamarans, at that time a new, exciting and extremely fast new form of racing boat. It says much for Peter that with little opportunity to try the boat beforehand, he came second in his race and also persuaded Prince Philip to try his hand in catamarans too.

Following his successful organisation of the sailing events at the 1948 Olympics it was inevitable that Peter would be drawn further into the sport's management. The body responsible for co-ordinating international sailing competitions was the International Yacht Racing Union (IYRU) which was managed from London under the auspices of the YRA. At one of the council meetings of the YRA, Peter suggested that the IYRU might benefit from having a constitution to regulate the issues that arose in international competitions, due to the differing rules of the various participating bodies. In a very short time Peter had been charged with formulating such a constitution and put at the head of a committee of the IYRU to bring the change about. In 1955, the president of the IYRU resigned and Peter, having decided to stand for election himself, duly became president, remaining in the position until 1969. The new Code of Racing Rules, the formulation of which Peter had initiated, took some time to evolve, but under Peter's guidance they were unanimously adopted in 1960. In 1956, as president of IYRU, he was appointed chairman of the international jury for the sailing events at the Olympic Games in Melbourne. Not one to waste an opportunity, Peter and Philippa, as we have seen, combined the visit with an extensive tour of Australia, New Zealand and New Guinea, filming wildlife for Peter's new *Faraway Look* series on the BBC.

Perhaps the pinnacle of Peter's sailing career came in 1964 when he was selected as skipper of the twelve-metre yacht *Sovereign* in the campaign that year to win back the America's Cup. Much of Peter's experience had been in dinghy sailing, but his winning record and his proven leadership skills tipped the balance and Peter was selected. An intensive period of training followed before the races themselves which were held at Newport, Rhode Island in the United States. In the event, *Sovereign* was heavily beaten by the American boat, *Constellation* which Peter acknowledged to be much superior to the British entry. What is most surprising about this episode is how Peter managed to find the time in his busy schedule to take part at all. Pre-race training was intense and lasted for three months, during which time, no doubt, many of Peter's other projects had to be put on hold. Shortly after the races finished, Peter and Philippa were en route to Tokyo where, once again, Peter was chairman of the international jury for the sailing events at the Olympic Games. These events coincided with Peter' burgeoning broadcasting career, his work at the Wildfowl Trust and the World Wildlife Fund, his lectures and his painting, which continued throughout this period. Somehow, he always managed to squeeze everything in.

Living at Slimbridge, sailing trips had to be planned in advance as Peter was too far away from the Solent or Norfolk to have a day's sailing on a whim. He was also very well aware that if he entered sailing competitions, his past triumphs would create a level of expectation among his associates. A win would be no more than expected while a failure to win might indicate he was over the hill. It was perhaps therefore inevitable that when the Bristol Gliding Club moved their headquarters to Nympsfield, just thirty minutes' drive from Slimbridge, Peter would be drawn into the world of gliding. The club had been based previously at Lulsgate Airport south of Bristol but now, in the spring of 1956, Lulsgate was being developed as Bristol Airport, and the gliding club had had to find a new home. The airfield at Nympsfield was developed from two undulating fields at the edge of the Cotswold escarpment. Peter first became aware of developments when a neighbour asked him if he had seen the gliders circling above the hills. Peter was intrigued, so half an hour after the conversation he had driven to Nympsfield where he was offered a flight by the club's chief flying instructor.

Peter was hooked. Here was a sport in many ways similar to sailing, a sport in which man used the currents of the air to get and stay aloft in an environment where the power of wind and heat thermals was harnessed to sail across the sky. Here at last Peter could come closest to the experience of his beloved geese in flight. Here also there were no expectations about his performance. As he wrote in *The Eye of the Wind*, 'In the new game I started at the bottom. I was not expected to be anything but a rather elderly clot, and many were the clottish mistakes I made.' After that first flight he decided to train to become a glider pilot. He was told that with his existing flying experience he would need to take about thirty flights before he could go solo. This would take quite a few weekends, given that he would have to take his turn with everyone else to get enough launches. In the event he made his first solo flight in just under ten weeks, on 9 June 1956.

Having learned to fly, Peter's main problem was the time he had to wait to get a flight in one of the club's gliders which were shared by all the members. Time was something Peter had very little of as he tried to juggle his demanding and varied commitments. The solution was simple, he bought a half share in a new Olympia 2 glider with fellow club member Harry Daniels. Now he was able to take to the air without having to wait. The following year, 1957, Peter decided to buy a glider of his own, a top of the range Slingsby Eagle which he christened *Sea Eagle*. *Sea Eagle* was a two-seater sailplane which meant that Philippa could accompany him on flights. In May 1957, while on a visit to Slimbridge, Prince Philip made his maiden glider flight in *Sea Eagle,* piloted by Peter Collier, who was chief flying officer at the club. The prince's security team had to remain on the ground, no doubt anxiously peering at the skies for the duration of the flight.

It might be thought that the idea of a sunlit afternoon spent soaring over the beautiful Gloucestershire countryside would be simply idyllic, but for Peter it was not enough to spend a relaxing afternoon swooping through the summer air. From the beginning, Peter wanted to fly higher and further every trip, and to do this meant flying his glider in rising air thermals underneath and within clouds to rapidly gain height. The local weather conditions inside summer cumulonimbus clouds can be extremely turbulent: flying within them can cause sensations which veer rapidly between exhilaration and fear, while the constantly changing temperature in the cockpit can cause considerable discomfort. Philippa went up with Peter several times but eventually decided that gliding was not for her. However, though she might have chosen not to go flying with Peter, her services as a driver were sometimes required when Peter knew he would have to make a landing away from Nympsfield, and the glider would need to be retrieved. Then she, or Peter's assistant Michael Garside, would drive with the aircraft's trailer in the direction of flight and eventually make contact with the downed plane, load it into the trailer and drive it, and Peter, home again.

The urge to compete both against the elements and against his fellow pilots was no different than that which had compelled Peter to the top of the world of sailing. The sport of gliding was governed by the International Aeronautical Federation which had established a range of certificates offering different levels of attainment for pilots who wished to improve their skills. Peter rapidly achieved the basic levels of A, B and C. The next two levels, Silver C and Gold C were much more challenging. For Silver C Peter was required to achieve three things: a flight of five hours' or more duration, a flight in excess of fifty kilometres and a flight which incorporated an ascent of more than 1,000 metres. These three things Peter managed to achieve in the first twelve months, whereupon he moved on to the Gold C challenge. For this he would be required to make a flight in excess of 300 kilometres and achieve an ascent of more than 3,000 metres. These challenges were more difficult, but the ascent was managed in July 1957 and the distance challenge in April 1958.

As he gained more experience, Peter realised his Eagle glider was being outperformed by another type of sailplane, the Olympia. In 1959 came the perfect excuse to upgrade. In May 1959, Peter crashed *Sea Eagle* on landing and it was sent back to the manufacturer for repairs which would take two months. Peter couldn't wait that long. He had just received a publisher's advance for his autobiography *The Eye of the Wind*, and used it to buy himself a new Olympia 419X. Having acquired his Gold C certificate, the next challenge was to attain the top award offered by the International Aeronautical Federation, known as the three diamonds. For the first diamond he was required to fly to a predetermined destination that was at least

300 kilometres away. In Great Britain, with prevailing westerly winds, this was not straightforward, but shortly after acquiring the Olympia, Peter arranged to be air-towed to a place several miles west of Nympsfield so that on release he could fly 300 kilometres to Great Yarmouth, which he succeeded in doing. The two remaining diamonds would require him to fly more than 500 kilometres in a single trip and, on a separate flight, to ascend more than 5,000 metres. In May 1960, he set out from Nympsfield aiming for an airfield north of Edinburgh. Achieving the 'distance' diamond in Britain was extremely difficult because of prevailing weather conditions and the shape of the country. It was therefore not surprising that Peter failed on this occasion. During the attempt however, he found himself in a weather system which permitted him to gain the 'height' diamond with an ascent that exceeded 5,000 metres.

The final diamond, the elusive 500-kilometre trip, might have evaded Peter altogether, but while visiting South Africa in 1962, he arranged to make an attempt there in a borrowed glider. Such an attempt, if successful, would still be valid, as the same standards of certification applied around the world. He was indeed successful, piloting his glider over a triangular course of more than 500 kilometres of unfamiliar terrain, a quite remarkable achievement. With his third diamond in the bag, Peter became only the seventh British pilot to gain all three diamonds.

As well as mastering the certificate system, Peter was also keen to compete against other pilots. The British National Gliding Championships offered such an opportunity, and Peter finally become national champion at his fourth attempt in 1963. This was, by anyone's standards, a quite remarkable achievement, only seven years after his first ever flight and at the age of fifty-three. Peter still wasn't satisfied however, setting himself the challenge of becoming British champion for a second time. He made several more attempts and bought several more gliders, each time choosing the most expensive and advanced model available. In 1968 he came second, while at his last, and seventh championships in 1969, he came eighth at the age of fifty-nine. That year was characterised by bad weather, seemingly endless rain and cancelled flying days. Peter had had enough and is supposed to have said to his assistant, Mike Garside, 'Sell the sailplanes and build a swimming pool!' That wasn't quite the end of Peter's connections with gliding as he had been elected president of the British Gliding

Association. He relinquished the post in 1970 due to the pressure of other commitments, whereupon he was elected vice-president, a post he held for the rest of his life.

A contemporary remarked that one of the reasons for Peter's success at gliding, apart from his sheer tenacity, was his attention to detail and his powers of observation. Once he knew what to look for, he could detect developing thermals or minute changes in weather patterns which might well escape those with less developed observational skills. During his gliding years, Peter rarely lost an opportunity to fly if he was at home at Slimbridge and the weather permitted. On more than one occasion, a visitor would turn up for a pre-arranged meeting only to be told that Peter had gone flying as the weather was good. In 1962, Peter played the same trick while attending an ornithological congress in New York. When he suddenly disappeared from the conference he was tracked down to a nearby airfield where he had asked to borrow a glider and headed into the blue. A pattern can be discerned perhaps in Peter's reluctance to miss an opportunity for fun if it presented itself. In the late 1920s and early 1930s the lure of the fens drew him constantly away from his studies, and while the mature man was very different from the student in so many ways, in his enthusiasm for escape, however briefly from the humdrum world of everyday life, he had hardly changed at all.

22

The Birth of Modern Conservation

When Peter formed the Severn Wildfowl Trust in 1946, the word 'conservation', in the sense of the protection and preservation of species and habitats, was little used. People were of course aware that through man's actions, individual species had become extinct. the dodo in Mauritius and the passenger pigeon in North America were well-known examples. However, few people had thought about the cumulative effects of species decline and extinction and what impact such events could have on the future of the world's wildlife and on man himself. Peter was one of the first naturalists to start thinking along these lines and certainly one of the first in the United Kingdom to start doing something about it.

Peter's fundamental belief in the importance of saving individual species had its origins before the Second World War. When he visited the Duke of Bedford at Woburn in the late 1930s, he was greatly impressed by the work that had been done to save the Père David's deer and wrote in *The Eye of the Wind*:

I remember being tremendously impressed by this. The vision of one man on the opposite side of the world had saved a Chinese species from extinction; and it was not some obscure animal barely distinguishable from its relations, but a magnificent great beast with antlers quite different in shape from those of any other stag in the world. This, I remember thinking at the time, was in itself an achievement to justify the work of a lifetime. Such was (and still is) my reverence for the evolution of species, and my horror of the extinction of any single one of them.

At the same time, Peter had also been thinking of a species closer to his heart than the deer, the nene goose in Hawaii, which he knew was threatened with extinction, but his early plans to do something to save the nene were scuppered by the outbreak of war.

The stated aims of the Severn Wildfowl Trust at its inception made no mention of conservation or species extinction. It is worth repeating these aims as recorded in the minutes of that inaugural meeting:

> To promote the study of wildfowl and to undertake any activity which, in the opinion of the Council, is calculated to promote knowledge of and interest in wildfowl and in particular to establish and maintain a wildfowl and research observatory at the New Grounds on the estuary of the River Severn which will provide facilities for:
>
> 1) A close study of the winter flocks of wild geese and other birds.
> 2) The ringing of wild ducks in the decoy pools and of wild geese on the marshes for the further study of migration.
> 3) The study of a comparative collection of live wildfowl.

Peter was clearly thinking about the wider issue of conservation however, and his pioneering work in saving the nene goose from extinction, with the first captive goslings reared in 1952, showed how practical steps could be put in place, species by species, if the will was there.

Eighteen months after the founding of the Trust, in April 1948, Peter wrote an article for the magazine *Country Sportsman* entitled 'The Wildfowl Problem: A New Research Station in Gloucestershire'. In it, he wrote that the Severn Wildfowl Trust had been formed for three reasons, and this time there was a clear shift towards the kind of aims which the Wildfowl and Wetlands Trust supports today. The three reasons for setting up the centre at Slimbridge, given by Peter in the magazine article were:

> First, because still very little is known about wildfowl, especially wild geese; and one of its objects is therefore to learn as much as possible about these elusive and wary birds. This objective is purely scientific – to add to knowledge.
>
> The second reason is that ducks and geese are decreasing in the world rather rapidly – and it would be a great pity if they were allowed to disappear altogether or even to become extremely rare.

To prevent that happening some sort of action is required – but what? Another of the Trust's objects is to find out where and when and how to take such action.

And the third reason is to interest people in wildfowl, partly because to deal with a problem like this – a problem of declining numbers – public opinion must be roused to a sense of responsibility about it; and partly because there is a wide field of interest and delight to be had from the study of birds – birds of all kinds, but waterfowl in particular – and education in my view still has easily the most important long-term influence on the future of our civilisation.

Here we can see, formulated for the first time, the three key objectives of the Trust: Research, Conservation and Education. In 1966, a fourth aim, Recreation, would be added to the list.

In 1956, Peter was a founder member of the Council for Nature in the UK. In the mid-1950s there were a number of organisations in the United Kingdom working for the protection of different groups of plants and animals, for example the Royal Society for the Protection of Birds, the Botanical Society of the British Isles, the Wildfowl Trust itself and a number of county Naturalists Trusts, but there was no single body that could represent and protect nature as a whole across the United Kingdom and so the Council for Nature was formed. Other founder members of the Council were close associates of Peter's, many of them also involved with the Wildfowl Trust, including James Fisher, Aubrey Buxton and Sir Julian Huxley. Lord Hurcomb was the first president and was succeed by Sir Landsborough Thompson who had been the first president of the Wildfowl Trust's Scientific Committee. The patron of the new organisation was Prince Philip. This sense for the need to consider nature as a whole, came at a time before the concept of biodiversity and habitat management had become part of mainstream thinking and shows that even sixty-five years ago, Peter and people like him were only too aware of the need to engage in conservation as a multi-species discipline. The Council for Nature did much over the years to promote conservation in the UK including the organisation in 1963 of the first National Nature Week marked by the issue of a series of commemorative postage stamps.

Elsewhere in the world, steps were being taken to tackle the growing problem of species loss and habitat decline. At Lausanne in Switzerland a new organisation was established in 1948, the International Union for the Protection of Nature (IUPN). In 1956, it changed its name to the International Union for the Conservation of Nature and Natural Resources (IUCN), becoming an organisation which, it was hoped, could foster programmes for the protection of the natural world that transcended national boundaries, providing more rigorous protection than could be achieved by schemes managed within the borders of individual countries. Members would be both government and civil society organisations and would harness resources and expertise from nations around the world. Today the IUCN has more than 1,400 member organisations and inputs from over 15,000 experts.

Peter's attendance and presentations at the conferences of the International Ornithological Union had raised his profile on the international stage, so it is perhaps not surprising that in 1956 he was invited to become a vice-president of IUCN as well as a member of the organisation's Survival Service Commission and of its Commission on Public Information. With his excellent interpersonal skills, his connections with ornithologists in Europe and the United States and his wide network of influential people in government and commerce, Peter was perfectly placed to assist in the development of international programmes targeting threatened species, and he set to work with his usual determination. Here was an organisation whose aims and objectives closely matched his own and his work on their behalf could not but help support the growing work of the Wildfowl Trust in these fields. It was a perfect fit.

Though Peter's work to this point had always focused on wildfowl he was well aware of the problems facing species of all kinds. In *Observations of Wildlife* Peter wrote:

> I was anxious not only about the wildfowl, for it was clear that all over the world a great number of other animal species – and plant species too – were threatened with extinction. These species were the current end-products of 40 million centuries of evolution – four billion years. This is how long it has taken for all the diversity of living creatures on our earth to evolve into what we know today; and, of course, the process is continuing. For me, one of the greatest fascinations in nature is the way that evolution has produced this diversity of species moulded by the particular environment they live in. Their study leads me to value each evolutionary creation, each species, very highly, and to look upon species extinction at the

hands of unthinking man – sometimes even by his deliberate choice – as wicked irresponsibility. Extinction is for ever. It is irrevocable, irreversible. We have a responsibility to prevent species extinction if it is in our power to do so.

One problem faced by IUCN over the years was where to focus their resources to achieve maximum impact. As more scientific evidence was gathered and as the evidence of decline of habitats across the world increased through the 1950s, it became obvious that a considerable proportion of the world's wildlife was at risk to a greater or lesser degree. Some of the most immediate questions were: What species were most at risk? Where do you begin to put out the fire? What are the most effective actions to deliver the most beneficial returns with the least amount of money spent? In order to attempt to answer these well-nigh impossible questions the IUCN had set up a division called the Survival Service Commission (later known as the Species Survival Commission). As noted, Peter had become a member of the Commission in 1956, but in 1963 they invited him to become its chairman, a post he would hold for sixteen years. His brief was to provide analysis that would assist the IUCN to effectively target responses to what was beginning to seem an unstoppable disaster on a global scale.

This was a task ideally suited to Peter's abilities; it played perfectly to his strengths, not least his analytical skills and the attention to detail which had proved so useful in his contribution to the planning leading up to the D-Day landings. Peter devised a scheme under which panels of experts called specialist groups would be established in every region around the world, each group composed of people with specialist knowledge in one area of the animal kingdom, from lemurs to whales and from snakes to flamingos. The members of each group were tasked with identifying the species that were most threatened and indicating the level of threat on a scale from one to five. The data were then fed back to the IUCN at Morges in Switzerland where a team, under Peter's direction, compiled detailed lists of endangered species and their level of risk from around the world. These were assembled in what became known as the red data books which continue to this day to record the ever-changing threat levels to species across the globe.

The first red data book covered mammals and was followed by books for birds, amphibians and reptiles, freshwater fish and flowering plants. The numbers of specialist groups grew steadily until by 1989 there were nearly 2,000 biologists working in eighty-four different groups. At the same time, individual countries, including Britain, Russia and China developed their own red data books, enabling them to focus more closely on problems in their own countries. Among other projects, the Survival Service Commission provided valuable support to the orangutan rehabilitation centre at Sepilok in Sabah which Peter and Philippa visited on the day after his sixty-ninth birthday in 1978. Peter was all too aware that they would not be able to save everything, the task was simply too daunting, but as he wrote to a colleague at the time, 'We shan't save all, but we'll save a jolly lot more than if we'd never existed.' The Wildfowl and Wetlands Trust continue to support this work; the specialist group for flamingos is based at Slimbridge which, at the time of writing in 2020, is the only place in the world where all six species of flamingo can be seen at one location.

With the scheme in place, the IUCN could more easily target those species to which funding should be directed. An improved understanding of the inter-relationships between species within habitats and wider ecosystems also meant that funding could be directed to habitats as a whole rather than individual creatures, thereby improving circumstances not just for target species but also for the whole collection of animals, birds, insects and plants supported by that habitat.

In 1959, a proposal was made to mark the centenary of the publication of Charles Darwin's *On the Origin of Species* by establishing a research station on the Galapagos Islands. During his visit in 1835, Darwin had discovered that certain species of finch on the islands had evolved subtly different characteristics which reflected local circumstances, in particular, the kinds of food available. The islands' remoteness in the Pacific Ocean had inhibited the arrival of species from South America making the groups of fauna and flora there truly unique. All sorts of creatures from birds to giant tortoises exhibited different characteristics from island to island providing an example in microcosm of the processes of natural selection that occur across the globe. The islands' unique fauna was at risk however. Over the centuries, visiting sailors had introduced goats, dogs and rats which decimated the local wildlife, the islands' original inhabitants having no defence against these alien predators. The giant tortoises unique to these islands had suffered a huge decline as they were taken by whaling ships for food. A giant tortoise could easily be kept alive for months onboard ship, providing a ready source of fresh meat on long voyages.

The proposed research station would offer new insights into the islands' fauna and flora, provide protection for the habitats that supported them and establish targeted breeding programmes in an attempt to save some of the rarer species from extinction. IUCN joined forces with the United Nations Educational, Scientific and Cultural Organisation (UNESCO), forming a committee under the chairmanship of Sir Julian Huxley to draw up plans for the new endeavour. Peter's appointment to the committee recognised his pioneering work in captive breeding and his growing profile as a conservationist; he himself relished the prospect, having long been an ardent admirer of Darwin's work. His father, too, had recognised the importance of *On the Origin of Species* and had taken a copy with him on his journey to the South Pole, so the book had additional resonance for Peter. Initially, money would be provided by UNESCO, but it was realised that it would be necessary to find additional funding elsewhere and that meant raising public awareness of the project. Peter had the perfect solution. He arranged with the BBC that he and Philippa would make a trip to the Galapagos to film the islands' extraordinary wildlife for *Faraway Look*. Tony Soper accompanied them as cameraman, and arrangements were made with the Ecuadorian navy to provide a ship which would take them round the islands. The diversity and abundance of life that they discovered on the islands fascinated Peter. The films that the team produced during the trip raised awareness of the islands and the unique fauna they supported at a time when people were much less aware of the islands than they are today. In 1959 there was no tourism in the Galapagos Islands, and the Charles Darwin Foundation, founded on 7 July 1959, was to play a major role in establishing the strict controls that would be imposed when tourism in the islands took off, sparked in part by the interest that programmes like *Faraway Look* engendered.

Peter visited Ecuador and the Galapagos Islands again in 1961, during negotiations between the Charles Darwin Foundation and the Ecuadorian government over the establishment of the research station. On this second visit, he was able to spend more time studying the wealth of wildlife on the islands. All the hard work eventually paid off when the Charles Darwin Research Station opened in January 1964. The work it has done since in pest eradication, captive breeding and habitat management has saved numerous species and helped to manage a carefully controlled, sustainable eco-tourism industry that provides a model for projects in other parts of the world, where the growth of tourism presents a serious threat to wildlife.

Peter was only too aware of the enormous debt he owed to all the organisations and individuals who had donated money over the years to the causes in which he believed so passionately. In 1978, with the Wildfowl Trust in good heart, he and Philippa decided to do something to try and redress the balance a little. Together they formed the Peter Scott Trust for Education and Research in Conservation. The aim was to provide modest funding for individuals wishing to undertake some form of research and for which they needed additional finance. Peter must have enjoyed reading the submissions for funding and have been pleased that he had found a way of supporting young people who, perhaps inspired by his example, were setting out on their own campaigns in support of the natural world.

It is clear that Peter's concern had gone beyond the threat to wildfowl such as the nene goose; he was now engaged in highlighting the danger faced by all life on the planet. While working at a global level, Peter continued to spread the conservation message at home through his writing, lectures and television appearances. In 1961 Peter wrote what he called a Conservation Creed, part of which read:

What man did to the Dodo, and has since been doing to the Blue Whale and about 1000 other kinds of animals, may or may not be morally wrong. But the conservation of nature is most important because of what nature does for man. I believe something goes wrong with man when he cuts himself off from the natural world. I think he knows it, and this is why he keeps gardens and window-boxes and house plants, and dogs and cats and budgerigars. Man does not live by bread alone. I believe he should take just as great pains to look after the natural treasures which inspire him as he does to preserve his man-made treasures in art galleries and museums. This is a responsibility we have to future generations, just as we are responsible for the safe-guarding of Westminster Abbey or the Mona Lisa.

It has been argued that if the human population of the world continues to increase at its present rate, there will soon be no room for either wildlife or wild places, so why waste time, effort and money trying to conserve them now? But I believe that sooner or later man will learn to limit his own overpopulation ... No one can tell when this will happen. I am concerned that when it does, breeding stocks of wild animals and plants should still exist, preserved perhaps mainly in nature reserves and national parks, even in zoos and botanical gardens, from which to repopulate the natural environment man will then wish to re-create and rehabilitate. These are my reasons for believing passionately in the conservation of nature.

All this calls for action of three kinds: more research in ecology, the setting aside of more land as effectively inviolate strongholds, and above all education. By calling attention to the plight of the world's wildlife, and by encouraging people to enrich their lives by the enjoyment of nature, it may be possible to accelerate both the change in outlook and the necessary action.

Almost sixty years on, matters have got progressively worse but there is still hope. The three kinds of action called for by Peter continue to be taken, not least by the Trust that he founded seventy-five years ago. Individual species are still being saved, most recently the Madagascar pochard, while head-starting programmes in the UK help to slow the decline of species such as the curlew and the black-tailed godwit. In the years immediately after the Second World War, Peter was almost alone in his concern to save threatened species from extinction; now there is an army of people round the globe working to save the world's biodiversity from the continuing threats identified by Peter and his colleagues all those years ago.

23

Enter the Panda

One of the most serious problems faced by Peter and his colleagues at IUCN was the lack of money. Identifying the creatures most at risk round the world was a vital step in tackling the challenge of species decline, but without funds to put the necessary programmes in place to actually halt that decline, the scientists were reduced to the role of spectators, albeit informed spectators, as the world's wildlife continued to disappear around them. Money to fund research and habitat management programmes had to be coaxed out of governments or sought from multinational companies and rich philanthropists, all of whom received numerous demands for support from a wide range of charitable organisations. How to raise awareness of the IUCN to ensure that the money so desperately needed kept rolling in? Peter was able to help here. With his rapidly growing international profile, his army of followers in the UK, his connections with people in high places, his enthusiasm and his charisma, Peter was an ideal mouthpiece for the organisation and its aims.

The real breakthrough came, as is often the case, almost by accident. In 1960, Sir Julian Huxley had made a tour of Central and East Africa on behalf of UNESCO and on his return he wrote a series of three articles about Africa's endangered wildlife in *The Observer*. Shortly afterwards, he received a letter from a man called Victor Stolan who felt it was imperative that some form of campaign to secure funds should be launched. Furthermore, he had some interesting ideas about how such a campaign should be managed; Stolan had little time for committees and organisations. His suggestion was a scheme under which small donations would be sought from a wide range of individuals to augment the money coaxed by people like Peter from large multinational companies. Stolan was convinced this could be achieved by a small group of people with determination and drive and without the need for complex organisational structures, which he felt impeded action.

Sir Julian Huxley discussed this with Max Nicholson, director general of the Nature Conservancy, and he in turn talked to Peter and to Guy Mountfort, a leading ornithologist and author of the *Field Guide to the Birds of Britain and Europe*, first published in 1954. Max Nicholson's original idea was to form something called an 'Ark Club' which would sign up 600 people of influence round the world, each of whom would donate £1,000. This idea was soon abandoned in favour of a series of more wide-reaching campaigns which would seek donations of any amount from the widest range of people as possible. The organisation would have its headquarters within the offices of the IUCN in Switzerland, with satellite branches in as many countries as possible, in each of which individual campaigns for funding would be launched. Peter, Max Nicholson and Guy Mountfort presented their plan to the IUCN, and it was readily adopted as the need for financial support was as pressing as ever.

The new organisation was given a name, the World Wildlife Fund (WWF). It needed a logo, and the panda was suggested as a suitable animal to feature on it. The panda was both charismatic and endangered and fitted the bill perfectly. Peter said:

> We wanted an animal that is beautiful, is endangered, and one loved by many people in the world for its appealing qualities. We also wanted an animal that had an impact in black and white to save money on printing costs.

From a sketch by Gerald Watterson, former secretary general of IUCN, Peter created what has become one of the most recognisable symbols on the planet. The original version was subsequently smoothed somewhat for digital representation. This apparently made Peter unhappy because he felt the panda no longer had a cheerful appearance, but the modern version is still undeniably recognisable as Peter's creation.

The organisation now needed a president, so Peter approached Prince Philip to ask him to become its head. Prince Philip, having read Peter's presentation to him, agreed he would be president, but only of the British branch of WWF. Peter was somewhat downhearted, but later the same day he received a phone call from the prince. He told Peter that Prince Bernhard of the Netherlands was visiting; Prince Philip had discussed Peter's proposal with him and Prince Bernhard might be willing to take on the international presidency but wanted to hear from Peter directly. Prince Philip added that Prince Bernhard was staying at Claridge's hotel and would be going out to dinner that evening at 7.30. Peter presented himself outside the prince's hotel at the appropriate time, and Prince Bernhard invited him to join him in his taxi en route to his dinner engagement. Twenty minutes later, Peter had his new international president, later recalling with some pride that he managed to get two princes in one day. Prince Philip did subsequently become international president, serving from 1981 to 1996 in the role. The organisation was now taking shape. Peter became one of two vice-presidents of the new organisation as well as chairman of the British appeal. In 1985 he was to become honorary chairman of the international board. Guy Mountfort became treasurer and Dr Fritz Vollmar, secretary general. At this stage the organisation still had no money so Peter and Max Nicholson each made an anonymous donation of £1,500, and a further £10,000 was received from businessman Jack Cotton.

In August 1961, came an additional and significant boost to the credibility of the new organisation. At an IUCN conference at Arusha in Tanzania, the formation of WWF was announced to the world and received the enthusiastic support of President-elect Dr Julius Nyerere. The idea that a group of white men from Europe and North America would be telling African leaders what they had to do to save their countries' wildlife would not sit well in post-colonial Africa, but to have someone of the stature of Julius Nyerere promoting the cause and encouraging his fellow leaders lent authority to the emerging movement, giving it an important and much-needed boost. It was during this trip that Peter paid his first visit to the Ngorongoro Crater and saw for himself not only the huge and diverse accumulation of animals on the crater floor but also the impact of the removal of forest on the crater rim by local tribesmen to create better grazing for their cattle. There were only four rhinoceros left at the time and one was killed by poachers on the same day as his visit. The crater represented in microcosm the problems facing Africa's wildlife as a whole, and it made a lasting impact on Peter.

Back in England, a sub-committee was formed to galvanise awareness of the huge problems faced by wildlife around the world. One of the members, a Scots businessman called Ian McPhail, was a friend of Hugh Cudlipp, editor of the *Daily Mirror*. McPhail asked Cudlipp to print an article on threatened wildlife and ask the public for donations to WWF. Cudlipp clearly saw the potential of a major campaign and the advantage it would bring to both WWF and his own paper. The *Daily Mirror* ran the feature, starting on the front page with banner headlines and running to several pages with dramatic photographs of species that were in peril. Money started to trickle in from concerned readers and the flow very quickly became a flood. WWF was up and running. Peter's name appeared in the *Daily Mirror* article and his association with WWF undoubtedly contributed to the success of this first British campaign. Through his *Look* programmes and other appearances on television and radio, Peter had become a hugely popular figure. Over the last ten years, thanks to his and David Attenborough's efforts, the nation had taken wildlife to its heart so that now, when they learned of the threat, they were ready to act. Julian Huxley's articles in *The Observer* and the feature in the *Daily Mirror* made the public aware as never before of the threat facing the world's wildlife; the campaign in the *Daily Mirror* raised £50,000, enough to get WWF off to a good start. Prince Philip was also involved in promoting the new organisation. He provided the narration for an hour-long *Survival* special on Anglia Television called *The New Ark*. The programme highlighted conservation issues in Africa and became the first *Survival* film to win international recognition, receiving the Golden Nymph award at the Monte Carlo Film Festival in 1963. The film was bought by NBC in the United States and became the first natural history programme to be networked on American television.

The United States appeal was launched at the end of 1961 at a banquet at which Prince Philip, Prince Bernhard and Peter all gave addresses. General Dwight D. Eisenhower agreed to become president of the US branch of the organisation. National appeals followed in the Netherlands, Germany, Austria and Switzerland. Peter worked tirelessly to promote the organisation and its campaigns, travelling thousands of miles, making speeches, entertaining potential donors at his home at Slimbridge and encouraging others to renew their efforts. Among the visitors to Slimbridge at this time was banker Ernest Kleinwort and his wife; Ernest Kleinwort became a major donor to projects both at the Wildfowl Trust and the World Wildlife Fund and a member of the Council of the Wildfowl Trust. The relationship between WWF and IUCN was mutually beneficial; WWF raised money for conservation work while IUCN provided scientific advice and information to help target the best use of the funds raised. From 1963, his work as head of the Survival Service Commission fed into the flow of information about endangered species around the world. Peter, with a foot in both camps, was sometimes required to intervene to make sure that the administrative links between the two organisations remained focused and effective; not always an easy task.

One of the problems faced by Peter and his colleagues was how to persuade people to donate to a cause established to save animals when there was so much human suffering around the world; shouldn't man seek to eliminate poverty and starvation before thinking about protecting the natural world? Peter's ideas about conservation had long espoused the view that by destroying habitats, man was not only imperilling the creatures that lived there but also threatening his own survival on the planet. He saw man as an integral part of the earth's web of life; in his view it was not possible to degrade the planet's resources without also threatening man's future existence as well. Peter encapsulated these thoughts in a concept he called the four pillars of conservation. The first pillar was one of ethics. What right did man have to destroy other species? The second pillar concerned aesthetics. The beauty of nature and the well-being it brings to mankind should not be denied to future generations. The third pillar was science; through the destruction of the natural world, potential new drugs and other as yet unknown scientific benefits would be lost. Finally came economics. A desire to experience the marvels of the natural world and to ensure that species and habitats were preserved channelled money primarily from rich countries to poor ones.

With the support of the general public in place, Peter and his colleagues could begin to put programmes in hand to save some of the most threatened creatures and habitats. WWF's first campaign was a plan to save the Coto Doñana nature reserve in southern Spain from further exploitation. The delta of the River Guadalquivir forms a huge area of marshes and wetlands that is home to a wide variety of water birds which winter there in great numbers. Over the years, the wilderness had come under threat as land was reclaimed for rice growing, while pollution up-river threatened to destroy what was left.

Funds were raised to buy several thousand acres, with the Spanish government a significant contributor. At the last minute the donations proved insufficient to buy the land and the project might have been lost were it not for the intervention of Prince Bernhard, who had a quiet word with General Francisco Franco.

The campaigns that followed were, in the main, high profile and highly publicised, focusing on animals whose endangered status, when brought to the public's attention, would be guaranteed to elicit a strong response. In 1961, the Arabian oryx was thought to number less than fifty animals in the wild. The Fauna Preservation Society established a breeding programme in three American zoos; starting with just four individuals a herd was gradually established with the support of WWF. The aim was always that the animals would eventually be released into the wild, but the threat of hunting was ever present and the risk of losing the carefully reared stock if they were released looked likely to doom the remaining animals to life in captivity. Then, in 1981, the Sultan of Oman agreed to establish a reserve which would provide a safe zone for the animals with round-the-clock protection from wardens, and so ten Arabian oryx were released back into the wild. In Philippa's study in the house at Slimbridge, a photograph on the wall shows her being introduced to the Sultan while Peter looks on, a proud moment for them both.

One of the highest profile campaigns was 'Save the Rhino' initiated in 1980. That we are all now very much aware of the threat to rhinos in Africa is a direct result of the WWF action. The rhino, once common across Africa, had suffered catastrophic decline in the twentieth century, largely due to the demand for rhino horn as an ingredient in traditional medicines in China and South-East Asia. The CITES convention, initiated by IUCN, was ratified in 1975 and forbids the traffic of wild animals and body parts across the world. The trade in rhino horn was so lucrative however that poachers defied any attempt to inhibit their activities and carried on killing rhinos in large numbers. WWF worked hard to persuade more governments to sign up to CITES and to urge existing signatories to do more to uphold its statutes. In addition work was undertaken with medical practitioners across Asia, pointing out to them that if they did nothing then the supply of rhino horn would very soon cease altogether. Of the two rhino species found in Africa, the black rhino remains most at risk and reached a record low of 2,400 individuals in 1995. Numbers have risen slowly but in the early part of the twenty-first century there were still 90 per cent fewer animals than three generations previously. The Javan rhino remains critically endangered with perhaps no more than fifty individuals left in the wild. Other species to benefit from WWF support included the Indian tiger, polar bear, Kashmir stag, mountain gorilla, peregrine falcon, whooping crane and the white-winged wood duck. Wider campaigns covered whole ecosystems; two examples were 'Save The Jungle' and 'The Seas Must Live'.

By May 1977, the Wildfowl Trust's *Wildfowl News* magazine, in an article about WWF, was able to report:

> Twelve million pounds has now been spent on conservation all over the world. This money, raised by 26 National Appeals has gone to 1,600 projects in 80 countries, to help establish national parks, nature reserves and sanctuaries, to support scientific studies of endangered species and their habitat as the basis for management plans; to provide equipment for the control of poaching; to support conservation education by training wildlife wardens and by forming wildlife youth groups.

The following year, when the twenty-sixth meeting of the WWF International Board of Trustees was held at Slimbridge, *Wildfowl News* reported an increase in activity with a new total of £15 million spent on 1,905 projects since 1961.

One of the greatest successes, and one of which Peter was particularly proud, came in 1979 when WWF became the first non-governmental conservation organisation to receive an official invitation from the Chinese government. China had announced the establishment of a WWF China committee, the twenty-seventh country to do so, and Peter went to China for a series of meetings and celebrations to mark the event. Particularly pleasing was that during Peter's visit, the Chinese announced that they would also be joining IUCN and would become a signatory to the CITES convention. This was a major boost to the campaign to save the rhino, given the prevalence of the practice of traditional medicine throughout China. Another major advance was the Chinese commitment to impose environmental impact assessments on all major developments in future. During the visit, Peter made a tour of Manchuria with Chinese officials where he saw, or at least was almost certain that he saw, three Chinese mergansers. This left only one species of waterfowl that he had not yet seen in the wild, the Brazilian merganser.

The following year, Peter and Philippa returned on a WWF mission to agree funding for a research station to study giant pandas, prevent their extinction in the wild and to determine best practices for future captive breeding programmes. This was a major investment for WWF which, after some negotiation, agreed an eyewatering $1 million donation to fund the project. For Peter, a major outcome of this agreement was not just the involvement of the Chinese government in protecting the giant panda in the wild but also their commitment to a range of other conservation programmes. Peter had urged the Chinese government to join the International Whaling Commission and this subsequently occurred. Through his patience, tact and goodwill, Peter probably did more for the conservation of wildlife in China than any other westerner, and the legacy of his work continues in China today with the recent creation of significant new coastal wetland reserves to protect migratory waders on the east Asia flyway. In particular, the spoon-billed sandpiper, a bird that the Wildfowl and Wetlands Trust is striving to save, is benefiting from these initiatives.

One of Peter's other great crusades was his work to save whales from extinction. Throughout the first half of the twentieth century, whale stocks had been plundered with impunity, while the whaling nations paid little heed to the fact that their own efforts looked set to put themselves out of business altogether as whale numbers plummeted. In 1946, the International Whaling Commission was established with the aim of conserving whale stocks and regulating the industry. The quotas they imposed proved ineffective and catches continued to rise as the numbers of surviving animals fell even further. Peter first became involved when, in 1963, the Survival Service Commission of IUCN, of which he had just been made chairman, set up a group to study the blue whale and nine other whale species. The plight of all of the species quickly became apparent, and Peter began to attend the annual meetings of the International Whaling Commission which WWF had now joined as a non-government organisation, expending a great deal of energy in pushing for a moratorium on whaling. In 1965, Peter became conservation adviser to the British delegation of the International Whaling Commission.

Peter's persistence seemed to bear fruit in 1972 when the United Nations Conference on the Human Environment in Stockholm voted by fifty-one votes to three for a ten-year moratorium on whaling to allow stocks to recover. Peter lobbied delegates hard prior to the vote and claimed to have persuaded eight members to change their vote in favour of a moratorium. Buoyed by his success, Peter took the conference recommendation to the annual meeting of the International Whaling Commission in London a few weeks later where he gave the opening address. It was to no avail however as the Commission voted fourteen votes to four against a moratorium. A less persistent lobbyist might have thrown in the towel at this point but Peter carried on. WWF were not alone in fighting for a moratorium as many other organisations, not least Greenpeace, joined the fray. Whereas Greenpeace's strategy tended to be confrontational, WWF, under Peter's guidance, chose a quieter and rather clever strategy. For a resolution to pass at a conference of the Commission it had to achieve three-quarters of the vote. As most member countries were whaling nations there seemed little likelihood that the requisite number could ever be persuaded to change their minds. However, the rules allowed any nation to join the Commission, and with a growing groundswell of opinion around the world, Peter set about encouraging as many nations as possible to join and throw their weight behind a moratorium. His plan bore fruit. Seychelles came on board followed by Oman and China, all through Peter's direct influence.

The urgent need for the conservation of whales was illustrated to Peter in 1979 while on a cruise in the ship *Lindblad Explorer*. In the middle of the South Atlantic, the ship had an unscheduled encounter with a Russian whaling ship in the act of catching and killing minke whales, an unpleasant spectacle for all on board. The encounter was a stark reminder to him of how important his work continued to be. By this time, support was growing, and later in 1979 Peter addressed a crowd of 12,000 people in Trafalgar Square who were protesting against the continued slaughter. Over the years the number of member countries in the Commission had risen from seventeen to forty-one, and so it was that at the Commission's annual meeting at Brighton in the United Kingdom in 1982, the moratorium was finally voted through. For Peter it was the culmination of nearly twenty years' work and he was justifiably pleased. It wasn't to be the end of the matter however as the moratorium would not take effect until 1985, and 'scientific' whaling would still be allowed, a large loophole through which the ships of several nations continued to sail with impunity.

Nevertheless, without the hard work of Peter and a number of other dedicated campaigners we might today be mourning the extinction of the blue whale, a species which survives still in the oceans of the world.

There has been a wide variety of innovative WWF campaigns over the years. In 1970, in an echo of Max Nicholson's idea of an 'Ark Club', Prince Bernhard was invited to be president of 'The 1001: A Nature Trust' to which 1,001 wealthy individuals were invited to donate $10,000 each; the scheme raised over $10 million in just three years. The money raised was used to fund the cost of running WWF, which meant that money raised from public appeals could be spent exclusively on conservation projects without having to divert part of the donations to administrative charges. In 1983, a scheme was set up under which postal authorities were invited to select endangered species to put on their postage stamps with a proportion of the revenue going to the Fund. Since its inception, 200 countries and dependencies have taken part. Peter's dedication to the work of WWF increased his workload significantly, and he was constantly in demand for meetings round the world. During his travels he mixed with everyone from kings and presidents to research workers and supporters and talked to all of them with the same confidence and charm. One of the highlights he recalled with pleasure was meeting Neil Armstrong, the first man to set foot on the moon, at the second World Congress of WWF in 1970. A more formal occasion was an audience with Pope Paul XI in 1969 when, at the head of a WWF delegation, Peter made a presentation of their work, taking care to make references to St Francis and his love of birds and animals. Despite Pope Paul's expressed view that animals were put on earth by God for the exclusive benefit of mankind, Peter felt that the meeting should improve the profile of WWF in those parts of the world where the Catholic Church was an important influence in daily life.

Not all of Peter's campaigning bore fruit. In 1974, he travelled to Saudi Arabia with Prince Bernhard of the Netherlands in the hope of persuading King Faisal to set up a foundation with a capital fund of £90 million to support conservation projects. They were unable to get an audience with the King and returned home without success. Peter was never one to give up however; further trips to the kingdom followed as he tried to persuade various members of the royal family and government officials of the benefits of such a fund. He gradually had to set his sights lower, and by the time of his eighth and final attempt in 1976 his proposal had reduced to a fund with a value of £50,000; even this proved to be unattainable.

In 1978, Peter became heavily involved in one of the most ambitious international conservation projects of the time. At a meeting of IUCN in Ashkhabad, USSR, he represented WWF in discussions on the draft for a new World Conservation Strategy. One of the perennial problems faced by both WWF and IUCN was that the projects into which they poured so much money and effort tackled conservation for one particular species or area. Worthwhile though these efforts were, the solutions provided did not address the wider and more serious problem of increasing loss of species and habitats on a global scale. The accelerating decline in biodiversity levels threatened not just the species concerned but man's future on the planet as well. The new World Conservation Strategy brought together critical research from a number of international organisations including IUCN, WWF, the UN Food and Agriculture Organisation, the UN Environment Programme and UNESCO. The new Strategy would, it was hoped, focus minds at an international level on the need to link the conservation of natural resources with sustainable human development and so mitigate the worst of the environmental disasters that appeared to be looming on the horizon. With his worldwide connections, Peter became a leading disciple for the cause. In 1979, during his visit to China for example, he worked hard to persuade the Chinese government to adhere to the new strategy which was in the final stages of preparation. The World Conservation Strategy was launched in 1980 and was endorsed by numerous leaders, organisations and governments. Over the coming years it would inform the national conservation strategies of more than fifty countries.

Peter's work did not go unrecognised. In 1973, he received a knighthood for services to conservation, a recognition which was followed by a succession of international awards and prizes. In 1977, Peter shared with Jacques Cousteau the United Nations International Pahlavi Environment Prize which was presented by the younger brother of the Shah of Iran. Peter received his award and a cheque for $25,000 from UN secretary general Kurt Waldheim at a ceremony at the United Nations Headquarters in New York. Peter gave an impassioned speech in response, which included the following:

When my father was returning from the South Pole in 1912, and was finally pinned down by a blizzard, with his companions in the tent in which they died, he wrote in a letter to my mother 'Make the boy interested in Natural History ... they teach it at some schools.' And so I became a naturalist and have been one ever since. It's one of the best recipes for a happy life. However all through it I have become increasingly concerned that all is not well with nature and our natural environment. I have been worried by the increasing rate of species extinction – species that are the current end-product of 30 million centuries – 3,000 million years of evolution since life began on earth. Many of them have been wiped out in a mere instant of geological time through the ignorance, carelessness or greed of mankind.

He went on to talk about whaling and energy wastage before finishing with an impassioned plea:

I would like to pinpoint one final area of concern – the Tropical Rain Forests of the world which are being cut down at the rate of 20 hectares per minute, day and night, day in – day out. They provide us with water and, when they are cut, erosion sets in and desertification follows. They represent an ecosystem which has changed little in perhaps 60 million years. They have a richness which is not yet half explored not half understood – and yet here we are sweeping them off our planet with all their amazing diversity of plant and animal species. It is the destruction of whole ecosystems in this kind of ignorance which holds the seeds of disaster for our species and our planet ... We need a greater reverence for our Blue Planet – the only home of man. We must develop a planetary loyalty – we must be geophiles – lovers of the Earth. I passionately believe in man's individual and collective responsibility for all life on earth. About this I care.

This speech, made before representatives of the nations of the world, is just one of hundreds of similar impassioned addresses that Peter made during his near thirty-year association with WWF. If it strikes a chord, and seems remarkably familiar, it is because man has continued in his reckless and dizzying downhill run to destruction almost without pause since this speech was made. Organisations like IUCN, WWF, Friends of the Earth, Greenpeace and WWT continue to fight against the tide, but the threats to man's future existence on the earth remain as real as they did in 1977. Peter gave 90 per cent of his prize money from the Pahlavi Environment Prize to conservation and with the remaining 10 per cent built the tower at his home in Slimbridge.

Other awards followed. In 1981, Peter received the IUCN John Phillips Gold Medal and a Twentieth Anniversary Special Award from the World Wildlife Fund. The year 1986 brought more recognition. In September he flew to the United States to receive the Getty Prize worth $50,000 at a ceremony at the Smithsonian Museum – this time all the money went to conservation causes. Another award received in the same year was the RSPB Gold Medal.

To celebrate the twenty-fifth anniversary of the founding of WWF, Prince Philip suggested the idea of an ecumenical service at Assisi in Italy. It so happened that Peter's birthday on 14 September coincided with the date in 1226 when St Francis preached to the birds. Peter was taken to Assisi in an aircraft of the Queen's Flight, piloted by Prince Philip, and received the World Wildlife Fund Gold Medal at a special ceremony. Shortly before his death in 1989, Peter received the Zoological Medal from Washington Zoo.

WWF changed its name in 1986 to the Worldwide Fund for Nature and has continued the work started by Peter and his colleagues. Since 1995, the organisation has invested over $1 billion in over 12,000 conservation projects around the world. Other organisations and individuals have taken up the baton. Greenpeace has done much to alter people's perceptions about the dangers we face from the pollution of our oceans, while a single broadcast by Sir David Attenborough in 2019 did more to alert the public to the dangers of plastics in the ocean than an army of commissions and scientists could have achieved in a lifetime. All is still not lost.

24

Beautiful Bewick's

Peter's heavy schedule resulting from his conservation work did not prevent him from engaging in research closer to home, indeed very close to home. The Bewick's swan, Europe's smallest swan species, is one of two sub-species of the tundra swan; the other sub-species, the whistling swan, is found in North America. The Bewick's swan breeds in the high Arctic tundra in northern Russia and winters in three locations far to the south of the breeding grounds. Of the current global population of around 98,000 individuals, 78,000 breed in eastern Siberia and winter in east Asia, 1,000 birds winter around the shores of the Caspian Sea, and a further group of around 18,000 breed in western Siberia and winter in Central and Western Europe with migrations in excess of 4,000 kilometres each autumn and spring.

The reasons for such extended migrations are complex but are determined primarily by the availability of food and lack of predators during the breeding season. In the far north of Russia during the summer months there is a ready availability of fresh green shoots for the swans and their cygnets to graze while the abundance of aquatic invertebrates is thought to provide a rich source of protein for the growing cygnets. The only predators of any size are the Arctic fox and the wolverine; in the continuous summer daylight experienced in high latitudes, a pair of swans working together can usually see off either of these threats. Conversely, in winter there is no readily available food and almost continuous darkness, so the birds have to migrate to safer and more comfortable quarters for the winter. The western flyway takes birds across the Baltic States and Poland, through Germany and the Netherlands and on into eastern England, with some birds continuing west to winter in Somerset and Ireland, though today, very few continue beyond the west of England.

When the Severn Wildfowl Trust was formed in 1946, there were few records of Bewick's swans wintering in the Severn Estuary on a regular basis, but in 1948 a single Bewick's swan landed in an enclosure in the collection at Slimbridge where there was a pair of whistling swans. Peter was not slow to take advantage. He caught the Bewick's swan, added it to the collection and acquired a mate for it from Rotterdam Zoo. The new couple were christened Mr and Mrs Noah, bred happily in the collection in the following years and in 1956 were responsible for the first Bewick's swans hatched in captivity anywhere in the world. Mrs Noah lived at Slimbridge for thirty-two years, dying in1983 at the age of at least thirty-four and having produced over thirty offspring. Over time, more individual Bewick's swans dropped in during the winter months, attracted by the Bewick's and whistling swans in the collection. In 1956, a group of sixteen birds spent some time on the Big Pen; by 1963, numbers wintering had increased to twenty.

In February 1964, Peter decided he would like to spend some time studying the visiting Bewick's swans and arranged to have the three captive swans currently in the collection brought from their enclosure and put on the lake outside the window. Shortly afterwards a wild female Bewick's swan arrived, but instead of joining its fellows on the lake outside the house, it flew into the collection pen in the grounds where the whistling swans were kept. The two sub-species are remarkably similar, the only difference being the smaller amount of yellow on the bill of the whistling swan. The wild Bewick's swan had clearly formed an attachment to one of the whistling swans, so Peter arranged for the four whistling swans also to be brought onto the lake in front of the window and sure enough, the wild Bewick's swan soon joined them. Because of her attachment to the whistling swan she was named Maud after a lady friend of Whistler, the painter. That day Peter made a careful painting of Maud, hoping to recognise her if she returned again.

That first evening, Maud disappeared into the night. The following day there was, once again, a wild Bewick's swan on the lake in front of the window. But was it Maud? Apparently not, because Peter, with his painter's eye for detail, saw at once that this new bird had a bill pattern that was slightly different from Maud's. Bewick's swans have bills which are mainly black with a wedge of yellow on either side, and sometimes a yellow patch on top of the bill. As more swans came to the lake, it became increasingly obvious that the bill of each bird was different. The differences between individual birds were slight but a distinction could always be made; we now know that each bird's bill pattern is as unique as a human fingerprint. This second swan was indeed a male and was christened The Major. That same day, four other Bewick's swans joined the group on the lake. Peter painted them all and gave them names for quick identification with his own brief additional notes: Ethel (the Speckled Hen), Rudy, Aristotle (Onassis) and Maria (Callas). The seven collection birds were already being fed a daily allowance of wheat grain, and Peter made sure there was enough food for the visitors as well. As the days went by, more birds came to visit, and by the end of that winter season, Peter had identified twenty-four individual Bewick's swans.

During the winter of 1964 to 1965, the Bewick's swans reappeared. Of the original group that had visited the previous winter, sixteen individuals returned to spend all or part of the winter at Slimbridge. Peter was delighted and wrote of the immense pleasure it gave him to see the same birds returning from a 5,000-mile round trip to rest and feed on the pond outside his house. The highest concentration on the lake that second winter was fifty-five swans, and over the whole season, sixty-eight individual birds were identified and their bill patterns recorded. The following year, the numbers were up again to a maximum count of 125 on the lake, with 147 individuals identified during the season. Peter was intrigued by this rapid increase in numbers. Prior to the start of the project, there might only have been thirty or so birds visiting the Severn Estuary throughout a winter season. Where did the additional swans come from? Evidently, the ones that had visited in a previous season remembered the ready availability of food. Peter speculated that as more birds began to return each year, other individuals would attach themselves to a group during migration and follow them to their winter food source. Individuals passing down the river valley would also be attracted by hearing or seeing the birds already gathered on the lake. Once they had spent a few weeks on the lake in winter, the swans would be very likely to return again in future years to what they recognised as a safe haven with a reliable food source.

From the very beginning, Peter kept meticulous notes, recording each day the birds that appeared on the lake, which birds were paired with which, how they behaved and the territorial and other displays between pairs and groups. All this information was recorded in what became known as the Swan Diaries, hard-backed quarto notebooks which still sit today on his desk by the window. Alongside the notebooks, in a small Perspex case, sits Thomas Bewick's telescope which Peter bought at auction. (The swan was named in honour of the British eighteenth-century naturalist after his death.)

Philippa now started to photograph the bills from three sides while Peter continued to paint each bird's bill pattern, joined by Dafila, a budding artist in her own right, who shared her father's fascination for the swans. As the project grew, Dafila and her parents were able to name over 200 swans on sight, but Dafila went on to even greater feats of memory and was subsequently able to remember and recognise over 1,000 different individuals. She had several favourite swans over the years, and in 1967 her father gave her, as a Christmas present, a painting of one of her favourite pairs, Peasant and Gypsy, with their cygnet. The painting still hangs in the studio in the house at Slimbridge.

The growing numbers of swans gave rise to another concern. Would a large group of swans grazing on the New Grounds impact the flocks of white-fronted geese on their most important British wintering grounds by reducing the amount of grazing available? Studies were undertaken that showed that the two species preferred different lengths of grass for grazing. This meant that by changing the pattern of cattle and sheep rotation during the summer months, grassland areas with sward lengths suitable for both species could be prepared, allowing them to graze happily together during the winter months.

When the monitoring of the swans on a daily basis became too much for Peter alone, the work was put onto a more established footing. Researchers were employed during the winter season to monitor the arrival of the swans, to conduct a roll call of birds each morning and record their behaviour during the day. One of the research team would be on duty every day in Peter's studio where a small door allowed them to access the left-hand window without disturbing Peter and whoever he might be meeting with. Only when the doctor was visiting were they excluded from the room. To ensure consistency of information, a template was developed with a formula for recording each facial characteristic, which meant that all records were completed in exactly the same way, thus minimising any potential confusion in identifying individual birds. Over time, the members of the research team became adept at recognising the swans and if Peter asked them to identify a particular bird they could usually do so at once without checking the records. Given that in later years there might be upwards of 400 swans on the lake at any given time, this was no mean feat. The record number of swans on the lake was 610 on 14 January 1979. One of the researchers, Eileen Rees, carried out work for the Trust until 2020; the expertise she built up over the years led her to write what became the definitive book on Bewick's swans, published by Poyser as part of their series of excellent monographs of bird species.

Bewick's swans mate for life and will resume their partnerships on the breeding grounds and at their winter quarters, even if separated during migration. First year cygnets make their first migration flight with their parents, and the family group will be maintained until the following breeding season. This meant that individual families could be studied together on the lake, and though individual identities are harder to establish in cygnets, it became possible to record family trees for many of the swans that visited each year. Close study of the swans at Slimbridge revealed new patterns of behaviour amongst individuals and between family groups. Since the study started in 1964, there have only ever been two 'divorces', while the longest partnership recorded was between two swans called Limonia and Laburnum who returned for twenty-two years between 1985 and 2007. Even this record was beaten by an individual male swan called Lancelot who arrived in the first winter of the project and visited Slimbridge for twenty-three consecutive winters thereafter. Lancelot was named after a fictitious character Lancelot Sage, who appeared in a regular column written for *Yachting World* magazine by Keith Shackleton; Lancelot Sage was apparently a thinly disguised caricature of Peter himself. Lancelot became so well known that his arrival each autumn was announced in *The Times*.

The start of the Bewick's swan study resulted in quite a lot of changes. As the numbers built up, it became apparent that the lake was not large enough to support the growing numbers of birds; they needed enough room to feed and sit for preening, but also space to land and take off. The lake had originally been seventy yards long by forty yards wide but was now lengthened by a further fifty yards to provide an adequate runway for take-off. The Rushy Pen which contained the lake had been open to the public since the collection was first started in 1946. Now it was closed off and became part of the wild reserve, creating an undisturbed space for the visiting flocks. Peter was always extremely anxious that nothing inside the house should disturb the birds, and Keith Shackleton recalled that people were told to move 'like the hands of a clock', i.e. very slowly, in front of the windows overlooking the lake. Any disturbance of the birds from either inside the house or beyond usually resulted in a demand from Peter to know what had caused the problem.

On one famous occasion, the problem was not caused by humans. One Saturday, in particularly misty conditions, a Bewick's swan coming in to land on the lake misjudged the situation and crashed through the window into the dining room. The Scotts were away at the time and the first any of the avicultural staff knew of the incident was when the housekeeper came running through the corridor from the house to seek help. The duty warden managed to catch the bird, though not before it had significantly rearranged the ornaments and pictures in the room. Unfortunately, the swan had cut its leg quite badly on the glass and none of the staff vets were on duty. Fortunately, a visiting friend of a member of staff was a surgeon who offered to sew up the wound if a sterilised needle and thread could be provided. All went well, the swan recovered and was named Harold after its saviour. It was some while later that the bird was discovered to be female and was therefore renamed Lady Harold.

In 1960, floodlights had been installed to illuminate the lake after dark. The impetus for this was a visit by Prince Philip when he had agreed to become president of the Wildfowl Trust; Peter thought that a floodlit display of the birds on the lake would please the prince. Now he found another use for them. During the early years of the project, the swans would spend the day on the lake, be fed in the early evening, then fly out to roost on the Dumbles, the salt marsh adjoining the estuary of the River Severn. In January 1972, a fox got amongst the roosting birds out in the fields so Peter decided to put the floodlights on every evening and introduced later feeds to encourage the birds to roost in the secure surroundings of the lake, which lies within the fox-proof fence. The plan worked, and the swans reversed their routine, spending their days on the Dumbles and coming in to spend the night on what was now called Swan Lake, the lights being left on until around 10 p.m. Peter and Philippa developed the habit of feeding the swans and the other waterfowl on the lake in the evening from the windows at each side of the big picture window in the studio. It pleased Peter in particular that the swans became accustomed to coming up to the window to be fed and yet remained truly wild birds that would take flight immediately in any other situation where a person was close at hand – he regarded it as a perfect partnership between birds and man.

Some years into the project, a problem was discovered. Research by Eileen Rees and others indicated that under natural conditions, the timing of the swans' annual migration is primarily triggered by the increase of daylight as spring advances. At Slimbridge however, the artificial light from the floodlights was interfering with the birds' sense of daylight length, causing them to start their migration earlier than they would under natural daylight conditions. The additional evening feeds possibly exacerbated the problem by encouraging the birds to remain under the floodlights and be more wakeful at a time when they should have been resting. The extent of the problem became clear in January 1978 when there was a mass departure of swans far too early in the year. Some days later, eighteen swans from Slimbridge were seen in Germany where they encountered severe weather conditions, whereupon fourteen of them returned to Slimbridge to wait until conditions improved. Since the problem was discovered, the lights have been turned off at 6.30 p.m. each evening and the birds have re-established their normal migration timetable.

With all the information that was being accumulated, it was inevitable that research should be undertaken into the life of the birds away from Slimbridge. Where exactly in northern Russia did the swans that visited Slimbridge breed? How long did it take them to complete their migratory flight? Where did they stop off en route and what threats did they face during their long migration? Peter was determined that these and other questions should be answered. One immediate concern was how the swans would be recognised away from Slimbridge. It was unlikely that ornithologists or researchers in other countries would be able to identify individual birds, even if the paintings of face patterns were supplied to them. It was a member of the Slimbridge team, Malcolm Ogilvie, who in 1968 came up with the idea of using plastic leg rings with large letters and numbers printed on them which allowed individual birds to be identified at a distance. Known as darvic rings because of the type of plastic used, this has become a universally accepted way of marking waterfowl for easy identification. In order to fit the rings, the swans need to be trapped, so in 1969 a swan pipe was built at one end of the lake; the pipe is used in the same way as a duck decoy to catch the swans. Since it was built, over 1,800 swans have been caught and ringed and their health checked. Through the use of X-rays it was determined that approximately a third of the swans caught had lead shot embedded in their bodies, highlighting the risk that the birds faced from hunting along their migration routes. In difficult light it was hard to see if a bird was wearing a ring so for several seasons birds caught in the swan pipe had their tails dipped in a solution of picric acid. This acted as a yellow dye to highlight the fact that they had been ringed and drew ornithologists' attention to the birds that Peter and his team wanted to follow – the dye disappeared when the birds moulted their feathers the following summer.

Dafila's interest in the swans continued to grow. In 1970 she was given a grant of £200 to travel to the Netherlands to observe the swans on migration and see if she could identify any individual birds that had wintered at Slimbridge – at that time the exact routes and stopping places of the Bewick's swans while on migration were still unknown. Dafila was thrilled when she first found a swan she recognised on a lake in Holland and told her companions what the code on its leg ring would be. The Dutch ornithologists with her were sceptical of her ability to identify a swan from its bill pattern; only when the swan emerged from the water and they could read the code on its leg ring were they convinced, and impressed. In all, Dafila recognised five swans that had wintered at Slimbridge and was delighted that among them were one of her favourite pairs, Peasant and Gypsy. Some years later she would study the swans for her PhD; her subject was the social behaviour of wintering Bewick's swans.

Gradually, the life story of the Bewick's swan was pieced together and the summer breeding grounds identified. In 1978 Peter, Philippa and Dafila were all part of a joint British–Russian expedition to the Yamal Peninsula in northern Russia to study the ecosystem on the tundra, to make a film for Anglia Television's *Survival* series and to attempt to find Bewick's swans that had been ringed at Slimbridge. Though they saw a good number of Bewick's swans on the trip, they failed to see any that had previously been ringed. Peter was particularly thrilled however to find the nest of a pair of Bewick's swans that had evidently just hatched their young a couple of days before and then moved away from the nest area. For the first time in his life he was able to see for himself the other end of the journey, the place where the Bewick's swans spent their summer. Back in Moscow at the end of the trip, various presentations were made. Peter was given an ornamental ceramic samovar which sits to this day in the glass cupboard in the dining room in the house at Slimbridge. Some years later, Dafila was to make another trip to the Russian Tundra with Eileen Rees when they became the first Britons to visit the Pechora River since the nineteenth century. The Bewick's swan project continues to this day and is one of the longest continuous studies of a single species of bird anywhere in the world. Over 12,000 individual Bewick's swans have been identified and recorded since the project started.

The number of Bewick's swans is declining however. In Britain, numbers fell by 70 per cent between 2015 and 2021, due to a succession of milder winters in Eastern Europe opening up good winter feeding sites nearer to their summer breeding grounds. Across the whole of Western Europe, numbers have fallen by around 40 per cent since the mid-1990s. A new project is underway to determine the reason for this wider reduction in numbers and to find ways of halting and reversing the decline. Initial findings suggest that the problems are occurring mainly along the migration routes and that, apart from the loss of wetland habitats, the main concern is the death of birds as a result of collisions with power lines and wind turbines. Bewick's swans migrate at a safe height, but they need to land regularly during their long journey to feed and rest, and it is at these points that the risk of injury and death is greatest. By encouraging authorities to mark power lines and turbine blades and, where possible, to avoid siting them near sensitive locations, it is hoped that the danger can be minimised.

An additional problem is illegal shooting. The number of birds found to have lead shot embedded in them is currently around 33 per cent. In addition, swans ingest particles of lead shot along with the gravel they swallow to help them break down and digest their food. The lead is highly toxic and just a few pieces of shot can cause death. A WWT expedition in 2016 named 'Flight of the Swans' saw the Trust's Sacha Dench fly a microlight aircraft along the migration route from northern Russia to Slimbridge. En route, she talked to as many people as she could about the Bewick's swans and their decline. In Russia, the team discovered that local nomadic hunters were unaware that it was illegal to shoot the swans and that the birds were at risk as a result of their activities. It is hoped that through further consultation and negotiation and with the support of people along the migration flyway, the decline in numbers across Europe can be halted. It would be sad if these magnificent birds no longer found their way during the winter months to their safe haven under the walls of Peter's house at Slimbridge.

25

A Mysterious Diversion

An additional and unusual diversion for Peter in the 1960s and 1970s came from his interest in, and association with, the search for the Loch Ness monster. For centuries there had been tales of a mysterious monster lurking in the depths of the loch, but interest quickened in 1934 when surgeon George Spicer took a photograph of what appeared to be a creature with a long, arched neck and small head, silhouetted above the surface of the water. The photograph caused a sensation, and the possibility of a large creature living in the loch became headline news. In 1957, Constance Whyte published a book entitled *More than a Legend,* in which she compiled details of over 100 sightings of the monster. Her credentials were enhanced by her husband's occupation: he was manager of the Caledonian Canal. Her book suggested that whatever was or was not lurking beneath the waters, the matter deserved rigorous scientific investigation.

Constance Whyte's book was brought to Peter's attention in 1960 by naturalist Richard Fitter, who had written the first of the 'Collins Guides' *The Pocket Guide to British Birds* and *The Pocket Guide to Wild Flowers.* Peter was intrigued by the possibility that a large creature unknown to science could be living undetected in Britain. As far as he was concerned, any investigation would have to be conducted on rigorously scientific terms, but with the popular media spotlight on events at Loch Ness and all the ballyhoo that surrounded the mystery, this would not be easy. In addition, the Natural History Museum had set out its stall firmly on the side of the sceptics, declaring that no large creature could possibly exist in Loch Ness. Denys Tucker, a member of the museum staff who subsequently expressed the view that it was impossible to say with certainty that the creature did not exist, was fired from his post. Any scientist wishing to keep their reputation intact would need to tread carefully.

Peter shared the view of Denys Tucker. While none of the evidence amassed provided conclusive proof of the creature's existence, nobody had been able to prove that it didn't, and therefore the matter was worthy of careful exploration. Working with Richard Fitter, he assembled a small team of eminent scientists to look at the evidence. The group included the professors of zoology from Oxford and Cambridge Universities, Desmond Morris the animal behaviour expert and Geoffrey Matthews from the Wildfowl Trust. At their first meeting, all agreed that the matter was worth investigating, but such a study would require funding. In 1961 Peter, Richard Fitter, Constance Whyte and David James MP, were among a group of people who set up a charity called the Loch Ness Investigation Bureau, managing to secure initial funding of £500. A monitoring programme was set up, led by David James, and for nearly twenty years observation sites were set up along the shores of the loch each summer to watch for the monster and to photograph and film any sightings.

Peter and Philippa joined the teams on more than one occasion. Peter was able to combine his interest in the search with two of his favourite pastimes. In 1963, he and two colleagues flew gliders north from Gloucestershire to assist the search team. From high above the loch, the pilots were able to observe a much larger area than the watchers on the shore, and the clear waters allowed them to see a short distance below the surface. In 1977, during another search expedition, Peter donned a wet suit and scuba gear to explore the loch to get a sense of the creature's habitat from below the surface. Inevitably his involvement was seized upon by those on both sides of the argument who hoped that such a high-profile individual would ultimately support their position.

In 1971, an American team led by Dr Richard Rines arrived at the loch to undertake a search using underwater sonar equipment and cameras. One of a pair of photographs taken underwater in 1975 showed what appeared to be a large diamond-shaped object that looked like a flipper. This single photograph more than any other piece of evidence drew Peter towards the conclusion that there was indeed some creature living below the loch's surface. The image suggested a large plesiosaur-like animal, and Peter felt that steps should be taken at once to protect the creature should it be proved beyond doubt to exist. The best way to do this would be to give it a scientific name so that if it were caught it would be covered by laws that protect British wildlife. Peter and Richard Fitter therefore proposed a name for it: *Nessiteras rhombopteryx* meaning 'the creature living in Loch Ness with rhomboid-shaped flippers'. They wrote a paper for the scientific journal *Nature,* laying out the evidence and announcing the name. It didn't take long for someone to work out that the name was an anagram of 'Monster Hoax by Sir Peter S', though as Philippa was to point out later, if he had wanted to create such an anagram it would have included his full name and not just 'Sir Peter S'. Ultimately, of course, the monster was never found and the focus of the world's press moved on. Peter never regretted his stance on the matter, and happily his investigations did not tarnish his reputation among the scientific community.

26

Wide Blue Yonder

One consequence of Peter's many commitments was that he began to travel more and more frequently, either to meetings of the various conservation bodies in which he was involved, or in support of projects at the planning or development stage in countries across the globe. In 1956, the year Peter was elected to the IUCN executive council, he travelled to Africa for the first time and his eyes were opened to the extraordinary wildlife spectacle that was to be found in sub-Saharan Africa. As was often to be the case, Philippa travelled with him; on this trip she was returning to the continent where she was born. In Uganda they stayed at Paraa where Peter officially opened the Murchison Falls National Park. In 1961, they returned to Paraa where they stayed in the same lodge before setting off on a tour of national parks in East Africa. In Kenya, Peter opened Nakuru National Park which was host to a vast flock of lesser flamingos on Lake Nakuru. From there they continued to Nairobi National Park and then on to Tsavo and Amboseli National Parks both well known for work in elephant conservation. They would return to Tsavo in 1971, when they spent a couple of days with David and Daphne Sheldrick whose foundation had pioneered a programme to rear orphaned elephants and return them successfully to the wild, a programme that continues to support elephant conservation in eastern Kenya today. On this trip Philippa recalled that they saw Kilimanjaro '... in all its glory: a wonderful sight. I would have liked to climb it'. Echoes in her mind no doubt, of Alpine days before the war.

In 1962, on a trip to South Africa, Tanzania and Sudan, Peter and Philippa spent a few days visiting Philippa's childhood home,

Beauchamp, at Westminster in the Orange Free State. It is obvious from Peter's diary that this was an emotional visit for both of them; Philippa had clearly been deeply attached to the place and had been unhappy to leave it when she had been taken to England at the age of twelve. Photographs of the house and its location indicate why. The ranch-style house sits on a low hill surrounded by trees, looking across a wide plain to distant mountains. The relatively cramped confines of a Sussex home must have seemed like a poor exchange to someone used to living in such magnificent surroundings. Nevertheless, the visit was a very happy one, and Philippa took great enjoyment in showing Peter around her childhood home.

Over the years, Philippa had become an extremely accomplished photographer, a skill which proved useful to Peter on many occasions during their travels. Peter was experienced with a cine camera and painted regularly wherever he happened to be, but while he was able to use a still camera he couldn't match Philippa's photographic skills, so it was she who maintained a photographic record of their travels. In 1962, they published *Animals in Africa,* a book full of the photographs Philippa had taken on their African trips. In 1980, Philippa was elected an associate of the Royal Photographic Society.

There were further trips to Africa. In 1969, the Scotts took the children on holiday to Zambia, Peter's first visit to the country. The family did the kinds of things people do on holiday, visiting Victoria Falls for example, but Peter was still absorbed by the wildlife and his diary for the trip is full of descriptions of the birds and animals they encountered. As this was an unofficial trip there were no meetings, receptions or lectures; nevertheless, Peter couldn't travel completely incognito. Because they had made prior arrangements to visit various national parks, the locals in some cases went out of their way to put on a good show for the great man. Not many children turning up to visit a game reserve have to wait while their father inspects a line-up of rangers and watches a display of marching, which was the case at Livingstone. Two further trips to Zambia in 1974 and 1977 were very different in nature. On both occasions Peter met with President Kenneth Kaunda to discuss conservation issues in the country. Kaunda recognised the importance of African wildlife both to the well-being and to the economy of his country. He was to become a valuable ally in the region for Peter and the WWF.

As previously described, towards the end of 1956, Peter and Philippa set off on an extended trip to Australia, New Zealand and Papua New Guinea. In Australia, Peter had to fulfil his duties as chairman of the international jury for the sailing events at the Olympic Games in Melbourne, but they found time to travel round the region filming for *Faraway Look*. The Scotts were away for Christmas and spent the holiday in Queensland in Australia. While there, Peter went snorkelling for the first time and his life changed for ever. In his diary he wrote:

> For a part of these three days I have been in a new world. Nothing I have done in natural history in all my life has stirred me quite so sharply as my first experience of skin-diving on a coral reef ... The dramatic threshold which is crossed as soon as one first puts one's face mask below the surface is, to a naturalist nothing less than staggering in its impact ... I cannot see how I can escape from its lure. I am already an addict and I have not yet used an aqualung.

At the age of forty-seven, Peter had found an entire new world to explore and he launched himself into it with his usual headlong enthusiasm. After this revelatory introduction, he began to fit scuba diving excursions into his foreign trips whenever possible. Thousands of new species were suddenly parading before him and he lost no time in starting to identify them and to paint and draw them, initially using a waterproof drawing slate below the surface and thereafter in the pages of his diaries. Peter was always an inveterate maker of lists and when it came to coral fishes he was no exception. His idea of heaven was to put on an oxygen tank and weights, sink to the bottom of some coral sea and sit there for an hour or so sketching fish and making a list of the Latin names of all the species he saw on a waterproof slate. He would then return to the surface, photocopy the slate, wipe it clean, grab a new oxygen tank and return to the seafloor. In Peter's files at Slimbridge were found page after page of these photocopied lists, each interrupted by thumbnail drawings of particular species. In 1972, he provided the illustrations for a guidebook entitled: *Fishwatchers Guide to West Atlantic Coral Reefs*. On a trip to Malawi in 1977, Peter was able to indulge his passion for diving by snorkelling in Lake Malawi. He was fascinated by the profusion of freshwater fish species and reflected on the conditions that led to such a wide variety of similar species in such a small area, comparing the micro-habitats in the lake to the islands in the Galapagos, where a similar divergence in bird species had led to Darwin's understanding of natural selection.

The trip to the southern hemisphere at the end of 1956 continued into 1957 when the Scotts flew to Fiji and from there to Hawaii. At this point, Peter's successful breeding programme of the nene goose had been running for five years at Slimbridge and Peter was anxious to see the projects that had been established to save the geese on their native islands. In the event he was unimpressed by the breeding centre at Pohakuloa and wrote a report afterwards suggesting (doubtless diplomatically) some improvements that could be made. While on the island of Hilo, Peter, Philippa and Charles Lagus, the cameraman who was filming for a *Faraway Look* programme, stayed with businessman Herbert Shipman and his sisters. Shipman had been keeping a collection of nene geese since before the war and it had been with his assistance that Peter had been able to start the breeding programme at Slimbridge. Peter now met him for the first time and found him a likeable if somewhat eccentric individual. Peter recorded in his diary that he lived in a house hidden among dark and dank vegetation making for an oppressive atmosphere. The house was full of boxes of priceless Chinese pottery, bronzes and jade pieces and also, rather more worryingly, all the Christmas presents he had ever received still wrapped in the original paper. Despite these idiosyncrasies, the two got on well. Herbert Shipman would subsequently visit Slimbridge on a number of occasions, receiving a warm obituary in the Trust magazine after his death at the age of eighty-four in 1977.

Some of Peter's trips saw him return to haunts of younger days. In 1969, he returned to Iceland, the first visit since his previous trips in 1951 and 1953 when he was ringing pink-footed geese. The summer breeding grounds that he had visited were now threatened by the building of a hydro-electric dam and Peter felt compelled to throw his weight behind the campaign to prevent it. The trip brought him into contact once again with his old friend Finnur Gudmundsson. There was a busy round of meetings, a visit with the president, a public lecture in the presence of the prime minister and finally a television interview. When Peter left after two hectic days, he had no idea whether he had succeeded or not, but fifteen years later he was able to record that the dam had not been built and that numbers of the British population of pink-footed geese that breed in central Iceland had grown from 30,000 in 1951 to 100,000 in 1984.

In 1936 and 1937, on his trips to Hungary, Romania and the shores of the Caspian Sea, Peter had failed to find the large flocks of red-breasted geese that he knew to exist somewhere in the region. In 1969, returning from the eleventh IUCN general assembly in India, Peter took the opportunity to divert via Beirut and Istanbul to Bucharest to visit a new wintering ground for this elusive goose. Once again, at the age of sixty, he was back in the wild, chasing geese. The trip must surely have reminded him of those heady and carefree days before the war when he was free to follow the geese wherever they led him. In his diary for 12 December he wrote with boyish enthusiasm, 'What a day of days!' and it was for him one of those very special occasions, because he and his companion came across a flock of 4,000 red-breasted geese feeding with around 3,000 white-fronted geese, something he must have reconciled himself to never seeing in his lifetime. He returned in 1971, bringing Philippa with him. This time his intention was more serious; to undertake a population study of the red-breasted geese, to photograph them and, if possible, to persuade the Romanians to take an interest in protecting the wintering grounds to ensure the numbers remained healthy. The Scotts returned again in 1973 to make a film for Romanian television and again in 1977, when they witnessed a huge flock of more than 17,000 white-fronted and red-breasted geese, and Peter got closer to the red-breasted geese than he ever had before. In his diary he wrote:

Today is the first time we have been within 60 yards of wild Red-breasted Geese – and the sun was shining. Nothing can take away the breathless excitement of those few minutes before the birds became aware of our presence.

On some trips, Peter found himself working very closely with organisations that had the potential to be some of the world's worst polluters. In 1969, he was commissioned by British Petroleum to advise them on the best route for the new pipeline in Alaska which would bring oil from Prudhoe Bay on the north coast to Valdez on the south. Peter was enough of a pragmatist to understand that sometimes it is better to work with big businesses rather than against them. Clearly the pipeline was going to be built, and it was going to have to run through some fairly remote and pristine habitats. In such a case, given the opportunity to help mitigate the impact of the pipeline, Peter felt compelled to offer his assistance. In his diary he wrote:

> BP no doubt selected me as someone who knew something about Arctic ecology and was closely involved with conservation. I made it plain that I was not ready to be 'nobbled'. In the event the pipeline was laid, but the plans were substantially modified in favour of wildlife conservation as a result of my recommendations.

Conservationists might (and did) argue that the pipeline should never have been built in the first place; the *Exxon Valdez* disaster in 1989, when a tanker spilled eleven million gallons of crude oil into Prince William Bay, seemed to vindicate that position. Nevertheless, without Peter's contribution, important breeding grounds for a range of migratory species might have been lost or damaged.

27

The *Lindblad Explorer*

In 1968, Peter was introduced to a Swede, Lars Eric Lindblad, who had recently started a travel company through which he planned to offer luxurious wildlife viewing holidays in some of the remoter parts of the world. He had commissioned a new ship, the *Lindblad Explorer,* which would be luxuriously appointed and equipped with everything that was needed to operate in remote locations, including a number of zodiacs, small but sturdy rubber boats equipped with powerful outboard motors. The ship would accommodate ninety-two passengers plus her crew and because of her small size would be able to access areas which could not be reached by larger cruise vessels. In order to provide his customers with the best wildlife viewing experience possible, he planned to commission expert naturalists to join the cruises to talk about the wildlife and the landscapes they were seeing and help with bird and animal identification. Peter was invited to join a trip which would take passengers to the Falkland Islands, then onward to cruise down the western coast of the Antarctic Peninsula. At this point the *Lindblad Explorer* was still under construction so Lindblad chartered a Chilean boat called the *Navarino* for the trip. Philippa accompanied Peter and the trip was a success.

With the commissioning of the *Lindblad Explorer* began a new and exciting part of Peter and Philippa's life. In the early days, they were booked by Lindblad for specific trips but later were permitted to choose which expeditions they joined, though the Lindblad company then asked them to take on two trips back-to-back each time, to help in expedition planning. The trips were a delight for Peter. He found he was being paid to travel to some of the most remote and interesting parts of the globe, many of which he would never have accessed under his own steam, or through his work with conservation agencies. In addition, there were no meetings with government officials, no worries about fundraising, no television and radio interviews, just the opportunity to study wildlife and talk about it with like-minded individuals. There was, of course, the additional advantage that the people he was spending time with were almost exclusively well-heeled and enthusiastic about conservation, and there were no doubt many opportunities to make connections or plant ideas in minds that would bear fruit later on. There were also occasions when Peter could use a Lindblad trip as a springboard to get to conferences or meetings on the other side of the world, thereby reducing the cost of the air travel that would have accrued had he travelled directly from home.

Philippa clearly loved the expeditions on the *Lindblad Explorer*. As with Peter, the trips gave her an opportunity to escape the high-pressure world which she shared with him, but her role onboard was slightly different. She, of course was not called upon to give talks to the passengers, though by now her identification skills had been honed on her many trips accompanying Peter round the world, so she was able to help in that area too. In her second autobiography, *So Many Sunlit Hours*, she wrote:

> … Peter and I were totally hooked on travel with the Lindblad Explorer. It was not just the ship, it was the exciting places she visited. Each trip was an expedition, with wild life as the core interest and the places off the beaten track. There was no doubt that Peter was a great asset as lecturer and it was my job to be nice to the passengers. That was, in fact, very good for me as I am not by nature a tolerant person.

In 1972, Peter and Philippa joined a Lindblad cruise to Norway, Spitzbergen, Greenland and Iceland and were joined on the trip by Keith Shackleton and Roger Tory Petersen as fellow lecturers. Their son Falcon was also able to join them as he had just finished school. During this trip, Peter and Philippa were pleased to be able to spend their twenty-first wedding anniversary in northern waters once again. The expedition started with a journey up the entire length of Norway's Atlantic coast to North Cape from where they headed west to Bear Island and then on to Spitzbergen. On Spitzbergen, Peter was delighted to sight a pair of barnacle geese at their nest site with three goslings. This was of significance because all of the barnacle geese that breed on Spitzbergen winter on the Solway Firth in Britain, so these adult geese were birds which would have visited the Wildfowl Trust reserve at Caerlaverock the previous winter. In Greenland he experienced the same elation when they sighted several hundred pink-footed geese in flight across a fjord. Peter wrote:

> The picture was utterly memorable. Recent snow had powdered the stratified mountains. The geese were 10 to 20 yards high above the sea ice – much of it showing glorious deep blues and greens. It was fascinating to think that these birds knew the Long Ridden at Caerlaverock, St Cerfs Island, Dupplin Loch and the gasometer at Southport.

Later on in the trip, they reached Reykjavik in Iceland, where they met up with their old friend Finnur Gudmundsson. Their arrival coincided with the famous world chess championship between Spassky and Fischer, so Finnur took Peter and Philippa that evening to see the great men playing. They were also able to show Falcon the former British Embassy building where they had been married in 1951. During this expedition, the ship reached the most northerly point ever achieved by a passenger ship at that time, 82° 12' north.

Many of the Lindblad expeditions they took part in were to tropical destinations, particularly in the Pacific; this meant that Peter could indulge in his passion for skin-diving and tropical fish. In 1973, the year after the trip to Spitzbergen and Greenland, the couple joined a Lindblad expedition to various groups of islands in the South Pacific. The *Lindblad Explorer* was the first cruise ship to reach the Marquesas Islands, where they visited the grave of Paul Gauguin. Arriving on Rarotonga in the Cook Islands, Peter was reminded of his father as it was here that his mother received news of his death while en route to be reunited with him in New Zealand. In Tonga, Philippa purchased a piece of Tapa cloth made from banana leaves, which still hangs over the door to the studio at the house at Slimbridge. During their travels, the Scotts bought a number of other local craft items which also remain on display in the house, along with the small model of the *Lindblad Explorer* which sits on top of Peter's bureau.

One of the most extensive double trips occurred in 1976 and took them initially from Prince Rupert on the west coast of Canada to Japan, then with a second group of passengers from Japan to Bali. Another two trips, in 1974 and 1976, visited the Galapagos Islands, where Peter was able to renew his fascination with their unique array of species. The last Lindblad trip, in 1986, when Peter was seventy-seven, almost ended in disaster. The voyage was on a chartered Yugoslav ship called the *Ambassador,* on board which the Scotts were assigned a small cabin without a window in the bowels of the ship. Initially, things went well, with some wonderful days' diving in the Maldives. Off Reunion however, they ran into a severe storm. Philippa recalled the chaos in their cabin as the wardrobe door fell off, the cold tap in the bathroom turned itself on and there was a continuous and ominous banging noise from the hull. The ship turned back and was fortunate to secure a berth at Reunion, where they stayed for several days. The noise turned out to have been the anchor which had broken loose and was crashing against the ship's hull.

Given the length of some of their trips, one might wonder how they managed to pack for such a wide range of weather conditions. The above trip for example, took them from the far north of Canada, across the equator and on to Bali. On another occasion, they included the Antarctic and Hawaii in the same trip. For anyone who has ever dithered over what clothes to take on even a fairly straightforward holiday, these journeys would represent an almost impossible challenge. With Peter, the answer, as so often, lay in meticulous planning. The shelves of the cupboard in his bedroom at the house at Slimbridge testify to this. A series of wide drawers stretching almost from floor to ceiling are still labelled according to their contents: 'socks, shirts, short-sleeved shirts, batik shirts, more batik shirts' – nothing was left to chance.

Throughout all of these trips, Peter would sketch and draw whatever he saw and wrote extensive notes about everything in his diaries. Philippa always had her camera to hand, and when Peter came to publish his *Travel Diaries* they were beautifully illustrated with his paintings and Philippa's photographs. Over the years they made twenty-six trips with Lindblad, each of them fascinating, each of them different. Peter's manuscript travel diaries extended to seventy-four volumes while Philippa amassed in excess of 45,000 images during her life with Peter, many of which were taken during their travels together. Each of those twenty-six trips would, for ordinary mortals, be the trip of a lifetime; Peter and Philippa were indeed fortunate to make so many wonderful journeys together. Small wonder he described himself in *The Eye of the Wind* as 'the luckiest of men'.

28

South

Throughout most of his life, Peter never envisioned visiting Antarctica. His father's extraordinary achievements and his heroic death in 1912 set Peter firmly against a life of exploration and fostered a determination to avoid the southern continent at all costs. Had he followed in his father's footsteps, he knew that however successful he might be, his life and his achievements would always be inextricably linked with those of his illustrious parent. As he wrote in his diary:

> From an early age I had been determined to make my way in life without trading on my father's reputation as a famous explorer. As I saw it, his achievements in the Antarctic precluded me from going there, and indeed from becoming knowledgeable about the continent and its history.

His determination to avoid any comparison with his father was absolute. In 1953 he was invited to unveil a plaque at the Royal Hotel in Cardiff where his father stayed before setting out for Antarctica on the *Terra Nova* in 1910. The plaque was to be placed in the room where Peter's father dined on the last night before setting sail. Peter declined and his secretary wrote on his behalf:

> Mr Scott ... has asked me to thank you very much for the invitation, but he does feel that he is not really the appropriate person, and says it might even be embarrassing for him. He says he feels someone not connected with the family would be more appropriate. I do hope you will understand this.

Peter remarked more than once that the Arctic was much richer in wildlife than the southern continent, which he was quite content to leave to others to explore. Just as early navigators in the Mediterranean would not pass beyond the Gates of Hercules into the unknown, Tierra del Fuego at the tip of South America became Peter's personal 'Ne Plus Ultra', the place beyond which he would go no further.

Antarctica would not leave Peter alone however. In 1948, Ealing Studios made a film about Robert Falcon Scott. Peter assisted with the production, visiting the set of *Scott of The Antarctic* on several occasions and welcoming the actress Diana Churchill, who played his mother, to his home in Edwardes Square when she was preparing to play the part. Peter received two tickets for the Royal Command Performance but was unable to attend as he was in America, so Philippa and Ray Gregorson (formerly Aickman) went instead. In her first autobiography, *Lucky Me*, Philippa recalled that at the time, velvet chokers were at the height of fashion, so Jane Howard made one for her to wear at the premiere. John Mills played Scott, and the cast included Peter's friend James Robertson Justice. The score was composed by Ralph Vaughan Williams.

The continent nudged its way back into his life in 1952, when Peter was invited to attend the annual 'swan-upping' ceremony on the River Thames at which swans are marked and divided between the Queen and the two livery companies entitled to own them. Also present at the event was the conductor Sir John Barbirolli, who told Peter that Vaughan Williams was converting his score for *Scott of the Antarctic* into a symphony, his seventh. He invited Peter to attend the premiere. This took place on 14 January 1953, shortly before Peter left for his South American trip. Peter was introduced to the composer, and after the performance Peter, Vaughan Williams, Barbirolli and the leader of the orchestra went to dinner with their wives. Peter wrote afterwards that he had not been a particular fan of Vaughan Williams prior to the concert but he found the music incredibly moving, doubtless because of the associations with his father. Like everyone who met him, Vaughan Williams was charmed by Peter and the composer came to visit Slimbridge from time to time. He was a regular at the Three Choirs Festival which was held every three years in Gloucester and confided with Peter that he had a dislike of Edward Elgar's *Dream of Gerontius*, which features regularly at the festival. To avoid having to sit through it he would come and see the ducks at Slimbridge or, if wet, go to the cinema.

Over the years, as Peter's career as a conservationist and artist developed and matured, his position on Antarctica began to change. He no longer feared comparison with his father; the danger of being thought to have used his reputation for his own advancement had passed. Through his own endeavours, Peter had achieved success and recognition in his own field, and his refusal to engage with the southern continent came to seem increasingly pointless. So it was that in 1966, when the BBC proposed making a film about Peter travelling to Antarctica to visit the scenes of his father's combined triumph and disaster, he decided to put his reticence aside and agreed to participate. Having made the decision, the gates to the great pristine wilderness in the southern hemisphere were unlocked for him – 'Plus Ultra' at last.

The team included BBC producer Christopher Ralling and cameraman Charles Lagus, with whom Peter and Philippa had travelled to Australia and New Zealand for *Faraway Look* in 1956. Philippa was not invited to accompany the team, as the bases where they would be staying were, at the time, limited to males only. The team flew from New Zealand to McMurdo in Antarctica in a Hercules transport aircraft, covering in just over eight hours a trip that would have taken his father a month. Peter's first journey to Antarctica took place fifty-four years after his father's death, during which time the situation in Antarctica had changed completely and forever. The alien world of extreme cold, ice and frost had been to some extent tamed by the presence of scientific bases which were now manned throughout the year. Yet fifty-four years seems hardly any time at all; this book is being written in 2020, exactly fifty-four years after Peter in turn made his journey south.

Peter was disappointed with the American settlement at McMurdo which he thought had been built without any sense of aesthetics, all the more frustrating given its position, surrounded on all sides by magnificent scenery. As a counterpoint was the knowledge that his father's hut from the 1902 *Discovery* expedition lay several hundred yards away at Hut Point. On a visit to the hut he found it in a derelict condition, with little remaining to remind him how it must have been when occupied during that first expedition. The New Zealand-run Scott Base he found more appealing than McMurdo, with more attractive buildings and lacking the sense that it had been dropped in from somewhere in the mid-west of North America. From the Post Office here, Peter took great pleasure in posting a letter to his son Falcon, linking three generations of Scotts with the Antarctic. The film crew were now hard at work, and Peter confessed that he found some of what they filmed rather artificial, or as he called it, phoney. The team would drive out across the ice for a few miles, make camp and pretend that they had been travelling for weeks across the wilderness – doubtless this would fuel Peter's fears of being seen to be pretending to be his father, the very idea that had kept him from Antarctica all his life. Nevertheless, he accepted that they needed to show what it was like to make a long journey in such hostile terrain, so he buttoned up his sensitivities and got on with the filming.

More enjoyable was a trip out to a research camp at Cape Crozier, where his friend Bill Sladen was conducting research into Adélie penguins. Left for the day in the camp, surrounded by penguins and other birds, Peter was reminded of his summer on the Perry River in Canada in 1949 and felt suddenly more at ease. Back at base, Peter phoned home. He recalled in his diary that when Philippa answered the phone and was invited to take a reversed charge call from Antarctica, her first response was to ask how much it was going to cost. She did accept the call, and Peter was delighted to learn that for the first time there were more than 100 Bewick's swans on the lake outside his window at home in Slimbridge.

Then, to the South Pole, again in a Hercules transport plane. The team stayed at what was then called South Pole Station, sleeping in the sick bay, as there was then no accommodation for visitors. Peter took photographs with his Instamatic camera, a very basic point-and-shoot device of the kind used for holiday snaps. To his credit, the photos he took with this simple camera are rather good. They show a basic arrangement of huts and sheds that would be unrecognisable to an inhabitant of the Amundsen-Scott Station at the South Pole today. A walk was taken to the Pole itself, some 400 metres away from the base. Numerous photos were taken, Peter again feeling self-conscious about all the fuss. He comforted himself with the thought that his father's party too had stood on the same spot taking photographs of themselves fifty-four years and four days previously. Looking around the Pole at the flat featureless landscape that stretched to the horizon on all sides, Peter reflected on the fact that after taking his photographs, his father faced an 800-mile walk across this most inhospitable of landscapes to reach safety. Peter had a walk of 400 yards. Back underground in the base, he had time to reflect on what his father would have thought about the facility in which he was sitting. In his diary he wrote:

> Since then the place has altered little on the surface, but underneath is the snug warm camp with all its machinery. I wonder if even in his most optimistic mood my father could have imagined flush toilets and computers, generators, and Club 90 under the snow at the pole. Surely not. The circumstances have changed too much. A plane will take us in less than three hours to Hut Point. No gnawing doubts about the lateness of the season, no appalling disappointment at Amundsen's changed plans, at his priority at the Pole, at the lost race, at the vanished daydreams. No dietetic problems with scurvy beginning to take its effect. No fears for personal survival.

Of one thing he felt sure: his father would have been delighted that there was now a permanent base at the Pole with scientists from many nations working together on projects which could safeguard the environment for generations not yet born. This was the kind of science that Peter most respected.

The day after they got back from the Pole, they took a helicopter up to Cape Evans to visit Peter's father's hut from the *Terra Nova* expedition in 1912. In contrast to the derelict state of the 1902 hut at Hut Point, the Cape Evans hut had a much more evocative feel. Many of the original contents remained, with tins of food, photographic supplies in the dark room and other bits of equipment stacked about. To Peter, the interior was familiar from the famous photograph taken by Herbert Ponting of his father sat at his desk. Now, Peter sat there in his place, writing his diary. At last he was able to let his true feelings show. He wrote, 'I do find it strange and rather moving to be sitting here in this alcove, having lived for so much of my life with the photo of my father sitting here.' Herbert Ponting had, in fact, taken a number of photographs inside the hut; what Peter didn't mention in his diary was that in one of the photographs, visible on the wall behind his father, is a photograph of his wife holding the young Peter in her arms. A copy of Ponting's photograph sits on Philippa's bureau in the house at Slimbridge today.

It is impossible to know what Peter expected before he set foot in the hut, but certainly he was moved by the experience and perhaps felt that a ghost had, at last, been laid to rest. The hut was and is, set in the most beautiful surroundings, with views of Mount Erebus at the centre of Ross Island. At 12,448 feet, Erebus is the southernmost active volcano in the world. On the wall of his studio in Slimbridge is a photograph of his father with the volcano in the background which would have been taken very close to where Peter now found himself standing.

The following day, back at McMurdo, they climbed Observation Hill behind the 1902 *Discovery* Hut. On the summit stands a cross carved with Tennyson's words: 'To strive, to seek, to find and not to yield', beneath which are carved the names of the expedition members who perished. This was the lookout post where, in 1912, members of the expedition waited in vain for a sight of the party returning from the South Pole. Before they left for home, Peter had time to write his final thoughts on the huts:

> Altogether, my father's hut at Cape Evans is an extremely beautiful place, and the old hut itself is of great interest. Somehow however the preservation of these huts is a new thought and the result is a new kind of museum piece. But it bears as much relation to the hut when it was in use as a stuffed bird does to a living bird – and is to the same extent depressing.

Nevertheless, he cannot fail to have been moved by his visit and to have seen the places so irrevocably entwined with his father's story.

Philippa recorded that two years later, in 1968, when Peter was first invited to join a cruise to the Antarctic as joint expedition leader for the Lindblad travel company, he was initially doubtful about taking up the offer but asked Philippa if she would like to go. She would indeed like to go, and Lars Lindblad was happy for her to join the team, so the decision was made. As previously mentioned, the boat was a chartered Chilean vessel called the *Navarino* as at this time the *Lindblad Explorer* was still under construction. Clearly the *Navarino* had seen better days, since on her previous trip south for Lindblad she had developed a steering fault off Cape Horn and had to return to port. Peter's friend, the ornithologist Roger Peterson, was the resident naturalist on board on that earlier voyage. Peter's party of around thirty people flew to Punta Arenas in southern Chile, where Philippa found herself very much in demand as she attempted to sort out various problems resulting from the convergence of their party with the one that had turned back off Cape Horn. Peter and his fellow leader, John Cadwallader, led a number of birdwatching excursions around Punta Arenas before they set sail, first to the Falkland Islands and then across to Antarctica to sail down the chain of islands along the coast of the Antarctic peninsula.

Peter's previous comparison between the wildlife in the Arctic and the Antarctic was forgotten, as they cruised past ice floes and islands alive with seals (four different species) penguins (three species) skuas, petrels, gulls and all manner of other animal and bird life. Peter was in his element, talking to the guests, leading parties ashore, painting and sketching and sharing with Philippa the magnificent scenery everywhere along the route. Peter's diary and Philippa's autobiography tell slightly different tales of the trip however. While Peter simply describes the journey and the birds and animals they saw, Philippa also describes the problems they faced keeping a mixed group of British and American passengers happy. There were differences of opinion about the itinerary, and people nearly came to blows when Peter issued an edict, not unreasonably asking the passengers and crew not to pick up young birds. Some American ladies were apparently insistent about cuddling penguin chicks. Philippa seems to have taken all this in her stride, though she did confess to taking herself off on a walk alone one day, simply to get away from the passengers.

At their most southerly point before turning north once more, they crossed the Antarctic Circle, the first passenger ship to do so on this side of the continent. The ship then sailed north across Drake Passage, returning up the Beagle Channel in beautiful weather to Punta Arenas in Chile. Peter was converted; he had fallen in love with this wild, remote, beautiful land which had for so long been an enigma to him.

The one location which Peter had not visited in Antarctica was, of course, the site of the tent in which his father and two of his colleagues perished. After the tent and the bodies had been found, they were left on the ice cap to make their slow but inexorable journey towards the sea. Peter had discussed the matter with a glaciologist at McMurdo in 1966, who told him that by then, the tent and the bodies would be fourteen miles to seaward of their original position and fifty feet below the surface of the ice. In 1968, the BBC decided to film a biography of the Norwegian skier Tryggve Gran. Gran had been a member of the 1912 *Terra Nova* expedition, his main role being teaching the British team members how to ski. When Scott failed to return from the Pole,

Gran was one of an eleven-man expedition which set out to look for the Polar party and eventually found their remains. A twelve-foot snow cairn was built over the tent and its occupants and a cross made of skis raised above it. For the return journey, Gran wore Scott's skis, reasoning that if Scott couldn't complete the journey, at least his skis would. The head of BBC2 at the time was David Attenborough, who felt that Peter should have the opportunity to see the film before it was transmitted, so a dinner was arranged with Gran and Frank Debenham, the only other remaining member of the expedition. Afterwards they watched the film. As Gran explained how he drew back the flap of the tent to discover the remains of the three men inside, David glanced at Peter who was quietly weeping.

In 1971, Peter and Philippa were invited to join another trip to the Antarctic, this time to the Ross Sea area where Peter had been in 1966. Dafila, who was recovering after an operation for appendicitis, joined them on the trip. Peter looked forward to showing them both his father's hut at Cape Evans. Peter's friend, Keith Shackleton, was on board as a fellow lecturer. This voyage was in the *Lindblad Explorer*, the little ship in which they made so many wonderful trips in different parts of the world. *Lindblad Explorer* sailed from New Zealand in February 1971 and after stopping at a couple of islands, arrived ten days later at Cape Evans on Ross Island, just off the Antarctic mainland. As they had not been able to get the key to the hut, which was kept at Scott Base, they were given permission to break in. Peter, Philippa and Dafila were allowed in first to share a few minutes alone before the rest of the party came in, then:

> ... the flashes started to flicker and the shutters to click ... Even the milling LE passengers could not spoil this enchanted place which had seen so many moods, in which men had been happy and bored, hopeful and heartbroken ... The aura of the Cape Evans has a quality which does not (at least for me) pervade the other huts to anything like the same degree.

Philippa found the visit to the hut 'moving and unforgettable, one of the very special experiences of my life'. Again, later, on Observation Hill, she was deeply moved by the thought of the expedition members waiting in vain and the little tent lost out in the frozen wastes to the south: 'the cold, the loneliness, the desolation, the beauty and the enormity of it all ...' The *Lindblad Explorer* sailed to Cape Royds where they visited Ernest Shackleton's Hut, which dates from his expedition in 1908. In the hut is a copy of the *Illustrated London News* with a full-page portrait of Herbert Asquith captioned 'the new Prime Minister'. Peter noted, 'I showed it to Dafila as "one of your grandmother's boyfriends and Kip's great grandfather."' (Peter's daughter Nicola had married Kip Asquith in 1963.)

Peter, once again, found himself analysing his feelings about the huts and his father's place in history. Back in 1966, he had visited his father's hut at Cape Evans alone, apart from the film crew; now he was with a group of tourists who were pointing their cameras in every direction and inspecting the tins and supplies left behind, imbued as they now were with a sense of historical significance. When did a tin of potatoes stop being an abandoned item of foodstuff and become an artefact? Did the sense that the hut was becoming a museum piece bother him? He had a long conversation with Keith Shackleton about it and wrote his conclusions in his diary:

> Of course it is impossible to ignore the influence of the explorers of the heroic age. For me the personal connection is almost cloying. I cannot read the diary messages and last entry without tears. Observation Hill and the Cape Evans Hut (and last time the South Pole) are the nearest topographical links with the diary. But even these places seem remote from the reality of 60 years ago. I suppose I am not cut out to be a historian. Or is it that I am leaning over backwards not to be inundated by the fulsome sentiment of the tourists? It is no good to pretend that I am not moved – and perhaps most of all by being able to show these lovely places to my beloved Phil and our darling Dafila. The places themselves are so real, so unmushy, so fantastically beautiful. Nothing can spoil them, but I am perhaps too busy trying to make sure nothing does. If that gives the impression that I am unmoved by these places then that is quite a false impression. But what is of most interest to me is what man is doing here now.

Peter was a man in whom the natural reserve of his generation – the dislike of fuss and the expression of sentiment – was often to the fore, but reading the above passage, nobody could doubt his true feelings, nor fail to admire his ability to express them in so candid a fashion.

In 1978, Peter and Philippa found themselves back on the *Lindblad Explorer* heading once more into Antarctic waters. Once again they were joined by Keith Shackleton as a fellow lecturer. This time they followed a similar route to that taken in the *Navarino* on their first Lindblad trip in 1968. With them on board were Prince Bernhard of the Netherlands and members of the WWF 1001 Club, all millionaires and major benefactors of the organisation. Also on board was Tenzing Norgay who, with Edmund Hillary, had conquered Everest in 1953. Unlike on previous trips, the weather was clear and calm and they experienced near perfect conditions as they travelled through the Lemaire Passage. Later, the ship was temporarily stuck in sheet ice, and the passengers and crew were able to descend onto the ice, drink hot punch, have a game of football and pretend to play golf when someone produced a golf club and ball (coloured red).

During this trip, Peter and Philippa had opportunities to engage in pastimes close to their hearts. Peter went skin-diving to look for penguins underwater, no small feat considering the temperature would have been close to freezing and he was sixty-nine years of age at the time. At Hope Bay, Philippa joined a small group with Tenzing to ascend a nearby mountain, Mount Flora. Though only 1,750 feet in height, this represented something of a challenge given the icy conditions, and they were forced to turn back before reaching the top, but Philippa was doubtless thrilled to make the ascent in the company of one of the most famous names in the history of mountaineering. Philippa wrote, 'That evening I had dinner alone with Peter, followed by dancing – what a happy day!' On this trip they once again visited the Falkland Islands and Philippa took advantage of the duty-free status of the Islands to purchase a new Olympus camera as recommended to her by Eric Hosking. The camera proved much lighter than her existing Nikon, and she was to use it for several years thereafter.

In 1979, Peter and Philippa made their final trip to Antarctica, again on the *Lindblad Explorer*. En route, they visited the Falkland Islands once more, where Peter had arranged to meet with a group of conservationists who had gathered from various parts of the world to discuss the developing threat to wildlife on the islands, foremost of which was the impact of the thousands of sheep, cattle and rabbits that had been imported in the nineteenth century. A Swiss benefactor had promised £40,000 as a pump-priming donation if some form of concerted initiative could be established. The group took a walk to see something of the problem for themselves. During this outing, Peter suggested the formation of a conservation foundation modelled on the Charles Darwin Foundation in the Galapagos Islands, which he had helped to bring into being. Fortuitously, one of the visiting conservationists was also a lawyer, so Peter asked him how long he thought it would take to set something up, imagining a period of months, if not years. 'We could do it today,' was the response, provided they had six people willing to sign the foundation document. So the agreement was drawn up that afternoon and signed, bringing into existence The Falkland Islands Conservation Foundation, of which Peter would become chairman when its office was established in London. The organisation that was born in a day soon began work on the ground, its activities only briefly interrupted by the invasion of the islands by Argentina three years later.

In contrast to the previous year, the weather in Antarctic waters was terrible. They were unable to refuel at McMurdo as planned so had to sail onwards with one engine to conserve fuel, spending twelve days at sea in atrocious conditions. It is worth bearing in mind that the *Lindblad Explorer* was similar in size to a modern cross-channel ferry, far removed from the slab-sided behemoths that currently trundle people round the Caribbean. Seas broke over the ship, and the pressure dropped to the lowest ever recorded in the Ross Sea, 939.61 mb, compared with an average of 990 mb for the region. Nevertheless, they were able to make landings at various points and cruise along a third of the Antarctic coastline before turning north to New Zealand. Once again, they visited Peter's father's hut at Cape Evans and were relieved to find it unchanged from their previous visit in 1971.

After leaving the *Lindblad Explorer* in New Zealand, Peter and Philippa flew to Hawaii prior to returning home. Here they had an encounter with whales that couldn't have been more different from their recent experience in the Antarctic, where they had seen minke whales being slaughtered. Peter had been invited to spend a few days with conservationist Dr Sylvia Earle on the island of Maui where research was ongoing into humpback whales which are plentiful round the island at that time of year. Their visit coincided with that of an IMAX film crew who were making a documentary about the whales. Peter and Philippa were invited to accompany them on their chartered boat. On that particularly memorable day, Peter and Philippa went into the water behind the film crew, being careful to keep out of shot.

Snorkelling on the surface, they witnessed several pods of whales at very close quarters in extremely clear blue water. Peter wrote of one encounter:

> Phil broke off to photograph them with her Nikonos. I swam closer as they came directly towards us, crossed slowly ahead of us and rolled slightly away from us to take a good look. I gazed into the eye of the nearer whale – it may have been 20 feet away – and the end of the pectoral fin was a good deal closer. As they passed ahead of Phil I saw the eye move from me to her and a crescent of white showed just behind the brown iris ... I am sure that it has to be one of the most stirring experiences of my life and to have shared the thrill with Phil was the very best part. Talk about euphoria – we were walking on air.

In the first published volume of Peter's *Travel Diaries* are two delightful watercolours of the whales painted at the time. Later Peter commemorated the event in a much larger oil painting, equally beautiful, a copy of which hangs in the hallway of the house at Slimbridge. In it can be seen two humpback whales, while above them, on the surface, swim two tiny figures in wet suits, one holding a camera. The title of the painting? *Self-portrait with wife and Humpbacks.*

29

Drawing and Drawing and Drawing

Throughout his life, as a backdrop to all the other endeavours in which he became involved, Peter's art was a constant; hardly ever would a day go by when he didn't pick up a pencil or a brush, however fleetingly. Peter's love of painting came early. In an interview he recalled his artistic beginnings, living with his mother in the house on Buckingham Palace Road and spending his time endlessly 'drawing and drawing and drawing'. It was inevitable, given his passion for nature, instilled by his mother at his father's behest, that Peter would concentrate on painting the natural world. There was no doubt that he had a natural talent and was certainly encouraged by his mother from an early age. Kathleen, as an artist herself, had very particular ideas about the development of artistic talent:

> My mother did not believe that art could or should be taught. There were perhaps some complicated techniques in art where time could be saved if you did not have to learn everything by trial and error. But the idea that anyone should be taught that there was a right and a wrong way to compose a picture, right and wrong combinations of colour, right and wrong ways of applying paint – this was to her a heresy, and liable to stifle the original artist, and perhaps disastrously influence the whole future of his art.

Nevertheless, she made no objection when, after finishing his degree at Cambridge, he went on to study fine art, first at the Academy of Fine Art in Munich and then, for two years, at the Royal Academy in London.

His acceptance by the Royal Academy was partly down to his mother's influence. She had invited the Keeper of the Royal Academy, Walter Russell, to lunch, during which he had admired a number of Peter's drawings on the wall, possibly placed there to achieve exactly that outcome. How far Peter's studies at these institutions improved his painting technique is hard to tell, particularly since he spent so much time away from his studies. What cannot be denied is that the quality of his painting gradually improved over time. As his work progressed, he developed a style of painting that was different from anything that had gone before. Painters admired by Peter included the Swede Bruno Liljefors and watercolourist Frank Southgate, who had died in the First World War, though neither of these men, Peter felt, understood their subjects quite in the way he did. For Peter, his connection with the birds he painted was almost visceral. The endless days and nights he spent, out in all weathers watching his subjects, gave him an instinctive understanding of how the birds looked in flight and at rest. One other painter who gave Peter advice was the remarkable bird artist Archibald Thorburn who, at the age of eighty-one, visited Peter at his home at Leinster Corner to view his work and offer advice.

During the winter of 1932 to 1933, much of it spent at the duck decoy at Borough Fen, Peter produced around forty paintings of geese and ducks in flight and these formed the body of work for his first one-man exhibition at the Ackermann Gallery in Bond Street, London. If Peter's talent and his developing style were uniquely his, his introduction to the world of the professional artist was largely a result of his mother's connections both in the art world and in society in general, as well as her determination to push him to make sure he succeeded. Kathleen herself had had several exhibitions at the Ackermann Gallery, and it was she who approached the owners to invite them to offer Peter a one-man exhibition. Knowing full well the importance of publicity, Kathleen hung a selection of Peter's new paintings in her living room and invited a cross-section of society to a drinks party. Thus cabinet ministers, ambassadors, captains of industry, a variety of artists and, of course, the owners of the gallery, were able to admire the paintings, together with some of her sculptures, over the canapés. The reactions were universally favourable, and Peter was offered the show. At this point in his life Peter was disinterested in the business side of things and was in Scotland when the party was held. His mother knew he would need to paint some additional works for the exhibition so phoned him the next day. Given a deadline of sixty days, he returned three weeks later with around a dozen new paintings. This was not a unique event. In 1936, while working at the lighthouse, Peter painted five paintings in four days and forty-eight in under six weeks.

The first exhibition was a complete success; all but half a dozen of the works were sold. Peter now knew for the first time that painting could become more than a passion: it had become a means of earning money. One result of his success was that he began to receive commissions for paintings. This was a completely new departure and one that required some adjustment. Until now, Peter had painted purely for pleasure. He painted what he wanted and when he wanted. If people wanted to buy his works at an exhibition that was an extra bonus. Now, the purchaser would be in control, and if Peter took the commission, he would have to paint what the client wanted and agree a time when it would be ready. In addition, the client might feel free to make suggestions for alterations while the painting was still in work. All these requirements would inevitably restrict the freedom he had enjoyed until now. One of his first commissions after the show was for a large painting, eight feet by five, considerably larger than anything he had done before. He was nervous about starting it and was still staring at a blank canvas when his client, assuming the painting was half-finished, said he was coming to see it the following week. In desperation, Peter got started but having left far too little time before the viewing, he enlisted his mother to paint the reedbeds which occupied the foreground of the painting. In the end, the client was very happy and the painting was completed.

Working to a deadline was always a problem for Peter, particularly in later years when he became so busy with his conservation work and other duties. Nevertheless, commissions became extremely important, particularly in times of financial hardship. Peter would sometimes offer a painting to a benefactor of the Trust or to someone else who had provided a service that would be expensive to repay. On one occasion, Peter promised someone two paintings. The first was completed fairly quickly but the second was forgotten amongst a welter of other priorities. In due course the recipient gently reminded Peter that he owed him a painting. He had been wondering, he said, what he might choose; he couldn't make up his mind between a painting of swans in flight or red grouse being driven over a moor. By return, Peter wrote to say that a painting of swans would be a much better choice, and he completed it shortly afterwards. Had the new owner insisted on the red grouse picture, the commission would have taken twice as long to get right whereas he could, by this time, have painted *Swans in Flight* standing on his head. Peter frequently found it difficult to schedule commissioned work among all his other commitments. He wrote about the difficulties in *Observations of Wildlife*:

> If the client is persistent and lucky the picture may be forthcoming within two years, even though it only takes three days to paint. Ideally I like to paint two or three such paintings from which the client may choose. This gives two spare paintings which can go to exhibitions or be acquired directly from my studio.

Other commissioned work was more commercial in nature, for example the set of cigarette cards of paintings of waterfowl that he prepared for Player's cigarettes. In 1966, working with other artists, Peter created a series of paintings for the Shell calendar which that year featured bird life in Britain with special emphasis on wetlands. Such commissions not only raised urgently needed funds but also brought paintings of waterfowl into the homes of hundreds of thousands of people who might otherwise never see them, raising awareness about the birds among the general public.

After the first solo exhibition, Peter went on to have another fifteen one-man shows at the Ackermann Gallery, each exhibition opened by a well-known figure including John Buchan, Hugh Walpole and G. M. Trevelyan. Receipts from the sale of his paintings became an important boost to the funds of the Severn Wildfowl Trust and to Peter's own finances; stories tell of how Philippa, working on the family accounts and noting a looming deficit, would open the hatch between their two offices and tell him he needed to create a couple of new paintings fairly promptly. As Peter became more well known, the value of his paintings increased, his work became more in demand and his clientele came to include the rich and famous as well as royalty – both Queen Elizabeth the Queen Mother and Prince Philip bought paintings. Indeed, as with gliding, Peter introduced Prince Philip to painting, and an oil painting of Caerlaverock Castle by the Prince now hangs at Caerlaverock, the Trust's centre on the Solway Firth in Scotland.

A lucrative development was the sale of prints of his paintings. In 1933, reprint rights were bought by the Medici Society for the large painting for which he was commissioned after his first exhibition. Ultimately titled *Taking to Wing*, the painting was sold in print format until 1959, achieving in that time 355,000 sales, which included framed prints, Christmas cards and table mats. After 1936, the Ackermann Gallery began to regularly make prints of selected paintings. Between 1936 and 1982 they sold limited edition runs of up to 800 copies of twenty-nine of his pictures. The royalties from these prints formed a significant revenue stream for Peter, all the more welcome because it was a steady flow of money. Peter later developed another way of making multiple copies of a painting for sale. From time to time he would make twenty photocopies on high quality paper in different tints from a pen and ink drawing. He would then paint each copy in different colours, arriving at a limited-edition print run, within which each copy was unique.

Peter continued to offer paintings to the Royal Academy for the Summer Exhibition, but with limited success. He felt, probably rightly, that commercial success on Bond Street worked against an artist in Royal Academy circles. He discovered that the paintings most likely to be accepted at the Academy were paintings with birds in flight and lots of sky – these could be hung high on the wall above other paintings, in spaces that were harder to find suitable pictures for.

From when he moved into the lighthouse in 1933, with the exception of the war years, Peter always had birds around him, which meant that he could closely study the arrangement and colour of their feathers and the shapes of the heads and bodies. What is remarkable is that, working from memory, he could also capture them in flight and make them look completely natural, something very few other people could master. Years spent watching them in the fens and later in Scotland, Romania, Iceland and elsewhere in the world had imprinted in his mind their disposition in flight. In his introduction to *The Art of Peter Scott*, Keith Shackleton described Peter's method of creating one of his portrait drawings. Instead of first sketching a rough shape to determine the perspective of the drawing and the arrangement of the features in relation to each other, Peter would simply start by drawing an eye in perfect detail then move on to the next feature. He had, it seems, an ability to fix in his mind the spatial relationships between objects and could put them down on paper one after the other in sequence, without having to worry about the overall effect. As his talent developed, he discovered that it was very easy to over-paint a canvas; the secret for him was speed and lightness of touch. It was this, together with his habit of working long into the night with lamps strapped to the sides of the canvas, that accounted for his prolific output during the 1930s.

Peter did not confine himself exclusively to painting birds. During his time at Cambridge he had taken up portraiture, having been commissioned to submit a few portraits of university figures to *Granta* magazine. It was suggested to him at one point that he might consider developing his work in this direction. After all, there were always people who wanted their portraits painting but how many had a taste for geese in flight? Peter's portraits tended to be more personal affairs and became largely confined to friends and family. There was an early self-portrait, drawings of John Winter and quite a few pen and pencil drawings of Jane Howard and later of Philippa. In 1947, he was granted permission to make portrait drawings of the royal princesses, Elizabeth and Margaret, at the palace; this was his first meeting with Elizabeth and though he was nervous, he recalled that both princesses were patient and charming. Subsequently, *Country Life* published his book *Portrait Drawings,* which included thirty-six of his best drawings.

Before the war, Peter had begun to experiment with abstract art and to think about alternative subjects and treatments, his head, as always, buzzing with ideas. But the war intervened and though he continued to paint during the conflict, when he had the opportunity, his subjects were the things that he missed and longed to return to – his beloved birds. In 1945, he had his first post-war exhibition at the Ackermann Gallery and now, all he wanted to do was continue painting what he loved. Despite his return to his pre-war style, he continued to experiment with techniques and with subjects. The paintings he hung in his studio at Slimbridge number among them works which, though they feature birds in flight, have an experimental, non-literal approach. Mallards in flight, for example, are surrounded by a thin orange halo. Over the fireplace hangs a painting of four geese in flight; three are a warm brown colour while the fourth is pale blue, all of them flying in a golden light. It is usually assumed that these are lesser snow geese, a species which has a distinctive 'blue phase' variety known usually as a blue goose. In actual fact, these are all pink-footed geese, but Peter decided on a whim that the painting would be improved if one of the geese was blue. He was right; Philippa liked the painting so much that he gave it to her, and it was hung over the fireplace, where it remains to this day.

Though the majority of Peter's paintings were of birds, he did occasionally find other subjects that interested him. One example has already been mentioned, the splendid painting of humpback whales off Maui in Hawaii; another superb painting of a humpback whale shows it at the point of breaching, arched above the sea's surface. There are other creatures, oleander hawk-moths, a giant panda and scenes of wartime naval engagements. Another painting sets out to bring substance to the Loch Ness monster, represented as a pair of plesiosaurs swimming in the peat-tainted waters of the loch. Then there are conceptual paintings, in which Peter attempted to express matters or issues that interested or concerned him. Perhaps the most well known of these is the painting called *The Natural World of Man* created in 1965. Here, Peter attempts to depict the problems facing mankind as pollution and over-crowding takes its toll on the planet. At the time it was painted, just three years after the Cuban Missile Crisis, western civilisation was much exercised by the threat of nuclear annihilation, reflected in this painting by a giant mushroom cloud towering in the distance. We see factories spilling out pollution, crop-spraying aircraft covering the fields in pesticides and the over-development of land for agricultural purposes. From above, stick figures representing people, pour in a cascade into this abstract world while a contraceptive pill hangs in the sky. In front stands man, represented in abstract form with one black hand and one white, transfixed, as Peter declared it, by the problems facing mankind. A copy of the painting hangs by the door in the hallway of the house at Slimbridge.

Opposite, hangs another semi-abstract painting titled *Peter and Philippa with some of their favourite animals*. In it, Peter and Philippa stand surrounded on both sides and above and below by birds and animals which, as an assembly of creatures, could stand as a pictorial biography of Peter's life. Here we find the head of a lesser white-fronted goose, the bird that first brought him to Slimbridge. Above it a giant panda and above that a nene goose, behind which is a Greenland white-fronted goose. Then an oleander hawk-moth, red-breasted geese, Bewick's swans in flight, pintails, a chameleon, a frog and a praying mantis, their beloved collie, 'Corrie' and a selection of tropical fish. Clearly this painting was one of Philippa's favourites as she used it as the illustration on the front of her second autobiography *So Many Sunlit Hours*. As for Peter's favourite painting, it wasn't any of the large canvases of flying geese or ducks for which he was so well know. His favourite was his study of a pair of mating oleander hawk-moths, creatures which had fascinated him since he was a small boy.

This huge body of work would be a respectable output for someone who spent his life doing nothing but painting. That it was produced by someone who was busy in so many other spheres of influence is simply extraordinary. Just as when he was a small child, in adult life Peter never stopped drawing and painting. At meetings he would doodle on his papers, producing drawing after drawing of heads of geese, ducks, birds in flight, lizards and insects. All too aware of the value of his drawings, he was always very careful to take all his papers with him once the meeting was over, but many examples of these remain in the files at Slimbridge and, it is rumoured, one or two of them are framed and hung on the walls at Buckingham Palace.

Peter kept detailed diaries of his travels over the years and he painted many of the birds, animals and reptiles that he encountered, building up an extensive library of drawings and paintings, which are both scientifically accurate and aesthetically pleasing, forming one of the most important collections of scientific wildlife illustration from the twentieth century. Peter filled over seventy notebooks with his travel diaries; the mystery is how on earth he found the time to write in such detail and paint with such profusion amid all the meetings, lectures and presentations. During the 1980s, Peter published three volumes of his travel diaries, documenting trips from Africa to Antarctic and from Russia to Tierra del Fuego. The volumes are lavishly illustrated with his drawings and paintings. The illustrations are mostly of a modest size and were created in whatever medium came to hand, most often pencil or watercolour. His birds in particular are beautifully painted, reflecting his brimming enthusiasm for everything he saw. Reviewing the first volume of the *Travel Diaries* in the Wildfowl Trust magazine, Keith Shackleton wrote:

> I have watched the gradual metamorphosis from a new, empty book straight out of the stationers into a unique wealth of illustrated records with maps, charts, photographs and clippings tucked in until with every page filled, it bulges with repletion against the restraint of a stout rubber band.

The other wildlife artist that comes to mind when leafing through Peter's diary paintings is Edward Wilson, Peter's father's companion on both of his Antarctic journeys and the man who may have inspired Robert Falcon Scott to urge his wife to 'make the boy interested in natural history'. The paintings of both men have an immediacy and a charm that conveys both a deep love for and a profound interest in their subjects.

Peter used every free moment when travelling to paint what he had seen that day, and this caused occasional friction between Peter and

Philippa. Philippa recalled an occasion in a hotel room in Buenos Aires when, having arrived very late, their luggage had failed to materialise. Peter wouldn't go to bed until the luggage was delivered so sat down to paint. Their bags appeared shortly afterwards but having started a watercolour painting he felt compelled to continue and painted into the night despite being, no doubt, desperately tired. Airport lounges were another place where the paints would come out. The work could not be hurried even after the flight was announced and everyone was headed towards the departure gate. Philippa wrote, 'His ability to sit down and paint anywhere at any time was amazing – and sometimes frustrating for me … I envied him his capacity for concentration and ability to "switch off".' Peter wasn't completely unaware of the impact his single-mindedness had on Philippa. Of an occasion in the Galapagos, when he continued to paint while Phil did all the packing, he acknowledged that she was quite right in pointing out to him that if he had wanted to complete his painting he should have started earlier, an exchange that will doubtless be familiar to a good number of readers of this book.

Throughout his life, Peter continued to hold one-man exhibitions at the Ackermann Gallery in Bond Street; his paintings continued to sell, and prices continued to rise. In 1966, the original paintings for volumes II – IV of Jean Delacour's magnificent four-volume work *Waterfowl of the World* were bound in two leather volumes and offered for sale with a reserve price of £10,000. At his penultimate sale in 1984, his larger paintings were selling for £4,000 to £5,000 apiece. In one day he sold seven paintings for a total of £27,000. His sixteenth and last one-man exhibition at Ackermann's was in March 1989. Prince Philip opened the exhibition and bought one of the paintings. All but four of the paintings were sold on the first day, a tribute to his enduring popularity and to a professional painting career that spanned over sixty years. Peter was doubtless pleased that his work continued to attract attention, but he had no expectation that his work would live on after his death, and he occasionally expressed regret that he had not experimented more when he was younger. Notwithstanding these occasional regrets, Peter had painted to live, just as much as he had lived to paint; the commercial success of his work was an ongoing support of his other activities. He need not have worried about his legacy; over thirty years after his death his paintings are still much in demand and doubtless will continue to be so for many years to come.

Peter's final painting stands on the easel in his studio at Slimbridge, unfinished at the time of his death. In 1989, Peter had been working on a proposal for a new WWT centre in London. Few, if any, conservationists had considered the idea of an urban wetland centre before. The idea of introducing wild nature into the middle of dense urban development presented a challenge that seemed just too difficult to accomplish. Peter knew through the work of the Trust and through the response to his wildlife television programmes that there was an innate desire in people to experience wildlife and the natural world at first hand. Many people living in big cities lacked the means to escape to places where such things could be found, so the answer to Peter was simple. If you can't get the people into the wild, bring the wild to the people. Thames Water possessed some redundant reservoirs and a series of water treatment beds in west London on land which was due for redevelopment, so Peter approached them with a plan to convert the reservoirs into a wetland centre. The resulting development was a partnership project between Thames Water, Berkeley Homes and WWT with Berkeley Homes providing substantial funding derived from housing developments on other parts of the site.

The Trust commissioned Peter to create a painting to show what the new centre would look like, and the artwork was well advanced when he passed away in August 1989. The painting shows wigeon flying in to land on a stretch of open water. At the time there were no wigeon on the reservoirs but ten years later, when the centre opened for the first time, wigeon had become regular visitors to the centre, just as Peter had known they would.

The painting was finished by Peter's friend Keith Shackleton, himself a marine painter of some distinction. Peter had painted the background and most of the wigeon in flight; Keith now painted the rest. The two friends had painted together before, aided by the fact that Peter was left-handed and Keith right-handed, which meant that they could both work on the same canvas at the same time, as Keith put it, '... our brush handles occasionally clacking together in the middle-ground like the bills of courting gannets'. Keith generously admitted that Peter was the better painter and spoke of times when, having nearly finished a painting, he would be worried about some aspect of it and show it to Peter for his advice. Often, rather than saying anything, Peter would pick up a brush and make some minor change or addition which invariably improved the whole effect, a process which Keith called giving the painting 'a Scotting over'. Keith signed the painting for Peter and himself, and after framing it has stood, ever since, on Peter's easel in the studio.

30

Evening Flight

Most people, as they enter their eighth decade, begin to take things a little easier, look forward hopefully to a slightly quieter life and determine to leave to others the pressures and strains of life's affairs. Not so Peter. As 1979 dawned, we found him returning from his fifth trip to Antarctica, founding the Falkland Islands Conservation Commission and swimming with humpback whales in Hawaii. For Peter, work was not something you could retire from. His life was his work, the two being inextricably intermixed, and he would have found the concept of retirement pointless and probably rather depressing. He could not hold back the advancing years however, nor their gradual impact upon him, but Philippa was always on hand to make sure, as far as she was able, that he did not overdo things.

Nevertheless, his programme of trips and lectures, meetings and committees, his fundraising, writing and painting continued unabated. Apart from the events mentioned above, 1979 was notable for a trip to Australia and Malaysia. The Australian leg of the trip lasted a fortnight and was a whirl of engagements with politicians and conservations, meetings and broadcasts, all part of the launch of WWF Australia. Flying to Malaysia, he was joined by Philippa. There were more meetings, including one with the prime minister, as well as time working with a group making an underwater film for WWF. It was on this trip that Philippa first went scuba-diving; previously she had only used a snorkel.

In 1979 the first computer was installed at the Wildfowl Trust, its arrival proudly announced in the Trust's magazine, *Waterfowl News*:

At the end of June the Research Department took delivery of one of the new generation of micro-computers. Taking up just a few feet of desk-top space, this machine has nearly the same capacity as one which a few years ago would have cost several times as much and which would have required a whole room to house. For the technically minded, what we have is a Research Machine 380Z with 32K bytes of memory.

By 1986, the single computer had become a network of eight machines. From today's perspective it is hard to imagine that for the first thirty-three years of the Trust's existence, all the information generated through research, for example the data underpinning the Bewick's swan project, was organised manually.

Peter's seventieth birthday, 14 September 1979, was spent quietly at home with his family. Two days later, there was a party for Peter and for Wildfowl Trust staff and other guests in the centre's foyer at Slimbridge, which Peter attended wearing a big brown wig; he was amused that some of the staff failed to recognise him. The Duke of Beaufort came, as did Max Nicholson, while Peter's old friend Keith Shackleton gave a very funny speech. The following day, Peter flew off to China for the series of events described in an earlier chapter.

In 1980, Peter was treated for prostate cancer and was forced, temporarily, to slow down a little. He spent the time at home writing and painting and completed his book *Observations of Wildlife*, a highly readable short recap of his life, richly illustrated with his paintings and drawings. One of the most charming of these is a line drawing of the house at Slimbridge with a tiny figure sat at the top of the tower. The caption reads 'Self portrait of an artist writing a book at the top of a tower. The Director's House at Slimbridge'.

Peter and Philippa continued to travel and to dive whenever possible. In August 1983, they were the guests of Hardy Jones, founder of the Living Ocean Society, joining him for a week in the Bahamas on the schooner *Cloudesley Shovell*. Hardy had been working for over five years with a group of spotted dolphins and had gained their complete confidence, giving Peter and Philippa the opportunity for some very close and extended encounters with them, something which gave both of them great delight. Peter dived frequently during the week and, as always, made extensive lists and notes on all the fish that he encountered. The year 1983 also saw the publication of his first volume of *Travel Diaries* which described some highlights from his travels round the world over a period of some seventeen years from 1956 to 1973. Drawn from his extensive collection of travel diaries, the book was lavishly illustrated with his paintings and drawings of the creatures he had encountered and with Philippa's splendid photographs. The book included a foreword by Prince Charles. Further volumes were to follow in 1985 and 1987.

In 1984, the Scotts were off on their travels again, this time to Sri Lanka to observe and swim with blue whales, at that time reduced to around 1,000 individuals worldwide. During the trip Peter began to suffer chest pains which were diagnosed as angina. Back home at Slimbridge, Philippa temporarily took over some of Peter's duties and was staying with Falcon in Yorkshire en route to open the new Wildfowl Trust centre in Washington when Peter suffered a mild heart attack at home. Falcon drove her straight back; Peter soon improved, though now it was clear that he needed to be more careful with his health in future, and he considered whether or not he should cut down on his travels or stop altogether.

He couldn't. While he still had the opportunity, he continued to do what he loved best, to paint, to work and to travel. November 1984 found Peter and Philippa on holiday on a diving boat in the Red Sea as the guest of the Marchioness of Hertford. Peter was not allowed to dive but had a wonderfully relaxing time away from the pressures of work. In 1985, the couple had a holiday cruising the islands of Indonesia with Keith and Jacq Shackleton. Peter was still banned from diving after his heart attack, but Jacq had learned to dive in the swimming pool at Slimbridge and she and Philippa dived together. Peter must have felt a little disconsolate at being denied access to the underwater world that he had come to love.

Another excursion later that year gave him great pleasure. At the invitation of Central Television, he and Philippa travelled to Grunau in Austria to spend some time with their old friend Konrad Lorenz and to be filmed in conversation. The two men had always agreed on so many things, and they hugely enjoyed each other's company. Philippa was fond of Lorenz too, remarking that he always treated her as a person in her own right and not just Peter Scott's wife.

Peter's health didn't hold up however. In June 1986, returning from a meeting of the International Whaling Commission in Sweden, Peter had a second heart attack and was forced to take an extended convalescence with the family at Slimbridge. Still he didn't rest completely, as he began making plans for a new, much bigger visitor centre at Slimbridge, plans which would ultimately bear fruit sixteen years later, when the current centre was built. In September of that year he was once again off on his travels, this time to New York to receive the £50,000 Getty Prize for conservation. And 1986 also brought another invitation that gave him great pleasure. The East Lighthouse at Sutton Bridge had been abandoned and fallen into disrepair after the war. Now, it had been bought by a Royal Navy commander, David Joel, who renovated it, painted it white and refurnished as it was in Peter's day. He uncovered a mural of flying geese under the plaster, installed an easel and re-dug the ponds outside, filling them once again with geese. He then invited Peter and Philippa and various friends to an opening party. Peter was delighted, and touched, to see his old home brought to life once more. The lighthouse subsequently became the centre of what was to be called the Snowgoose Wildlife Trust and while, at the time of writing, it is not open to the public, various species of geese, including nenes, feed around its walls.

In 1987, Peter and Philippa organised a diving expedition in Australia. They chartered a boat from friends in Cairns and found a group of divers who paid to take part in the trip. The diving on the Great Barrier Reef was spectacular; Peter spent a lot of the time snorkelling and watching the divers below him. He was, however, allowed to have a single dive using Philippa's equipment for the purpose. At the end of the dive, he wrote on his white board, 'It's so beautiful, I don't want to go.' On the way back to England they stopped off in Muscat to present a joint IUCN/WWF report on conservation in the Sultanate of Oman.

The year 1987 brought further recognition for Peter when he was made a Companion of Honour to Her Majesty the Queen. Peter had been at Hampton Court for a dinner for members of the WWF 1001 Club in the presence of Prince Charles when news reached him that the prime minister had recommended Peter for the position. Peter was extraordinarily proud and pleased, and his happiness was completed later in the year when he was made a Fellow of the Royal Society. This for Peter was deeply rewarding, recognising as it did his contribution to science and to international conservation. With this honour came the additional distinction of being the first (and still the only) Fellow to have won an Olympic medal. When asked to comment on these two signal offers, his response was to say he'd received them because he was old. Of course, that wasn't the case, and it is pleasing that he was recognised in this way in his own lifetime, fully aware of how his contribution was valued at the highest levels.

Also in 1987, Peter was a co-founder with Christopher Parsons of 'Wildscreen', a conservation charity with the aim of encouraging and recognising excellence in natural history film making. The charity built on the work of the Wildscreen Film Festival which had started in 1982 as a collaboration between Anglia Television, the BBC and WWF, offering the famous 'Panda' awards at their annual awards ceremony.

In 1988, Her Majesty the Queen paid another visit to Slimbridge to open the Yuen-Peng McNeice Observatory. She had lunch in the house, and Philippa was able to tell her the story of the 'Queen's Bedroom' which she duly inspected. Both Prince Philip and Prince Charles had slept in it but the Queen never had. Philippa described the event as very light-hearted; the formal opening in the afternoon went off very smoothly. Today, the Peng Observatory is in use every day, particularly in winter when visitors gather each evening to view the Bewick's swans being fed outside on the Rushy Pen.

By this time, Peter had received a number of other honorary awards including being made a Doctor of Law by five universities and a Doctor of Science by three more. But one award bothered him. Some years previously he had been given Iceland's highest honour, the Order of the Falcon. Now, in 1988, Iceland precipitated a break with the international whaling moratorium, announcing the intention of catching and killing 120 whales, ostensibly for research purposes. This was too much for Peter, and sadly, he returned the medal, sadly because Iceland was where he had made his breakthrough in his research on the pink-footed goose and where he and Phil had had such happy times and been married.

Despite his determination to carry on regardless, Peter could not but be aware of his advancing years, particularly in light of his body's attempts to slow him up. He knew that he shouldn't overdo things, but equally he wanted to continue to live his life to the full as long as he could. He wrote that he was not afraid of dying, he just didn't want to be a nuisance to people. He was not a religious man in the strictest sense. In the BBC broadcast for American radio listeners transmitted in 1953 he had said:

My picture of the power and glory that unites humanity is not the Bible's picture. I believe in the basic greatness and goodness of man.

I believe in a lot of simple things, beliefs which are common to most of us – that good ends do not justify evil means, that love and tolerance and kindness make the world go around. (Kindness, how important that one is); and above all, and this I believe implicitly, that in the evolution of the human race, as in lesser fields too, good must ultimately triumph over evil. If I didn't believe that I should be a much less happy man than I am.

Some years later, writing in *The Eye of the Wind*, Peter had already given his thoughts on death and his legacy, stating that he did not believe in life after death but that people could live on 'in the creations of their art, in the memories of the living and in the persons of their descendants'.

In 1989, the year in which he would turn eighty, Peter showed few signs of slowing down. In May he was due to receive the Zoological Medal from Washington Zoo, so he and Philippa decided to have a short break in the British Virgin Islands first. Shortly after their arrival, Peter became ill with a viral infection which triggered his angina. Philippa was anxious about how to get Peter to Washington quickly as medical facilities were limited on the island where they were staying. In the end, nearby resident Richard Branson came to the rescue, offering them his helicopter to fly to San Juan in the American Virgin Islands from where they were able to get a direct flight to Washington. Here Peter was able to receive medical attention; a few days later he was well enough to receive the award. Nevertheless, this was a real warning sign to them both.

Other events that year harked back to earlier times. In June, Peter and Philippa attended the annual meeting of the Captain Scott Society at the Royal Hotel in Cardiff, where Robert Falcon Scott stayed before setting out for Antarctica on the *Terra Nova* in 1910. The same meal that had been served in 1910 was served in the room where Peter's father dined on the last night before setting sail and where, years before, Peter had declined to unveil a commemorative plaque; Peter, in old age, was finally at ease with the memory of his father and was attending the event for the second time. A visit to the National Maritime Museum at Greenwich brought him back together with his old friend John Winter for the presentation to the museum of their sailing dinghy *Thunder and Lightning*, in which they had confounded their critics and won the Prince of Wales Cup all those years ago in 1938.

At the Wildfowl Trust, changes were in the air. Two new centres, at Llanelli in Wales and Castle Espie in Northern Ireland were due to open. In addition, a suggestion had been made to change the name of the organisation to The Wetlands Trust, partly to reflect the organisation's increasing role in habitat development and the growing realisation of the importance of wetlands around the world. Peter, Philippa and the rest of the board members were unhappy with the proposal, as they feared that members might think the Trust was losing interest in wildfowl, so in the end the new name was changed to The Wildfowl and Wetlands Trust. Nevertheless, the work of the Trust was increasingly involved with wetland habitats as well as individual waterfowl species. In 1989, a new department was formed, the Wetland Advisory Service, the aim of which was to provide consultancy on wetland habitats, visitor centres and water treatment systems. Now called WWT Consulting, the operation is still an important component of the work of the Wildfowl and Wetlands Trust. Peter worked on all these projects and also further developed his plans for a new visitor centre at Slimbridge. The announcement of the change of name for the Trust was to take place at the Natural History Museum in London. Peter was to make a short address but was taken ill shortly before the event and was taken into hospital in London; his place at the launch was taken by his daughter Dafila who read his presentation.

Back at Slimbridge, Peter was involved in the preparation of a major retrospective exhibition of his work to celebrate his eightieth birthday, which was to be mounted at Cheltenham Art Gallery and Museum. Peter was heavily involved with the selection of paintings, and a book was produced to accompany the exhibition which included a series of testimonials from his friends and colleagues. Preparations were also being made for his birthday party on 14 September.

As things turned out, Peter would not live to see his eightieth birthday. Another heart attack proved to be fatal and he died in hospital in Bristol on 29 August, after two days in intensive care. It is some consolation perhaps that the book accompanying his retrospective exhibition had already been prepared, so he had been able to read what his friends had written about him and his extraordinary life. There were contributions from Keith Shackleton, John Winter, Gerald Durrell, Christopher Dreyer, Richard Fitter, Desmond Hawkins, Michael Garside, Max Nicholson and Nigel

Sitwell, each writing about a different aspect of his life. Gerald Durrell wrote:

> Peter during his multi-faceted lifetime has probably done more for world conservation than any other one man. To be born with all Peter's gifts is a wonderful thing; what is even more wonderful is the way he has managed to share these gifts with so many people all over the world.

Peter himself had written the preface:

> To have a retrospective exhibition, which I have not had before, is very flattering and agreeable to an octogenarian naturalist, and to have a book in which many of the works are reproduced makes it even better because books last longer than exhibitions. It is also very nice to find a biographical section, a bibliography, and contributions from nine of my life-long friends. From these you may gather that my life has been hugely enjoyable, fortunate and happy. For the last forty years of it, I have to praise and thank my adored wife Philippa, my three children and seven grand-children.

Here was, by accident, a kind of personal epitaph for a good life, well lived. None of us can know when our time will come but this passage, written when it was, must have brought some comfort to Philippa and the children. But then, perhaps, they had always known that Peter was, as he often claimed, the happiest and most fortunate of men.

The House Reborn

In 2016, the Wildfowl and Wetlands Trust announced a major new initiative, heralding the largest development programme at Slimbridge for forty years. The Heritage Lottery Fund had offered £4.6 million for a project to highlight Peter Scott's life and work, and to ensure that his passion for, and commitment to, wetland conservation should not be forgotten, especially by those people who were not old enough to remember the heady early days of the World Wildlife Fund and his appearances on radio and television.

As one of a legion of volunteers at the Trust, I was only too aware that Peter was disappearing from people's memories. Leading guided walks around the collection I would pause by Peter's bust and ask how many people knew about him and about his work. Invariably, most older people remembered him and often mentioned the *Look* television programmes and the view from the studio window, but many of the younger people in the group had no knowledge of his life and work. The new project aimed to address this. Initially called the 'Sir Peter Scott Living Legacy Project – Slimbridge 2020' the title was very soon shortened to 'Slimbridge 2020'. The Trust engaged in some serious fundraising and was able to add a further £1.4 million to the Heritage Lottery Fund contribution. Planning could begin in earnest.

Slimbridge 2020, was conceived and developed as a series of mini-projects, each one designed to illuminate an aspect of Peter's life and work and the need to protect and conserve wetlands around the world. The biggest single project was the construction of a huge wetland aviary and theatre where the Trust could showcase some of the most charismatic waterfowl species and demonstrate aspects of bird evolution and behaviour in a way that was currently not possible. Another project would explain how captive breeding and habitat protection can bring species back from the brink – the nene geese would be centre stage here. A part of the site was cleared to recreate a section of tundra landscape (not easy in the middle of Gloucestershire) and a hut was constructed which was an exact replica of the hunting lodges in northern Russia used by the Trust's researchers when studying Bewick's swans and other species on their summer breeding grounds. Here, young people would be able to get a feel of what life out in the wilderness was like, identify geese and swans on the 'tundra' and take part in simple experiments, including identifying what birds eat from looking at their poo.

The old Holden Tower, beloved by many but cold, draughty and damp in winter was replaced. The new Estuary Tower overlooking the famous Dumbles beside the River Severn has two levels, including a rooftop terrace and a lift to enable disabled visitors to share in the magnificent winter spectacle of thousands of birds feeding on the salt marsh and in the wet fields where Peter first saw those lesser white-fronted geese seventy-five years before. The summer walkway was widened to enable wheelchair access to the shore, while the old goose hut, once a shelter for the rich and famous, was rebuilt exactly as it had been during the days when the Berkeley family came here in winter to shoot the geese. The Berkeley New Decoy was dredged and repaired and new screens erected; following renovation, the decoy was put back into regular use with demonstrations of decoying with a dog and handler.

At the heart of all this new development was Peter Scott's house. Slimbridge 2020 included a scheme to renovate the house, catalogue its contents and open it as a museum to allow the public to see for themselves Peter's studio and the view through that famous window that had appeared in so many television broadcasts in the 1950s and 1960s. This part of the project presented significant challenges as the house was in need of considerable renovation, was in an area of the grounds not usually open to the public and contained a huge amount of material in need of varying levels of conservation. But what had happened to the house in the intervening years since 1989?

In the days after Peter's death, Philippa felt the numbing shock and grief that such a bereavement brings, but she also felt a growing imperative to continue with his work as he would have wished. Among the welter of affairs in which she became engaged, she found time to deal with the huge volume of letters of condolence that had arrived following Peter's death. She continued to manage the Trust's affairs, which she was determined should be conducted as they would have been had Peter not passed away, and she also took upon herself the task of organising Peter's memorial service, which was to be held at St Paul's Cathedral. In this huge task she was assisted by her brother, Evelyn, who was working as a volunteer guide in the cathedral. Philippa recalled later that the dean was surprised that she wanted to use the main nave of the cathedral, but she knew what she was doing and might even have thought back with a wry smile to the day when Peter decided to hire the Royal Festival Hall in 1953. Of course, she was proved right, and the cathedral was full. Philippa had wanted a service that was uplifting, even cheerful, a celebration of Peter's life. And so it was. Keith Shackleton gave the address and Prince Philip read Psalm 104, his own choice. A further remembrance service was held in the church at Slimbridge, so that his co-workers and friends from the Trust could remember him too in the village that came to mean so much to him.

After Peter died, Philippa continued to live in the house and altered it very little. His books, photos and other belongings remained where he had left them, except for a little tidying. Philippa continued her involvement with WWT, and, with the agreement of council and the Chief Executive Officer, took on the title of Honorary Director, which Peter had held for many years. She continued to sit on council and to have regular meetings with council members including Martin Spray who took over as CEO in 2004. An apocryphal story relates that when he was interviewed, he was instructed to crawl across the floor of the studio to the interview chair to avoid disturbing the Bewick's swans on the lake outside the window, something she and Peter had been known to do in winters past. After Philippa passed away, the house became the property of WWT. Peter and Philippa's children naturally took away some personal possessions and objects of family significance, but they took care to leave most of the house contents untouched. Following discussion with the family, Martin Spray decided to use the studio as his office, and his secretary took up residence in Philippa's old room next door. To his great credit, Martin also took care to leave Peter's things as they had been.

This continuity of use and the care taken not to disturb many of the objects in the rooms, meant that in opening the house as a museum, the Trust had a significant advantage. It would not be necessary to recreate the room settings as they might have been; the house had never really changed since Peter and Philippa's time and could therefore be viewed as it actually still was, unchanged; there would be little need for reinterpretation. When the house was finished in 1954 its furnishings and contents were the most modern, comfortable and convenient for the period. The Scotts entertained regularly and a well-equipped kitchen was essential. Once established in the house however, Peter and Philippa saw little need to change anything unless it needed repairing or replacing. They obviously had little interest in changing the design of the rooms or redecorating – they were too busy doing other things. What we see today therefore is something of a time capsule. The kitchen is particularly interesting, with the fitted cupboards and surfaces that were installed when the house was first built in 1953 still *in situ*.

In 2017, the Trust recruited eight volunteers to be trained to go methodically through the house and clean and catalogue every item, from the teaspoons in the kitchen drawers to the memorabilia, books and awards in the studio. The programme was run by Helen Clark who had extensive experience in preserving historic buildings and their contents for the National Trust, with the support of Claire Rees from the centre office at Slimbridge. Each object was cleaned, given a catalogue number and entered into the catalogue with a brief description. Often the nature and provenance of an object was obvious, but there was sometimes need for further research. As a team of volunteers we came from different backgrounds. Some of us were already working for the Trust and knew something of Peter's life and work. Others came from a background of volunteering for the National Trust and brought with them valuable knowledge about antiques and fabrics. Between us, slowly, we pieced together the history of the contents of the house. Equally slowly, Peter's life and work began to come more clearly into focus.

The conservation and cataloguing work began in the kitchen in July 2017. At the time, Martin Spray and his secretary were still working at the other end of the house, but in March 2018 they moved to new offices in the administration block. For the first time since it was built in 1954, the studio was no longer the nerve centre for the Trust. In early 2018, Helen McConnell-Simpson was appointed as the museum's curator. Later that year, all work on the house's contents ceased as the builders moved in to undertake essential repair work. The roof and windows were replaced, though not the studio window, and essential damp-proofing work was carried out. During preliminary inspections it had been discovered that the water in the swimming pool was rising and falling in tandem with the water in the lake outside, so it was decided to fill it in and convert the room into a splendid curved meeting room. The first floor of the house was completely re-modelled as it was to become a holiday-let, where people would be able to stay and enjoy the magnificent views of the lake and the estuary beyond. The house was extensively rewired and new blinds added to the windows facing the lake so that in winter, activity in the house would not be seen by the swans outside. All of the exterior work had to be completed during the summer of 2018 to avoid disturbing the swans during the coming winter months.

February 2019 saw the volunteer team return to the house. Now the race was on to complete our work before the house opened, an event which was planned for September that year. The studio still needed to be catalogued and the team set to with a will. All of the rooms in the house have a good feeling about them but the studio in particular always feels particularly welcoming. Maybe it is the proportions, or the view from the window, the range of books and objects scattered around or simply the feeling that Peter has just popped out to see someone for a few moments and will be back shortly – whatever it is, almost everyone entering the studio for the first time comments on what a lovely room it is. In cataloguing its contents, we all felt a responsibility to ensure that everything was returned to its exact position, and that though we had cleaned and catalogued every object in this historic space, the room itself would look no different.

It was always planned that Scott House would be a living museum. There would be no cabinets with objects on shelves, no ropes holding people back, no Perspex screens separating visitors from everything on view. It would therefore be necessary to arrange to show groups of visitors around the house with volunteer guides to talk about Peter's life story and the objects in the house but also to make sure that everything stayed secure. Early in 2018, a small number of trial tours were conducted. Led by Slimbridge 2020 project manager Jackie Harris, these trial events gave us a good idea of how the tours could be organised and what we should include in telling Peter's story. More particularly, we learned that we were on the right track; people's reactions to the tours were invariably favourable. A number of people shared memories of seeing Peter on television or remarked on how similar the kitchen was to that of their parents. In February 2019, an open day was held to recruit new volunteers to help with several of the 2020 projects but more immediately to become volunteer guides in the house. The plan was to run three tours a day in the summer months and two in winter. With two volunteers accompanying each tour, there was obviously a need for a large pool of people on which to draw. In the end around thirty people signed up, including most of the eight people already working in the house.

Tour notes were written and learned. Everyone went through several days of training to become familiar with the house and its contents and to sharpen up our presentation skills. We also continued to work in the studio, cataloguing and cleaning in advance of opening. During this time, one matter was very much in people's minds as the house slowly evolved into a museum; what would Peter and Philippa's children think about what we were doing? Nicola, Dafila and Falcon had always retained an interest in the Trust's work while pursuing careers of their own. Slimbridge 2020, a project aimed at promoting Peter's life and work and strengthening his legacy, was doubtless appealing to them, but opening the house as a museum might seem a step too far. This was, after all, their childhood home. How would they feel about hordes of people tramping through the house to look at their parent's belongings? During the process they were kept informed of what we were doing and Dafila came to visit during the run up to the opening to see what had been done. All three of them generously donated objects to the museum; Dafila gave us her father's painting chest in which he kept all his paints and brushes, from Nicola came four boxes of possessions including photographs and other memorabilia and Falcon gave the museum his father's leather backed chair.

In mid-2019, the holiday-let upstairs was opened. Christened Bewick's Lodge, it very quickly began to attract guests keen to stay in the historic house. In the month before opening the downstairs rooms, we ran tours for members of staff from the Trust so that we could practise our skills on real people and get used to moving groups of visitors safely through the house. Finally, after two years of intensive work, we were ready to open the doors to the public and on 2 September 2019, the first tour of the museum took place. At last the museum was open and Peter's story was being re-told; it was a splendid moment for everyone concerned. Saturday, 14 September would have been Peter's 110th birthday, but it also coincided with the National Heritage Open Days on which buildings are opened to the public across the country, so the doors of Scott House were opened as part of the scheme. Volunteers were stationed in every room and the public were free to wander at will. Nicola, Dafila and Falcon and members of their families stayed in Bewick's Lodge for the weekend, and we were proud to host three generations of the Scott family at the open day event.

Over the ensuing months, the tours have been extremely popular, and we have on occasion found that people on the tour know more about the house than we do! More than once, someone has revealed that they worked for Peter or knew him through his work. I was particularly pleased one day to discover that one of the original swan researchers was amongst the party I was conducting round the house. Mary Matthews remembered the Bewick's swan project very clearly and entertained us all with the tale of Lady Harold, the swan that flew through the dining room window. Another visitor was a friend of Martin Davis, the son of Howard Davis who first brought Peter to Slimbridge in 1945. We contacted Martin and he came to visit us, bringing with him his father's letters and photographs, including the sketch of the lesser white-fronted goose that Peter had drawn on that long ago morning. Almost without exception, people have been fascinated by the house, its contents and the amazing story of Peter's life that we are now able to retell.

I do sometimes wonder what Peter would make of it all. As we know from his comments about his father's huts in the Antarctic, Peter had no time for history. He was interested in the present and the future, not in the past. He would, I have not the slightest doubt, have loved the new wetland aviary, the Arctic Adventure Hut, the nene exhibit and the new Estuary Tower with its lift to enable people in wheelchairs to share the spectacle of winter waterfowl. But the house? I sometimes wonder. I don't think he would bother for a moment about all the people coming through, as long as they didn't disturb the birds on the lake, but he might wonder what was the point of his house becoming a museum. However, if he knew that by telling his story in this way, future generations would be inspired by the huge contribution that he made to world conservation, then, perhaps, he might smile and say, 'Go on then.' I certainly hope so.

Sources

Attenborough, David, *Life on Air* (London: BBC Books, 2002)

Cook, Tony and Pilcher, R. E. M., *The History of Borough Fen Decoy* (Ely: Providence Press, 1982)

Davis, Martin, *The Farmer and the Goose with the Golden Eyes* (Bristol: Redcliffe Press, 2009)

Delacour, Jean, *The Waterfowl of the World*, 4 vols. (London: Country Life, 1954)

Durrell, Gerald, *The Drunken Forest* (London: Penguin Books, 1958)

Howard, Elizabeth Jane, *Slipstream* (London: Pan Macmillan, 2002)

Huxley, Elspeth, *Peter Scott Painter and Naturalist* (Golden, Co. USA: Fulcrum Publishing, 1993)

Marren, Peter, *The New Naturalists* (London: HarperCollins, 1995)

Scott, Kathleen, *Self-Portrait of an Artist* (London: John Murray, 1949)

Scott, Peter, *Morning Flight* (London: Country Life, 1935)

Scott, Peter, *Wild Chorus* (London: Country Life, 1938)

Scott, Peter, *Wild Geese and Eskimos* (London: Country Life, 1951)

Scott, Peter, *Faraway Look I* (London: Cassell & Company Ltd, 1960)

Scott, Peter, *Faraway Look II* (London: Cassell & Company Ltd, 1960)

Scott, Peter, *The Eye of the Wind* (London: Hodder and Stoughton, 1961)

Scott, Peter, *Observations of Wildlife* (Oxford: Phaidon Press, 1980)

Scott, Peter, *Travel Diaries of a Naturalist*, 3 vols. (London: Collins Harvill, 1983–87)

Scott, Peter and Fisher, James, *A Thousand Geese*, (London: Collins, 1953)

Scott, Peter, et al, *Sir Peter Scott at 80*, (Gloucester: Alan Sutton Publishing, 1989)

Scott, Peter and Scott, Philippa, *The Swans Fly In*, (Slimbridge: The Wildfowl and Wetlands Trust, 1983)

Scott, Philippa, *Lucky Me* (London: The Kenilworth Press, 1990)

Scott, Philippa, *So Many Sunlit Hours* (Slimbridge: The Wildfowl and Wetlands Trust, 2002)

Scott, Philippa and Shackleton, Keith, *The Art of Peter Scott* (London: Sinclair-Stevenson, 1992)

Sitwell, Nigel, *Happy The Man* (London: Sphere Books, 1967)

Thoreau, Henry David, *Walden* (London: Penguin Books, 1854)

Walkden, Paul, *Peter Scott, Collected Writings 1933–1989*, (Slimbridge: The Wildfowl and Wetlands Trust, 2016)

Williams, Gareth, *A Monstrous Commotion* (London: Orion Books, 2016)

Acknowledgements

I am extremely grateful to the large number of people who have provided me with assistance and advice during the writing of this book. First and foremost, I would like to thank the Scott family, in particular Peter and Philippa Scott's daughter Dafila, who has given me permission to quote from her parents' works and to include her mother's images in the book. I thank her also for writing the foreword for the book and for the helpful suggestions and corrections she provided. Nicola Starks also kindly read an early draft of the book and provided some very useful corrections.

The Wildfowl and Wetlands Trust generously allowed me access to Peter Scott's correspondence in the archive at the Scott House Museum and has kindly given permission for me to quote from it. I am grateful to the Trust for allowing me to reproduce a number of images from their archives. I particularly wish to thank Jackie Harris and Claire Rees at WWT, without whose encouragement and support this book may never have seen the light of day. Also at WWT, Angela Rosser kindly assisted in sourcing the images I needed, while Eileen Rees, Mary Matthews and Kevin Peberdy provided helpful information. Paul Walkden threw light on his experiences as Peter's bibliographer and Gina Dorkins at WWT Martin Mere assisted with commercial arrangements.

I owe a debt of gratitude to Martin Davis, son of Howard Davis who invited Peter Scott to Slimbridge in 1945. Martin made his collection of documents available to me and kindly permitted me to reproduce a sketch by Peter Scott and a photograph and to quote from Peter's correspondence with his father.

Acknowledgements

Frank Bowles at Cambridge University Library kindly tracked down the source of a number extracts from Kathleen Scott's diaries and correspondence and Peter Scott's correspondence, while Lisa Barr, Susan Miles, Nicholas Milton, Dan Todman and Cathy Williams all helped in locating copyright sources.

Grateful thanks go to my friends and former colleagues, Richard Tucker and Nick Ford. Richard is, I suspect, one of Peter Scott's greatest fans and both he and Nick provided unstinting support in my search to find a publisher for the book. Many thanks too to the team at Quiller Publishing, especially Connor Stait, Nicola Embery and Angeline Wilcox.

The author and publisher would like to thank the following people and organisations for their kind permission to reproduce items in this book as listed below:

Dafila Scott: Extracts from the published works of Peter and Philippa Scott.

The Wildfowl and Wetlands Trust: Extracts from bulletins, magazines and correspondence.

Lee Durrell: Extracts from her husband Gerald Durrell's writing and correspondence.

Piers Nicholson: Extract from his father Max Nicholson's correspondence.

David Hosking: Extract from his father Eric Hosking's correspondence.

Andrew Jamieson: Extract from his grandfather Archibald Jamieson's correspondence.

Helen Blackmore: Extract from her grandfather Thomas Hinton's correspondence.

Jasper Shackleton: Extracts from his father Keith Shackleton's writing.

The Liddell Hart Centre for Military Archives: Extract from the correspondence of Lord Alanbrooke.

Country Life magazine: Extract from Country Life, 29 September 1955.

The British Broadcasting Corporation: Extracts from radio programme What I Believe broadcast on 10 June 1953.

Index

Index